Series Editors:
Robert C. Pianta
Carollee Howes

D1473932

The
Promise
of Pre-K

The Promise of Pre-K

edited by

Robert C. Pianta, Ph.D.
Dean, Curry School of Education
Novartis US Foundation Professor of Education
Director, National Center for Research on Early Childhood Education
University of Virginia
Charlottesville

and

Carollee Howes, Ph.D.
Director, Center for Improving Child Care Quality
Department of Education
Professor
University of California–Los Angeles

with invited contributors

Baltimore • London • Sydney

Paul H. Brookes Publishing Co.
Post Office Box 10624
Baltimore, Maryland 21285-0624
USA

www.brookespublishing.com

Typeset by Barton Matheson Willse & Worthington, Baltimore, Maryland.
Manufactured in the United States of America by
Versa Press, Inc., East Peoria, Illinois.

The individuals described in this book are composites, pseudonyms, or fictional accounts
based on actual experiences. Individuals' names have been changed and identifying details
have been altered to protect confidentiality.

Supported in part by the Institute of Education Sciences, U.S. Department of Education,
through Grant R305A060021 to the University of Virginia. However, the content does not
necessarily reflect the position of the U.S. Department of Education, and no official
endorsement should be inferred.

Library of Congress Cataloging-in-Publication Data
National Center for Research on Early Childhood Education. Leadership Symposium
(1st : 2007 : Washington, D.C.)
   The promise of pre-K / edited by Robert C. Pianta and Carollee Howes ; with invited
contributors.
       p. cm. — (NCRECE series ; v. 1)
   Papers originally presented at the National Center for Research on Early Childhood Edu-
cation first Annual Leadership Symposium, which was held in Washington, DC in February
of 2007.
   Includes bibliographical references and index.
   ISBN-13: 978-1-59857-033-5 (pbk.)
   ISBN-10: 1-59857-033-1 (pbk.)
   1. Education, Preschool—United States—Congresses. I. Pianta, Robert C. II. Howes,
Carollee. III. Title. IV. Series.

   LB1140.23.N375 2009
   372.210973—dc22   2009006879

British Library Cataloguing in Publication data are available from the British Library.

2012   2011   2010   2009

10   9   8   7   6   5   4   3   1

Contents

Series Preface vii
About the Editors ix
About the Contributors xi
Foreword *Richard M. Clifford* xiii
Preface xv
Acknowledgments. xxi

Section I   National-Level Concerns

Chapter 1   An Overview of Prekindergarten Policy in
the United States: Program Governance,
Eligibility, Standards, and Finance
*W. Steven Barnett, Allison H. Friedman, Jason T. Hustedt,
and Judi Stevenson-Boyd* 3

Chapter 2   Assessing the School Readiness Needs
of a State
Thomas Schultz 31

Chapter 3   Models for Financing State-Supported
Prekindergarten Programs
Anne W. Mitchell 51

Chapter 4   Comparing Universal and Targeted
Prekindergarten Programs
*Aryn M. Dotterer, Margaret Burchinal, Donna M. Bryant,
Diane M. Early, and Robert C. Pianta* 65

Section II   Implementation at the State Level

Chapter 5   Research Evidence About Program Dosage
and Student Achievement: Effective Public
Prekindergarten Programs in Maryland and
Louisiana
Craig T. Ramey, Sharon Landesman Ramey,
and Billy R. Stokes................................. 79

Chapter 6   Georgia's Prekindergarten Program:
Bright from the Start
Marsha H. Moore................................ 107

Chapter 7   North Carolina's More at Four
Prekindergarten Program: A Case Study of
Funding versus Quality and Other Issues in
Large-Scale Implementation
Carolyn T. Cobb................................ 123

Chapter 8   Implementing Large-Scale Prekindergarten
Initiatives: Lessons from New York
Moncrieff Cochran............................... 145

Chapter 9   Emerging Issues in Prekindergarten
Programs
Youngok Jung, Carollee Howes, and Robert C. Pianta..... 169

Index... 177

Series Preface

The National Center for Research on Early Childhood Education (NCRECE) series on the future of early childhood education addresses key topics related to improving the quality of early childhood education in the United States. Each volume is a culmination of presentations and discussions taking place during the annual NCRECE Leadership Symposium, which brings together leaders and stakeholders in the field to discuss and synthesize the current knowledge about prominent issues that affect the educational experiences and outcomes of young children. Most important, it is the aim of these symposia, and the related series volumes, to be forward-looking, identifying nascent topics that have the potential for improving the quality of early childhood education and then defining, analyzing, and charting conceptual, policy, practice, and research aims for the future. Topics to be addressed in subsequent volumes include the nature and quality of publicly funded preschool programs and the integration of Quality Rating Systems, early childhood competencies, and models of professional development.

The series is designed to stimulate critical thinking around these key topics and to help inform future research agendas. The series should be of interest to a broad range of researchers, policy makers, teacher educators, and practitioners.

Robert C. Pianta, Ph.D.
Carollee Howes, Ph.D.

About the Editors

Robert C. Pianta, Ph.D., is Dean of the Curry School of Education, Novartis US Foundation Professor of Education, Director of the National Center for Research on Early Childhood Education (NCRECE), and Director of the Center for Advanced Study in Teaching and Learning (CASTL) at the University of Virginia, Charlottesville. A former special education teacher, Dr. Pianta is particularly interested in how relationships with teachers and parents as well as classroom experiences can help improve outcomes for at-risk children and youth. Dr. Pianta is a principal investigator on several major grants including MyTeaching Partner, the Institute of Education Sciences Interdisciplinary Doctoral Training Program in Risk and Prevention, and the National Institute of Child Health and Human Development (NICHD) Study of Early Child Care and Youth Development (SECCYD). He was also a senior investigator for the National Center for Early Development and Learning (NCEDL), and served as Editor of the *Journal of School Psychology*. He is the author of more than 300 journal articles, chapters, and books in the areas of early childhood development, transition to school, school readiness, and parent–child and teacher–child relationships, including *School Readiness and the Transition to Kindergarten in the Era of Accountability* (with Martha J. Cox and Kyle L. Snow, Paul H. Brookes Publishing Co., 2007) and Classroom Assessment Scoring System (CLASS; with Karen M. La Paro and Bridget K. Hamre, Paul H. Brookes Publishing Co., 2008). Dr. Pianta consults regularly with federal agencies, foundations, and universities.

Carollee Howes, Ph.D., is Director of the Center for Improving Child Care Quality, Department of Education, and a professor of the applied developmental doctorate program at the University of California–Los Angeles (UCLA). Dr. Howes is an internationally recognized developmental psychologist focusing on children's social and emotional development. She has served as a principal investigator on a number of seminal studies in early child care and preschool education, including the National Child Care Staffing Study; the Family and Relative Care Study; the Cost, Quality, and Outcomes Study; and the National Study of Child Care in Low Income Families. Dr. Howes has been active in public policy for children and families in California as well as across the United States. Her research focuses on children's experiences in child care, their concurrent and long-term outcomes from child care experiences, and child care quality and efforts to improve child care quality. Dr. Howes is the author of *Teaching 4- to 8-Year-Olds: Literacy, Math, Multiculturalism, and Classroom Community* (2003, Paul H. Brookes Publishing Co.).

About the Contributors

W. Steven Barnett, Ph.D.
Board of Governors Professor
Director
National Institute for
Early Education Research
Rutgers University
120 Albany Street, Suite 500
New Brunswick, NJ 08901

Donna M. Bryant, Ph.D.
Senior Scientist
FPG Child Development Institute
The University of North Carolina at
    Chapel Hill
College Box 8180
Chapel Hill, NC 27599

Margaret Burchinal, Ph.D.
Senior Scientist
FPG Child Development Institute
The University of North Carolina at
    Chapel Hill
521 S. Greensboro
Carrboro, NC 27576

Carolyn T. Cobb, Ph.D.
Former Executive Director
NC Office of School Readiness
Department of Public Instruction
4701 Metcalf Drive
Raleigh, NC 27612

Moncrieff Cochran, Ph.D.
Professor Emeritus
Cornell University
Interim Director of Early Childhood
    Education
Eliot Pearson Department of Child
    Development
Tufts University
105 College Avenue
Medford, MA 02155

Aryn M. Dotterer, Ph.D.
Assistant Professor
Child Development and Family
    Studies
Purdue University
1200 W. State Street
West Lafayette, IN 47907

Diane M. Early, Ph.D.
Visiting Scholar
FPG Child Development Institute
The University of North Carolina at
    Chapel Hill
College Box 8180
Chapel Hill, NC 27599

Allison H. Friedman, Ed.M.
Research Project Coordinator
National Institute for Early
    Education Research
Rutgers University
120 Albany Street, Suite 500
New Brunswick, NJ 08901

Jason T. Hustedt, Ph.D.
Assistant Research Professor
National Institute for Early
    Education Research
Rutgers University
120 Albany St., Suite 500
New Brunswick, NJ 08901

Youngok Jung, M.Ed.
Doctoral Student
University of California–Los Angeles
8118 Math Sciences Building
Post Office Box 951521
Los Angeles, CA 90095

Anne W. Mitchell, M.S.
President, Early Childhood Policy
    Research
1250 Honey Hollow Road
Climax, NY 12042

Marsha H. Moore, B.S., MPA
Honorable Past Commissioner of
    Bright From the Start
North Georgia College and State
    University
President, Marsha H. Moore and
    Associates, Consulting and
    Training, Inc.
School of Education
82 College Circle
Dahlonega, GA 30597

Craig T. Ramey, Ph.D.
Distinguished Professor and
    Director, Center on Health and
    Education
Georgetown University
3700 Reservoir Road NW
Washington, DC 20057

Sharon Landesman Ramey, Ph.D.
Susan H. Mayer Professor of Child
    and Family Studies
    and Director, Georgetown
    University Center on Health and
    Education
Georgetown University
3700 Reservoir Road NW
Washington, DC 20057

Thomas Schultz, Ph.D.
Project Director, Early Education
    Accountability
Pew Charitable Trusts
1025 F Street NW, 9th Floor
Washington, D.C. 20004

Judi Stevenson-Boyd, Ed.M.
Research Project Coordinator
National Institute for Early
    Education Research
120 Albany Street, Suite 500
New Brunswick, NJ 08901

Billy R. Stokes, Ed.D.
Executive Director and
    Cecil J. Picard Endowed Fellow in
    Child Development
Cecil J. Picard Center for Child
    Development
University of Louisiana at Lafayette
220 Hebrard Boulevard
Lafayette, LA 70503

Foreword

The United States, like most of the industrialized countries of the world, is experiencing a major shift in the education and care provided to children prior to and entry into elementary school (Clifford & Crawford, 2009). Unlike many countries, the United States has a very complex and disjointed set of preschool and child care programs. Our federal government does not even collect data on many of these programs and is unable to fully describe the nature and extent of services to children; instead, it relies primarily on studies by public and privately funded researchers examining relatively small samples of the population in question.

In writing about early childhood services here in the United States for policy makers and service providers in other countries, I have referred to our nonsystem as much like parallel play that we see in young children (Clifford, 1995). Early in their development, young children play mostly by themselves, but occasionally bump into other children, which sometimes results in conflict. Here, we have had programs for young children operating very much like this. We have Head Start, child care centers, paid and public preschool programs (public, nonprofit, and for profit), and other informal types of services for children and their families prior to entry into kindergarten. These providers of services are funded in different ways, are governed and regulated by different parts and even by different levels of government, and view themselves as having different goals and purposes.

It appears that our set of service delivery providers may be maturing. Over the past two decades, prekindergarten (pre-K) programs, funded primarily through state and local education agencies, have emerged as a leading force in serving children in the year or two prior to entry into the mostly public K–12 education system. As documented in the chapters of this book, now more than a million children are in state-funded pre-K programs alone, with many more served in related programs. It appears that we are in the beginning stages of shifting to universal access to educationally oriented programs for 4-year-olds and possibly, in the longer term, to a similar situation for 3-year-olds as well. Other countries are already in or have experienced such a transition.

This book offers excellent insight into the current situation in the United States, with the best-available evidence regarding the services provided in pre-K programs, how programs are financed, and the outcomes that can be expected as a result of these emerging program types in our country. Once these programs are fully in place, it will be extremely difficult to change them in substantive ways, as evidenced by the failure of most K–12 school reform efforts. So, it is absolutely critical that we look objectively and thoroughly at what we are doing that works and doesn't work at this point in implementing pre-K so that we may make the best possible decision as we expand toward universal services. The editors and chapter authors are to be highly commended for their important contributions to this end.

Richard M. Clifford, Ph.D.
Senior Scientist
FPG Child Development Institute
The University of North Carolina at Chapel Hill

REFERENCES

Clifford, R.M., & Crawford, G.M. (Ed.) (2009). *Beginning school: U.S. policies in international perspective.* New York: Teachers College Press.
Clifford, R.M. (1995). Párhuzamosságok: Napközbeni kisgyermekellátás az Amerikai Egyesült Államokban [Public policy, public need, and varieties of non-parental child care]. In K. Mihály (Ed.), Napjaink Szociálpolitikai és Társadalmi Igénbyei a Kisgyermekek Napközbeni Ellátásában, Bölcsödék Országos Módszertani Intézete, *Budapest*, 62–75.

Preface

Half a century ago, American schools added a kindergarten year for our youngest children. Kindergarten was to be a gentle way of introducing children to the rigors of "real" school; it was to help children be ready for school. Kindergarten was not necessarily to be housed within the public schools.

We both have vivid memories of our pathways into school as young children. One of us (CH) has memories of her mother in the 1950s first organizing a parent cooperative kindergarten for her next-to-youngest child and then with other mothers, convincing the public school to incorporate this kindergarten, making it universal 3 years later. The youngest brother was in the first kindergarten class in their tiny rural public school. For the other editor (RP), the first day of school was the first day in first grade in a new town. There was no kindergarten in the prior community in which he lived as a 5-year-old, and on moving, he started school as many children did in the 1960s and (believe it or not) many still do today, by entering first grade. Clearly, society has invested in—since the pathway blazed by CH's mother—a graduated, developmentally supportive system of early education aimed at fostering social and emergent academic competencies that serve children well as they move into the elementary grades.

The same rationale—investing in early education settings that support children's readiness for school—is the promise of the current pre-K movement. We characterize this as a promise for a good reason; advocates, scientists, and policy makers are aligned in identifying early education programs, such as publicly funded pre-K, as an investment that will pay dividends to society, and to individuals, a promise. More often than not, this promise is framed as even more relevant to the futures of children reared in less-advantaged homes and communities. Perhaps due to increasing academic accountability of early elementary school, and perhaps due to the detrimental effects of poverty and dis-crimination, our poorest children, often children of color, tend to strug-gle in their earliest school experiences and fail to catch up to their more advantaged peers (Winsler et al., 2008). The promise of pre-K is all the more important for these young citizens.

Despite considerable public investment in pre-K programs and the evident interests of the public schools in their success, pre-K programs are not necessarily within the public school system. Pre-K programs are funded through diverse sources, and funding often attempts to lever-age capacity in existing preschool and early childhood education offer-ings. Thus, adding a pre-K year is a decision made at a state, county, or in some cases individual school district level. As a result, pre-K pro-grams are stunningly diverse, varying on dimensions including chil-dren served, location of the program, length of the day, staffing, and curriculum and programming (Clifford et al., 2005). It is indeed the case that society now *expects* early childhood education to deliver on its promise of fostering social and emergent academic competencies that, in turn, assist young children in adjusting to the demands of "real school." With publicly funded pre-K programs, the most recent and most compelling examples of this expectation, however, approaches to building a system of effective programs for 4-year-olds are so varied and so new that we are only beginning to understand how to do this well. It is the aim of this volume, which is a synthesis of conversations and presentations at a 2007 symposium sponsored by the National Cen-ter for Research on Early Childhood Education (NCRECE), to take stock in the promise of pre-K by describing and evaluating the organizational diversity embedded within this first generation of publicly funded pre-K programs that have operated at scale since the mid-1990s.

The volume is divided into two sections: 1) national concerns, and 2) implementation at the state level. Despite the promise of pre-K, the authors of the chapters in the national level concerns section do not paint an optimistic picture. Although there is a great deal of activity at the federal level in the areas of designing standards for children's learning and for program standards in the areas of assessment and ac-countability, there is no national level funding for implementation of programs. In general, pre-K programs are not uniformly of high qual-ity nor do they have high impacts on children's outcomes. States are designing pre-K program initiatives and program standards and are providing funding in many different ways. At a state level, much is promised for these programs, but rarely is a program universally im-plemented even if promised to be universal, and rarely are programs funded at adequate levels. Most state-level programs do not have a dedicated funding stream. And the universal versus targeted programs do not provide different experiences for children or impacts on children's gains in pre-academic skills.

The National Institute for Early Education Research conducts a yearly survey of states, and Chapter 1 rests on the 2006–2007 results. Barnett and colleagues report that in 2006–2007, 38 states and the District of Columbia funded pre-K programs that served more than 1 million children and spent more than $3.7 billion on these programs—a sixfold increase since 1980. Describing the modal pre-K program is difficult, however. Most programs intend to educate 4-year-olds who are typically developing and who are in classrooms at least 2 days per week. However, variations in state goals for programs, such as education, child care for working parents, and parenting skills, contribute to program differences between states. There is also large variation in collaborative governance and in whether programs must be located in public schools. For example, only 68% of states locate their pre-K programs administratively within state departments of education. States often have more than one program, and there is considerable variation within and across states on eligibility (although programs are primarily for low-income families), programs standards, ancillary services, and in-state monitoring and accountability practices.

In Chapter 2, Schultz describes the policy context for early childhood programs and examines how disparate federal and state agencies implement varied approaches to standards-based assessments of programs and children. The policy contexts that argue for pre-K programs are the achievement gap, brain research, and cost-benefits of early childhood education (ECE). The existing federal funding incentives for pre-K programs are for learning standards and assessment rather than for services and implementation. Policy makers expect early childhood programs to demonstrate their worth over and over again and in new and different ways. The chapter provides numerous state-level cases of child and program assessment and accountability.

Chapter 3 (Mitchell) focuses on how state preschool programs are funded. She discusses the revenue sources used by the states to fund preschool, raises questions and challenges about these different revenue generating methods, and assesses the outlook for preschool finance strategies in the next decade. The vast majority of states fund preschool with general revenue, but through a grant/contract method. These funds are in almost all cases inadequate to support quality services.

Dotterer and colleagues (Chapter 4) compare universal and targeted state pre-K programs using the Multi-State/Sweep data sets. These data sets describe child and classroom experiences and children's gains in preacademic skills in state pre-K programs. The states represented in the data set all had pre-K programs that were funded publicly and operating at-scale. This chapter presents findings that variability *within* the universal and targeted programs is far greater than *between* the two types of programs. There are inconsistent differences between the two types of programs in classroom characteristics. Although universal programs had longer classes, teachers with more years of education, a greater proportion of white children per class, and a lower proportion of children from low-income families, observed classroom quality was higher in targeted programs. Neither universal nor targeted programs were consistently related to greater child gains during the pre-K experience.

Section II describes implementation at the state level. Chapter 5 (Ramey, Ramey, and Stokes) describes state-level pre-K programs in Maryland and Louisiana. Pre-K programs in Georgia are described by Moore in Chapter 6 and in North Carolina by Cobb (Chapter 7). Finally, in Chapter 8, Cochran describes New York's pre-K program. Each of these chapters provides a rich description of program implementation.

Chapter 8 raises a set of issues wider than program descriptions, however. Cochran argues that pre-K programs have to be viewed within the context of the social and economic realities of American family and community life and an encompassing infrastructure, which includes health and safety-oriented regulation and support by public agencies, economic subsidies to families and providers, the professional preparation and training of caregivers, and both policy and program oversight by appropriate state departments. As Cochran notes, state pre-K program success at finding eligible children, getting them into appropriate settings, and providing them with experiences through which they learn what is needed for success in kindergarten will depend heavily on "the extent to which they are designed to recognize and acknowledge existing systems of family support and utilize those systems to attain their policy goal."

From a systems point of view, states have conceptualized pre-K goals as part of the formal K–12 education framework, yet have built pre-K programs outside of state education systems for which state departments of education have responsibility. For the most part, programs are not part of state education funding, monitoring, standards, or accountability infrastructure. From a systems point of view, pre-K programs look more like child care or early childhood education intervention programs. Unlike in K–12, pre-K program participation is not a family entitlement. Moreover, the ages of the children move pre-K programs into the arenas of conflicting cultural ideas about who is responsible for young children, what the role of the state is in serving young children, and the needs of working parents versus nonworking parents.

We believe that taking stock of pre-K by relying on a corpus of solid evidence gathered as programs emerged and scaled over the last decade is critical to advancing the scope, quality, and effectiveness of what could be an important asset for individual children and families, for communities, and for the nation. Clearly, the evidence supports the promise of pre-K in terms of its benefits, yet at the same time indicates quite strongly that for too many children, families, and communities, the promise of pre-K is not being fulfilled. As one of us (RP) has argued, although for many, "school" quite clearly starts at age 3, the rather haphazard funding, monitoring, and programmatic organization and infrastructure supporting efforts to foster young children's developmental competencies in various settings undermines the capacity to deliver on that promise. Yet, it is precisely this loose organization and infrastructure that affords us the opportunity to learn from variation and to experiment with novel policies and program options, and by so doing, to lead in the design and structuring of educational settings that really work for children and youth. As just one example, Mitchell's chapter describes the concept of "Quality Rating and Improvement Systems," frameworks that states are building to monitor the quality of education programs and link monitoring to incentives and improvements for which teachers and administrators are held accountable. There is no question that applying this type of policy and program development framework to a system of private and public programs provides an opportunity for early childhood education to develop and test ideas that are far ahead of the K–12 accountability approaches.

As this book went to press, many of the policy and financial conditions that shape the nature and effectiveness of pre-K programs and early childhood education more generally are changing rapidly. President Obama has made early childhood education a priority in his administration, but at the same time it is not clear exactly what his plans are for enhancing early learning and development opportunities for our young citizens. The economic stimulus package signed into law in February 2009 includes funds for Head Start, data system infrastructure, employment opportunities and workforce training, and health care for poor children. On the docket are efforts to develop new ways to improve teacher performance and build better assessments and standards that reflect knowledge and skills both broader and deeper than those currently assessed by state tests.

Clearly, the attention and resources being devoted to bolstering education, improving the health and well-being of families and young children, and addressing economic challenges through training and workforce development all have profound implications for pre-K and early child education more generally. Every one of these potential futures builds on the frameworks described in this book. Moreover, as policy makers debate these futures, the lessons presented in this volume can be extraordinarily helpful so that we can make the most of what is likely to be an unprecedented investment in young children that can return benefits to them, their families, and their communities.

We are convinced that the promise of pre-K, strikingly evident in the lives of many children, can be more fully realized through careful analysis of evidence and the kind of thoughtful policy making and program development described in the chapters to follow.

REFERENCES

Clifford, R.M., Barbarin, O., Chang, F., Early, D., Bryant, D., Howes, C., et al. (2005). What is pre-kindergarten: Characteristics of public pre-kindergarten programs. *Applied Developmental Science, 9*(3), 126–134.

Winsler, A., Trana, H., Hartmana, S.C., Madiganc, A.L., Manfrab, L., & Bleiker, C. (2008). School readiness gains made by ethnically diverse children in poverty attending center-based childcare and public school pre-kindergarten programs. *Early Childhood Research Quarterly, 23*, 314–329.

Acknowledgments

We recognize that this book would not be possible without the dedication and hard work of the very wide and diverse range of people working in the field of early childhood education to support the development of young children. Scholars, child care professionals, teachers, parents, and administrators have all contributed to the "promise of pre-K" and should be remembered and appreciated daily for their work.

We also acknowledge the support of the Institute of Education Sciences, U.S. Department of Education, through Grant R305A060021 to the University of Virginia. We have been fortunate to have received support for the work involved in putting this volume together, and we especially recognize our program officer, Caroline Ebanks, for her help and advice.

To our friend and colleague, Dick Clifford,
whose dedication to the field of early childhood education
and to the quality of teachers' and children's
experiences helped make possible
the promise of pre-K for so many children

National-Level Concerns

Chapter 1

An Overview of Prekindergarten Policy in the United States

Program Governance, Eligibility, Standards, and Finance

W. Steven Barnett, Allison H. Friedman,
Jason T. Hustedt, and Judi Stevenson-Boyd

The education of young children has dramatically changed over the past several decades, and state prekindergarten (pre-K) has played an important role in that change. In 1960, approximately 10% of the nation's 3- and 4-year-old children were enrolled in any type of classroom (Barnett & Yarosz, 2007). Less than a half century later, most children enroll in a preschool classroom prior to kindergarten. In 2005, 74% of children attended a preschool program the year prior to kindergarten, and 51% entered a program classroom 2 years prior to kindergarten (Belfield, 2008). One of the accompanying changes has been the growth of state-funded pre-K (Barnett & Yarosz, 2007). To some extent, this growth is a response to increased public demand for preschool education, and some children would otherwise attend private programs if state pre-K was not available. State pre-K, however, enrolls many children from low-income families that might find private programs unaffordable. Although it is difficult to judge how much state pre-K has increased enrollment (and not just shifted enrollment from the private to the public sector), it is clear that state pre-K has altered the early education landscape and changed the educational experiences of young children across the country.

This chapter provides an overview of state-funded pre-K programs, with particular attention to enrollment, program standards and policies, and funding. In the mid-1960s, states began to create programs for children in poverty or otherwise determined to be at high risk of poor academic progress, but only six states and the District of Columbia funded preschool programs prior to 1980 (Mitchell, 2001). By 1988, this number had increased to 27 states plus the District of Columbia, with an enrollment of about 290,000 children. State spending totaled about $190 million per year (Mitchell, 2001). Moving forward to 2000, at least 34 states and the District of Columbia funded pre-K programs, enrolled approximately 740,000 3- and 4-year-olds, and spent more than $2 billion annually (Bryant et al., 2002). The most recent figures we have are for 2006–2007, and in that year, 38 states and the District of Columbia funded pre-K programs that served more than 1 million children. State governments spent more than $3.7 billion on these programs (Barnett, Hustedt, Friedman, Boyd, & Ainsworth, 2007).

DATA SOURCE

To describe the status of state pre-K, we rely on data collected by the latest of five annual surveys of state pre-K programs conducted by the National Institute for Early Education Research (Barnett et al., 2007). This survey consists of 64 primary questions, although there are many subparts to questions. The survey is administered over the Internet using a computer-aided design that facilitates collecting accurate information. Typically, the survey is completed by the state administrator most directly responsible for the program. These state administrators have worked with us to construct the survey. Responses are reviewed for possible errors, ambiguities, and inconsistencies, which are then discussed with the respondents to clarify their answers. After we have compiled and interpreted all of the answers, the resulting data set for each state is reviewed by the respondents. In addition, responses are checked against public information and subject to verification by key informants in the states. Only a small part of the data collected can be discussed here, and readers who seek further information about the survey and its results are referred to the complete report (Barnett et al., 2007).

Any discussion of state pre-K programs must begin with a definition. States fund a wide range of preschool programs that are expected to contribute to children's early learning and development. The primary purposes of these programs vary and include educating young children, providing child care for working parents, and improving parenting. In addition, some states supplement the federal Head Start program. All of these efforts have a goal of improving children's learning and development, and the distinctions between these programs can become quite blurred. We do not consider all of them to be state public education programs, however.

We define *state pre-K* as programs funded and administered by the state with a primary goal of educating 4-year-olds who are typically developing and who are in classrooms at least 2 days per week. A program's age range may include younger and older children. State pre-K programs can include children with disabilities, but if this population is a program's primary focus, then it is considered a special education program and not state pre-K. Child care programs that determine eligibility based on maternal employment status and that do not guarantee children at least 1 school year of services are not included. State programs that operate through supplements to the federal Head Start program are counted as state pre-K if they are designed to increase the number of children and the state has some role in administration of the program. Minor state supplements that enhance quality or otherwise support Head Start without any significant increase in enrollment are not counted. In 2006–2007, 38 states and the District of Columbia funded 50 different programs that met this definition of state pre-K. Tables 1.1 and 1.2 summarize much of the information discussed in this chapter. The data is presented individually for each program but is summarized across programs for each state (e.g., total spending) where appropriate.

GOVERNANCE

Governance of state pre-K is more complex than is the governance of public provision of K–12 education. Table 1.1 identifies the state agencies responsible for administering each program. In 26 states (68%), pre-K programs are solely administered by the state Department of Education. Other states administer their pre-K programs entirely through other agencies, including new agencies specifically created to administer pre-K, departments of human services, and governors' offices. Some states jointly administer one pre-K program across as many as three agencies or have two or more pre-K programs each in a different agency. Joint administration by education and human services agencies is the most common form of collaboration. Many states fund and administer programs directly through a grants process that is separate from the

Table 1.1. State pre-K program administration, income eligibility, and enrollment by number and percentage served

State (program)[a]	Year program began	Auspice	Percent in public schools (%)	Income eligibility	Number served at 4 years old	Percent of state's 4-year-olds (%)	Number served at 3 years old	Percent of state's 3-year-olds (%)
Alabama	2000	Other[d]	49	None	1,062	2	0	0
Arizona	1991	DOE	90	185% FPL	5,076	5	0	0
Arkansas	1991	Collab	57	200% FPL	8,148	21	4,068	11
California	1965	DOE	74	75% SMI[i]	56,254	11	26,318	5
Colorado	1988	DOE	57	185% FPL[i]	9,784	15	2,084	3
Connecticut	1997	Collab	24	75% SMI[i]	6,625	16	1,907	4
Delaware	1994	DOE	46	100% FPL[i]	843	8	0	0
Florida	2005	Collab	21	None	124,390	57	0	0
Georgia	1995	DOECE	43	None	74,155	53	0	0
Illinois	1985	DOE	NR	None	47,108	27	32,711	18
Iowa	1989	DOE	56	130% FPL[i]	1,515	4	518	1
Kansas	1998	DOE	100	130% FPL[i]	5,971	16	0	0
Kentucky	1990	DOE	NR	150% FPL	15,808	29	5,815	11
Louisiana	—	—	92	—	14,543	24	0	0
LA 8(g)	1988	DOE	100	None	3,327	6	0	0
LA LA4	1992	DOE	100	185% FPL	10,063	17	0	0
LA NSECD	2001	Gov office	0	200% FPL	1,153	2	0	0
Maine	1983	DOE	89	None	2,263	16	0	0
Maryland	1979	DOE	96	185% FPL	24,825	34	849	1
Massachusetts	1985	DOECE	16	100% SMI[i]	8,047	10	7,153	9
Michigan	1985	DOE	80	250% FPL[i]	21,801	17	0	0
Minnesota	Unknown	DOE	0	100% FPL[i]	1,245	2	864	1
Missouri	1998	DOE	79	None	3,262	4	1,710	2

Nebraska	1992	DOE	70	185% FPL	977	4	496	2
Nevada	2002	DOE	80	None	799	2	140	0
New Jersey	—	—	44	—	28,240	25	17,259	15
NJ Abbott	1999	DOE	34	None	20,521	18	17,117	15
NJ ECPA	1996	DOE	96	None	7,194	6	142	0.1
NJ ELLI	2004	DOE	72	185% FPL	525	0	0	0
New Mexico	—	—	40	—	2,497	9	242	1
NM CDP	1991	CYFD	8	None	303	1	242	1
NM SPK	2005	DOE and CYFD	50	None	2,194	8	0	0
New York	—	—	53	—	83,505	35	1,155	0
NY TPK	1966	DOE	100	185% FPL[i]	18,733	8	1,155	0
NY UPK	1997	DOE	39	None	64,772	27	0	0
North Carolina	2001	DOE	54	75% SMI[j]	17,961	15	0	0
Ohio	1990	Collab	82	200% FPL	4,979	13	1,870	1
Oklahoma	1980	DOE	88	None	34,375	68	0	0
Oregon	1987	DOE	20	100% FPL[i]	2,235	5	1,203	3
Pennsylvania	—	—	100[e]	—	10,329	7	3,255	2
PA EABG	2004	Collab	100	None	3,341	2	962	1
PA HSSAP	2004	Collab	NR	100% FPL[i]	3,487	2	2,293	2
PA SBPK	1993[b]	Collab	100	None	3,501	2	0	0
South Carolina	—	—	100[f]	—	21,367	38	349	1
SC 4K	1984	DOE	100	185% FPL[i]	18,126	32	349	1
SC CDEPP	2006	Collab	NR	185% FPL	3,241	6	0	0
Tennessee	1998	DOE	86	185% FPL[i]	12,293	16	753	1
Texas	1985	DOE	NR	185% FPL[i]	170,313	45	16,925	4
Vermont	—	—	57[g]	—	2,908	45	1,028	16
VT ADM	1987[c]	Collab	NR	None	2,358	36	679	10

(continued)

7

Table 1.1. *(continued)*

State (program)[a]	Year program began	Auspice	Percent in public schools (%)	Income eligibility	Number served at 4 years old	Percent of state's 4-year-olds (%)	Number served at 3 years old	Percent of state's 3-year-olds (%)
VT EEI	1987	Collab	57	185% FPL[i]	550	8	349	5
Virginia	1995	DOE	NR	None	12,501	13	0	0
Washington	1985	DEL	59	110% FPL[i]	4,671	6	1,163	1
West Virginia	1983	Collab	NR	None	9,586	46	1,073	5
Wisconsin	—	—	0[h]	—	24,878	36	550	1
WI 4K	1873	DOE	NR	None	24,097	35	0	0
WI HdSt	Unknown	DOE	0	100% FPL[i]	781	1	550	1
District of Columbia	1960s	Public schools	69	None	3,170	49	1,757	27
Total					880,309	22	133,215	4

[a]Program names are listed for states with multiple programs.

[b]Estimated as the PA Kindergarten for 4-Year-Olds, now called PA School-Based Pre-K, which was started in the early 1990s.

[c]In place since 1987, but formalized with the passage of Act 60 in 2000, Act 68 in 2004, and Act 62 in 2007.

[d]Office of School Readiness within the Department of Children's Affairs.

[e]Includes only PA EABG and PA SBPK programs.

[f]Includes only SC 4K.

[g]Includes only VT EEI.

[h]Includes only WI HdSt.

[i]Some exceptions allowed.

[j]There is no income eligibly requirement for the MA UPK program.

Key: NR = not reported; DOE = department of education; Collab = collaboration; DOECE = department of early childhood education; DEL = department of early learning; CYFD = children, youth, and families department; FPL = federal poverty level; SMI = state median income

8

Table 1.2. State pre-K program structure and expenditures

State (program)[1]	Length of day	Teachers required to have a bachelor's degree	Teacher specialized training required	Staff–child ratio	State spending	State per-child spending	Total per-child spending	Cost of quality Half-day estimate	Cost of quality Full-day estimate
Alabama	FD	Yes	Yes	1:9	$5,369,898	$5,056	$6,931	$3,837	$7,033
Arizona	PD	No	No	1:10	$12,077,496	$2,379	$2,379	$4,012	$7,354
Arkansas	FD	Lead teachers	Yes	1:10	$58,775,935	$4,316	$7,194	$3,604	$6,607
California	PD, FD	No	Yes	1:8	$295,104,549	$3,486	$3,486	$4,801	$8,801
Colorado	PD	No	Yes	1:8	$28,965,099	$2,047	$3,194	$4,200	$7,699
Connecticut	ED, FD, PD	Public	Yes	1:10	$65,755,670	$7,707	$9,577	$4,816	$8,828
Delaware	PD	No	Yes	1:10	$5,685,800	$6,745	$6,745	$4,454	$8,164
Florida	PD (FD summer)	Summer	Summer	1:10	$290,406,902	$2,335	$2,335	$4,055	$7,432
Georgia	FD	No	Yes	1:10	$309,579,383	$4,111	$4,114	$4,300	$7,882
Illinois	PD	Yes	Yes	1:10	$283,020,000	$3,322	$3,322	$4,520	$8,286
Iowa	DL	Public	Public	No limit	$6,800,000	$2,966	$8,966	$3,667	$6,722
Kansas	PD	Yes	No	1:10	$15,500,000	$2,596	$2,596	$3,705	$6,792
Kentucky	PD	Yes	Yes	1:10	$75,127,000	$3,474	$4,637	$3,868	$7,091
Louisiana	—	—	—	—	$74,719,738	$5,138	$5,275	$3,797	$6,960
LA 8(g)	FD	Yes	No	1:10	$12,494,431	$3,755	$3,755	$3,797	$6,960
LA LA4	FD	Yes	No	1:10	$55,000,000	$5,466	$5,664	$3,797	$6,960
LA NSECD	ED	Yes	No	1:10	$7,225,307	$6,267	$6,267	$3,797	$6,960
Maine	DL	Yes	No	1:15	$4,247,915	$1,877	$3,575	$3,656	$6,702
Maryland	PD, FD	Yes	Yes	1:10	$74,910,729	$2,918	$6,132	$4,735	$8,680
Massachusetts	DL	Public	No	1:10	$65,816,357	$3,681	$3,998	$4,765	$8,735
Michigan	PD, FD	Yes	Yes	1:8	$90,850,000	$4,167	$4,167	$4,275	$7,837

(continued)

Table 1.2. *(continued)*

State (program)[1]	Length of day	Teachers required to have a bachelor's degree	Teacher specialized training required	Staff-child ratio	State spending	State per-child spending	Total per-child spending	Cost of quality Half-day estimate	Cost of quality Full-day estimate
Minnesota	PD	No	Yes	1:10[2]	$19,100,000	$7,251	$7,251	$4,233	$7,758
Missouri	PD, FD	Yes	Yes	1:10	$12,631,001	$2,540	$2,540	$3,961	$7,261
Nebraska	DL	Yes	Yes	1:10	$3,677,596	$2,273	$6,888	$3,704	$6,789
Nevada	DL	Yes	Yes	1:10[3]	$3,152,479	$3,322	$3,322	$4,357	$7,986
New Jersey	—	—	—	—	$477,466,737	$10,494	$10,494	$4,947	$9,068
NJ Abbott	ED	Yes	Yes	2:15	$445,309,362	$11,831	$11,831	$4,947	$9,068
NJ ECPA	PD, FD	Yes	Yes	1:25	$30,000,000	$4,089	$4,089	$4,947	$9,068
NJ ELLI	PD, FD	Yes	Yes	2:20	$2,157,375	$4,109	$4,109	$4,947	$9,068
New Mexico	—	—	—	—	$8,149,234	$2,975	$2,975	$3,841	$7,040
NM CDP	FD	Public	No	1:12	$1,413,666	$2,594	$2,594	$3,841	$7,040
NM SPK	PD	Yes	Yes	1:10	$6,735,568	$3,070	$3,070	$3,841	$7,040
New York	—	—	—	—	$292,413,929	$3,454	$3,454	$4,899	$8,980
NY TPK	PD	Yes	Yes	1:9	$47,808,117	$2,404	$2,404	$4,899	$8,980
NY UPK	PD, FD	Public	Yes	1:9	$244,605,812	$3,776	$3,776	$4,899	$8,980
North Carolina	FD	Public	Yes	1:9	$84,635,709	$4,712	$7,401	$4,134	$7,577
Ohio	PD	No	Yes	1:14[4]	$19,002,195	$2,515	$2,515	$4,134	$7,577
Oklahoma	PD, FD	Yes	Yes	1:10	$118,003,070	$3,433	$6,731	$4,194	$7,688
Oregon	PD	Public	Yes	1:10[2]	$27,000,000	$7,853	$7,853	$3,682	$6,749
Pennsylvania	—	—	—	—	$55,648,261	$5,519	$5,519	$4,173	$7,650
PA EABG	DL	Public	Public	1:10	$15,648,261	$3,637	$3,637	$4,002	$7,335
PA HSSAP	DL	No	Yes	2:17	$40,000,000	$6,920	$6,920	$4,173	$7,650
PA SBPK	PD, FD	Yes	No	1:10	NR	NR	NR	$4,173	$7,650

South Carolina	—	—	—	$34,747,844		$2,702	$3,947	$7,235
SC 4K	PD	Yes	1:10	$21,832,678	$1,600	$2,477	$3,947	$7,235
SC CDEPP	FD	Public	1:10	$12,915,166	$1,182	$3,985	$3,947	$7,235
Tennessee	FD	Yes	1:10[3]	$55,000,000	$3,985	$5,295	$4,025	$7,378
Texas	PD	Yes	No limit	$532,687,148	$4,168	$2,836	$4,333	$7,942
Vermont	—	—	—	$10,206,693	$2,836	$2,577	$3,704	$6,789
VT ADM	PD	Yes	1:10	$8,904,484	$2,577	$2,932	$3,704	$6,789
VT EEI	PD	Yes	1:8	$1,302,209	$2,932	$1,409	$3,704	$6,789
Virginia	PD, FD	Public	1:9	$44,713,471	$1,409	$5,633	$4,740	$8,689
Washington	DL	No	1:9	$35,083,000	$3,577	$6,010	$4,548	$8,336
West Virginia	DL	Pre-K	1:10	$47,338,791	$6,010	$6,724	$3,708	$6,796
Wisconsin	—	—	—	$81,012,500	$4,441	$4,665	$4,156	$7,618
WI 4K	PD	Yes	DL	$73,800,000	$3,178	$4,635	$4,156	$7,618
WI HdSt	DL	Public	1:10[2]	$7,212,500	$3,063	$5,185	$4,156	$7,618
Washington DC	FD	Yes	1:10[5]	NR	$5,185	NR	$5,380	$9,862
Total				$3,724,382,129	$3,642	$4,134		

[1] Program names are listed for states with multiple programs.

[2] Staff–child ratio for 3-year-olds is 2:17.

[3] Staff–child ratio for 3-year-olds is 1:8.

[4] Staff–child ratio for 3-year-olds is 1:12.

[5] Staff–child ratio for 3-year-olds is 2:15.

Key: DL = Determined locally; FD = Full day; PD = Part day; ED = Extended day; NR = Not reported

K–12 regular education system. These grants are sometimes competitive. Three states (Connecticut, Florida, and Vermont) have regional or local councils that share in the administration of pre-K. Some state pre-K programs are funded and administered through the public schools much like kindergarten (e.g., Oklahoma, the Wisconsin 4K initiative).

Governance of state pre-K is further complicated by the public–private delivery systems employed by most programs. With the exception of Kansas, every state allows private providers (often including Head Start grantees) to participate in one or more of its state programs, typically through direct grants from the state. In 11 states, only public school districts are eligible to receive funds directly, and the participating districts are permitted to contract with private providers. As noted earlier, a few states use other intermediate agencies. The percentage of state pre-K children served in the public schools varies across the states from 0% to 100%. Although most children in state pre-K are served in the public schools, the percentage served in private programs is large and growing. In nine states, more than half of the state pre-K children are enrolled in private programs. These nine include several with relatively large enrollments—Georgia, Florida, New Jersey, and New York.

The private providers of state pre-K include for-profits, nonprofits, religious organizations (although not every state permitting private provision allows organizations with religious affiliations), and Head Start grantees. Private programs have executives of various sorts as well as proprietors, stockholders, and various types of boards that oversee policies and operations. Some are part of larger multipurpose agencies or chains. Head Start grantees have their own governance structure locally (e.g., parent councils) and are subject to federal Head Start regulations and oversight. How much choice parents have and the extent to which they (and others) participate in governance varies greatly across (and, perhaps, even within) the different types of public and private arrangements. Issues that arise from these arrangements are the loss of local democratic governance when local school districts are bypassed, the potential for conflicts of interest to arise when local boards of education or other school officials award contracts to private pre-K providers, how bargaining and competition might be used to improve outcomes or reduce costs, and the potential for inequalities to arise if parents do not have equal access to all of the public and private providers.

ELIGIBILITY AND ENROLLMENT

Across the nation, just over 3% of all 3-year-olds and nearly 22% of all 4-year-olds were enrolled in state pre-K in 2006–2007. Behind this average is a tremendous variation in enrollments among the states, however. Twelve states did not fund a state pre-K program at all, and most of the 38 states with state-funded pre-K programs focused on enrolling children who are at risk or who have special needs.

Age is the most common eligibility criterion, and most programs limit eligibility to children who will turn 4 by the birth date cutoff for kindergarten entry. Nearly half of the states permit enrollment at age 3. Most states do not allow any exceptions to the age requirements, but some permit older children with disabilities to attend pre-K, and a few leave exceptions to local discretion. California permits up to 10% of the children enrolled to be over age.

As shown in Table 1.1, most states set an income limit for pre-K eligibility, and most often this is the federal poverty level (FPL) or some multiple of that level, although in some states it is a percentage of the state median income (SMI). This means test (income-based eligibility criterion) may not apply to all children who enroll. For example, Connecticut requires that 60% of the children served have family incomes below 75% of the SMI, and North Carolina requires that 80% fall below 75% of the SMI. Sixteen states and the District of Columbia (44%) allow children to participate regardless of income. Although some of these states limit eligibility with other risk criteria, others leave the specific risk criteria for eligibility to local discretion. Yet, other states have "universal" programs but continue to prioritize applicants for limited spaces based on risk or need so long as funding is inadequate to enroll all applicants. New Jersey is unusual because it allows universal access at age 3 in 31 designated school districts that have high concentrations of children from low-income families. Other states, however, have universal enrollment in districts that choose to participate in the state program. Risk factors other than income that are commonly used to determine eligibility include disability or developmental delay, low parental education level, non–English-speaking family members, teen parents, and homelessness or unstable housing.

The states that have committed to providing access for all 4-year-olds are Florida, Georgia, Illinois, Iowa (after 2006–2007), New York, Oklahoma, and West Virginia. In addition, Illinois has committed to provide access to all children at age 3. These states vary greatly in their enrollment and their pace toward achieving the goal of universal access. Only Oklahoma and, perhaps, Florida can say that they have fulfilled that commitment. In Oklahoma, nearly every school district offers pre-K, and the state has a 68% enrollment rate at age 4. When children in special education and Head Start programs are taken into account, Oklahoma's enrollment in public preschool education at age 4 is 90%. Florida's voters amended their state constitution to require that high-quality pre-K be offered to all 4-year-olds. Although the state has rapidly increased enrollments, it is still not truly universal, and the data on standards and funding in Tables 1.1 and 1.2 raise questions about quality. Lack of quality may be one reason that Florida's enrollment is not higher. Georgia's universal program appears to be limited by the amount of money available from the state lottery and the willingness of providers to offer a program with the funding level provided by the state. Combined enrollments across state pre-K, special education, and Head Start programs likely top 70% in Florida and West Virginia and 60% in Georgia.

Another eight states have at least one program that is, in theory, open to all children in participating districts. This brings up to 15 the number of states with a pre-K program that does not limit eligibility by income. Seven of these ranked in the top 10 for enrollment. Not all of these states, however, have appropriated sufficient funds to ensure that every applicant to a program can enroll. Five states with programs that do not use income as a criterion for eligibility enrolled less than 10% of their 4-year-olds in state pre-K (New Mexico, Pennsylvania, Missouri, Nevada, and Alabama). In addition, Iowa has just initiated its universal program, and its progress toward universal access remains to be seen.

Expulsion from state pre-K is an issue related to eligibility and enrollment and was raised as a concern by a survey of teachers in state pre-K (Gilliam, 2005; Gilliam & Marchesseault, 2004). Although teachers in that survey were not asked about expulsion per se, and some cases reported by teachers may have been transfers from one classroom or program to another, any significant number of children expelled as preschoolers raises concerns. Our survey found that in 2006–2007, most states had no regulations regarding expulsion and left this up to local discretion. Eight states explicitly permitted expulsion from pre-K under specified conditions and procedures, typically including behavior problems (although in Colorado expulsion is permitted only due to parental behavior and not child behavior). Another eight states prohibited the expulsion of preschool children under any circumstances.

PROGRAM SCHEDULE

State pre-K programs vary as much in their required operating schedules as they do in their eligibility criteria and enrollment (see Table 1.2). The majority of state pre-K programs nationwide operate on a part-day schedule, and they may offer fewer than 5 days per week. Of 50 state initiatives (including the District of Columbia), only 13 require programs to operate more than 5 hours per day. Three state programs have provisions for expanded days and hours so that they essentially provide full-time child care in conjunction with state pre-K, although this may be accomplished with multiple funding streams. Many states' regulations leave the number of hours and days per week up to local discretion. In these states, local authorities have the option to provide full-day programs, but the extra costs required would be borne by the local school districts. At the other extreme, some states permit programs to provide fewer than 10 hours per week and to operate only 3 or 4 days per week.

LEARNING STANDARDS

Statewide early learning standards provide guidance to pre-K programs with regard to how they address specific content areas of children's learning and development. When early learning standards are adopted at the state level, all pre-K programs funded by that state are provided with a common set of standards. Since 2003, the vast majority of states have adopted new early learning standards or revised existing standards to make them more comprehensive. The National Education Goals Panel (NEGP; 1991) identified five broad content areas as fundamental: physical well-being and motor development, social-emotional development, approaches toward learning, language development, and cognition and general knowledge. During 2006–2007, 42 of 50 pre-K initiatives had early learning standards that encompassed all five NEGP domains and were specific to pre-K. In 17 programs, standards were offered as guidance, but the state did not require that programs follow the standards. In most programs, the early learning standards are linked to child assessment in pre-K, most commonly some type of observational assessment of performance in the classroom. In two states it is linked to assessments at kindergarten entry— Florida employs a standardized assessment and teacher ratings, and Maryland employs a portfolio-based performance assessment.

PROGRAM STANDARDS

Some of the most difficult decisions faced by policy makers in designing state pre-K programs surround setting requirements related to program structure. After deciding on the appropriate starting age and hours per week, the decisions that most strongly affect program cost are staff qualifications and compensation, class size, and ratio. Yet, guidance from research regarding these decisions is mixed (Dowsett, Huston, Imes, & Gennetian, 2008; Early et al., 2007; Finn, 2002; Howes et al., 2008; Kelley & Camilli, 2007). Correlational research methods typically used in studies of the effects of program structure are subject to serious errors, which may be one reason for the mixed results (Rothstein, 2007).

Given these concerns, it is useful to look at the characteristics of the programs found to be highly effective and that yield high economic rates of return in rigorous studies, especially in randomized trials. These programs have had highly qualified, well-trained, and well-compensated teachers and assistants with relatively small classes and high staff–child ratios (Barnett & Belfield, 2006; Barnett & Masse, 2007; Gormley, Gayer, Phillips, & Dawson, 2005; Schweinhart et al., 2005; Temple & Reynolds, 2007). This formulation is consistent with an analysis of what experts believe that teachers should know and be able to do with children in order to produce strong gains in learning and development (Bowman, Donovan, & Burns, 2001). In our view, if programs depart from this formulation, then they run a high risk of failing to produce large gains for children. We believe, however, that this structure by no means guarantees that programs will be well implemented so as to produce large gains.

Teacher Preparation and Professional Development

State pre-K initiatives vary in the importance they attach to teachers' educational backgrounds. In 28 of the 50 pre-K programs operating during the 2006–2007 school year, all lead teachers were required to hold a bachelor's degree. In 14 more, lead teachers were required to hold a bachelor's degree under certain circumstances. These state pre-K initiatives typically employed tiered systems that required bachelor's degrees only for those teachers working in public school settings. The remaining eight state pre-K initiatives did not require bachelor's degrees in either public or private settings. In 37 of 50 programs, teachers were required to have specialized training in teaching preschool children. For teachers with bachelor's degrees, this was most commonly addressed through licensure, certification, or an endorsement in early childhood education. When a bachelor's degree was not required, the specialized training requirement most often was a Child Development Associate (CDA) credential. In general, state pre-K has placed less emphasis on qualifications and training requirements for assistant teachers. Degree requirements for assistant teachers have tended to be minimal. During 2006–2007, only 12 of the 50 pre-K initiatives required assistant teachers to have at least a CDA or equivalent training.

Continuing professional development activities, monitoring, providing supervision, and offering feedback on performance also contribute to effective teaching (Bowman et al., 2001; Frede, 1998; Fukkink & Lout, 2007). States vary in their continuing education requirements from none at all to 45 clock hours per year and 6 credit hours over 5 years. During 2006–2007, 38 of 50 programs required teachers to receive at least 15 hours of annual in-service training. Much of the responsibility for monitoring and supporting effective teaching resides at the local level. Three quarters of state initiatives, however, have policies that provide for some on-site monitoring of program quality and external accountability, as we discuss next.

Class Size and Staff–Child Ratio

Setting maximum class sizes and staff–child ratios are among the most important decisions when designing a state pre-K program. These have large consequences for program cost, and there are reasons to believe that smaller classes and better ratios are associated with more effective education (Barnett, 1998; Bowman et al., 2001; Finn, 2002; Frede, 1998; National Association for the Education of Young Children, 2005; National Institute of Child Health and Human Development Early Child Care Research Network, 1999). Our sense is that a classroom for 3- and 4-year-olds should have a maximum of 20 children, which is generally considered acceptable by professionals in the United States. There also seems to be general agreement that classrooms should have at least 1 teacher or assistant for every 10 children. In 2006–2007, 42 of the 50 state-funded pre-K initiatives capped their class sizes at 20 or fewer children. Staff–child ratio requirements were closely related to those class size requirements, and 43 of the 50 state pre-K initiatives capped the staff–child ratio at 1:10 or better.

Comprehensive Services

Preparing children for success in school involves not only their broad cognitive development but also their physical health and social-emotional well-being. Additional support services that pre-K programs offer to preschoolers and their families can help promote learning and child development. Types of services may include parent conferences or home visits, parenting support or training, referral to social services, and information relating to nutrition. For some children, preschool provides the first opportunity to detect vision, hearing, and health problems that may impair a child's learning and development (Meisels & Atkins-Burnett, 2000). Good nutrition is essential for children's healthy development and learning, and programs attend to this by educating children and families about healthy eating, helping them to develop healthy eating habits, and providing healthy snacks and meals (Shonkoff & Phillips, 2000). Programs vary in their policies and practices, but all of them address the issue in some way, and half require at least one meal regardless of length of day. Some of the most effective programs have also partnered with parents (Bowman et al., 2001; Frede, 1998), and our survey finds that parent support and education requirements are commonplace (about 75%) in state pre-K. Thirty state programs require two or more parent–teacher conferences each year, and others require conferences but do not specify how many.

MONITORING AND ACCOUNTABILITY

There will always be implementation challenges in state-funded pre-K, regardless of how carefully states specify the features and operation of the program. Some administrators and teachers will unintentionally fail to implement statewide policies as intended, and sometimes they will even intentionally disregard state policies. In addition, no state would attempt to fully describe the teaching practices it wishes to see implemented. That would require a level of detail that simply is not feasible, and states do not have that level of control over implementation in any case (Weick, 1976). There are ways, however, in which states can increase the influence of policy on practice (Odden, 1991). Thus, it is important that states take what steps they can to ensure that programs are meeting the intended standards and that effective teaching is taking place.

States engage in a wide array of activities to monitor and support effective program implementation. All states have some form of monitoring, although Maine, Maryland, Vermont, and Texas leave much or all of it up to local education agencies. Programs are monitored with respect to accountability for finances, safety, and enrollment, and most require some kind of documentation of children's learning. Representatives of the state conduct site visits for monitoring purposes in 39 programs, and 27 require structured observations of the classroom. The frequency of site visits varies from several per year to once every 6 years, with most states requiring visits between 2 times a year and once every 4 years. Child learning in pre-K is most commonly monitored with observational assessments (e.g., The Work Sampling System [Meisels, Jablon, Marsden, Dichtelmiller, & Dorfman, 1994], High/Scope Child Observation Record [Schweinhart, McNair, Barnes, & Larner, 1993]). The Dynamic Indicators of Basic Early Literacy Skills (DIBELS; Good & Kaminski, 2002), however, is the most frequently required assessment at kindergarten entry. States use this information to both support and sanction programs. The most commonly reported uses are to inform professional development and technical assistance, take corrective action, and inform funding decisions (e.g., in awarding grants).

In addition to routine monitoring, formal program evaluation is quite common, with most states conducting or planning evaluations.

California, Maine, Minnesota, and Pennsylvania are the only states reporting that they have not evaluated their programs and have not yet planned an evaluation. Pennsylvania has only recently revised its programs, so it may be too early to evaluate them. Two other states have had no evaluation since the mid-1990s—Texas and Colorado. Evaluation approaches have varied widely across the states, and the methods used have not always been sufficiently rigorous (Barnett, 1998; Gilliam & Zigler, 2001). Many have provided useful descriptive information about program implementation (e.g., LoCasale-Crouch et al., 2007), however, and there are examples of rigorous and innovative approaches to estimating effects on children's learning and development (Barnett, 1998; Frede & Barnett, 1992; Gormley et al., 2005; Wong, Cook, Barnett, & Jung, 2008).

TRANSPORTATION

The availability of transportation services to state pre-K programs is often an overlooked issue. The provision of transportation can be a factor in some families' decisions about whether their children attend a state pre-K program. This may be a more common issue for programs that do not offer wraparound child care or otherwise accommodate parent work schedules in ways that facilitate parent pick up and drop off. It may be more of an issue in rural areas than in more densely populated cities and suburbs, as well. Typically, state pre-K programs permit the use of funds for transportation, but it is much less frequently provided. Budgets tend to be tight even without the addition of transportation costs, as discussed in the next section. In 2005–2006, all but five of the state-financed pre-K initiatives allowed providers to use state pre-K funds for transportation services (Barnett, Hustedt, Hawkinson, & Robin, 2006). In 18 state pre-K initiatives, transportation to pre-K was a required service under certain circumstances—most typically for children with an individualized education program or receiving special education services. Even in those programs, however, transportation was rarely provided to other children enrolled in state-funded pre-K.

SERVICES TO ENGLISH LANGUAGE LEARNERS

A rapidly growing number of young children face the challenge of learning English as a second language, with the vast majority from homes where Spanish is the primary language (Tabors, Paez, & Lopez, 2003). In the United States, Hispanic children already account for more than 20% of all children under the age of 5 (Collins & Ribeiro, 2004). Children who are English language learners (ELLs) are even more highly represented in populations eligible for state pre-K because they are more likely to be from low-income families and because some state pre-K programs include a home language other than English as a factor in determining eligibility. Access to preschool education is particularly important for these children because many would otherwise have limited opportunities to learn English prior to kindergarten. Preschool programs can be specially designed to best help children master English as a second language while helping them learn and maintain their home language. For example, dual language preschool education can be as successful as monolingual English preschool education in promoting school readiness in English, while offering important added benefits to all children in mastering a second language such as Spanish (Barnett, Yarosz, Thomas, Jung, & Blanco, 2007). In 2006–2007, 26 pre-K programs allowed preschool bilingual or monolingual non-English classes, 20 programs required information to be presented to parents in their primary language, and 12 required translators or bilingual staff for children who do not speak English. No states require English-only instruction in pre-K. Fifteen pre-K programs in 14 states do not have state policies regarding services for children who are ELLs, including Arizona and Florida, which have large ELL populations.

Of the pre-K programs that have eligibility requirements other than age, 17 mention a non-English home language as a risk factor that can be used to determine eligibility. Support for children who are ELLs is a more prominent issue in some states than others because of large variations in the percentage of these children in the population. Fifteen states reported the number of children who are ELLs enrolled in state pre-K programs during 2006–2007. Unfortunately, some states with large ELL populations—including Arizona, California, and Florida—did not report the numbers of children who are ELLs served in their pre-K programs. Of those that did report, Nevada had the highest percentage (59%) of children who are ELLs, although it serves relatively few children overall. Texas reported the next highest percentage (40%), or nearly 79,000 children who are ELLs of the 198,000 children served. Texas has a large Hispanic immigrant population and a focus on serving children who are ELLs.

SPECIAL EDUCATION

All state pre-K initiatives have classrooms open to children receiving special education services, although in 12 initiatives, children receiving special education were not included in state pre-K enrollment counts.

Nearly all state pre-K programs reported blending state pre-K money with other sources, including federal Individuals with Disabilities Education Improvement Act (IDEA) of 2004 (PL 108-446) funds to serve children receiving special education services in state pre-K. Kentucky had the largest special education enrollment in state pre-K in 2006–2007. The Kentucky program is offered to all 3- and 4-year-olds in the state with disabilities, and special education students made up 60% of the total enrollment. Kentucky also has the nation's second highest rates of special education for preschoolers—14% at age 4, 8% at age 3—because it has a broad definition that includes developmental delays. (Wyoming, which does not offer a regular state pre-K program, has the nation's highest rates for preschool special education.) In no other state is it likely that even one third of the children in the state pre-K program are special education students. There are many states, however, where preschool special education enrollment is large (sometimes overwhelmingly so) relative to state pre-K enrollment, presenting both opportunities and challenges.

The most obvious policy issue for state pre-K and special education is overlapping governance and administration at federal, state, and local levels. These differences in administration produce differences in standards for programs that can be incompatible. When pre-K is administered by a state department of education, regular pre-K and special education pre-K are at least within the same state agency, although this does not necessarily ensure easy collaboration and coordination. Furthermore, states may have separate standards for pre-K operated by the public schools and pre-K operated by private providers. Problems of collaboration and coordination can become even more difficult when pre-K is administered by another state agency. These difficulties become apparent even when trying to simply count how many children are served in state pre-K programs and how many of those are included in the special education enrollment figures reported to the federal government.

Despite the administrative challenges, including children with special education needs in state pre-K classrooms provides opportunities to improve services for all children through collaboration and coordination of preschool education services (Guralnick, 2001; Odom, 2002). State pre-K programs offer opportunities for more easily educating children in the least restrictive environment and for identifying the special needs of children who might otherwise not even be screened for problems prior to kindergarten. Special education programs offer opportunities for regular classrooms to draw on the expertise of specialists for children whom teachers find challenging due to developmental delays or behavior problems but who do not have a disability. Integrating special and general education staff and facilities also has the potential to make services more cost effective.

Nevertheless, there are also many challenges to program coordination and inclusion beyond administration (Gallagher, Clifford, & Maxwell, 2004). Teachers and other staff can have different qualifications and preparation and schedules can be quite different as well, leading parents and others to question whether state pre-K programs can provide the necessary quality and quantity of education that constitutes best practice for children with special needs (Odom et al., 2004; Stahmer, 2007). Differences in preparation can also result in different perspectives on curriculum and teaching practices that make collaboration difficult (Buysse, Wesley, & Keyes, 1998). Developing an accountability system that adequately accommodates all teachers and children can also be challenging (Harbin, Rous, & Mclean, 2005).

RESOURCES

The amount of funding allocated to state preschool initiatives limits the number of children served, the amount of services children receive, and/or the quality of the services children receive. Policy makers and program administrators inevitably face trade-offs—additional money can increase enrollments; extend program hours or days; or seek to enhance quality through class size reductions, higher salaries, increased in-service education and coaching, or expanded services to children and families beyond the classroom. Only a few states guarantee preschool education to all children who are eligible and make funding automatically available for every child who is enrolled. In most states, the pre-K budget is discretionary and must be fought for in each legislative session. Moreover, as with K–12 education, states typically provide only a portion of the funding for state pre-K, with substantial funding allocated at the local level. As a result, an approximate accounting of the resources available to state pre-K programs requires information about local expenditures as well as state expenditures (see Table 1.2).

Since 2001–2002, total funding for pre-K by the states has increased each year, even after adjusting for inflation. Based on this trend, we predict that states will have spent more than $4 billion on pre-K in 2008, about double what states spent at the beginning of the decade. As might be expected, states vary tremendously in how much each contributes to total spending on pre-K. Table 1.2 shows that states' annual expenditures on pre-K programs vary by more than two orders of magnitude, from barely more than $3 million in Nevada to $533 million in Texas. These differences in state spending reflect both the size of each state's population and the percentage of children each state chooses to serve. Other influences on expenditures are the percentage of the full cost paid for at the state level, program standards, salary and benefit levels, and cost-of-living differences among the states. New Jersey, for example, spends nearly as much as Texas despite its much smaller population because New Jersey enrolls a relatively large percentage of children at age 3 and has a high cost per child. Five other states—Georgia, California, New York, Florida, and Illinois—each spent in the neighborhood of $300 million per year on their preschool initiatives. These seven large states account for more than half of all state spending on pre-K. At the other extreme, 12 states spent nothing at all on state-funded preschool education, as we define it.

Per-Child Spending

State expenditures per child are less variable than total spending but still vary appreciably. Differences in spending per child reflect key differences in decisions about schedules, quality, the state–local split of costs, and cost-of-living differences that make it more expensive to provide preschool education in some states than in others. In contrast to total state spending, per-child spending by states has declined since 2001, when adjusted for inflation. States spent an average of $4,342 per child in 2001–2002, and spending per child decreased each year through 2005-2006, falling to $3,610 per child (in FY 2007 dollars). In 2006–2007, states spent an average of $3,642 per child, marking at least a pause in the downward trend. Despite that pause, per-child spending remained $700 below the 2001–2002 level.

Although real (inflation-adjusted) per-child spending averaged across all of the states has decreased since the 2001–2002 school year, individual states have followed different patterns. Twenty-two states decreased real per-child spending, ranging from less than $100 to almost $4,000 per child. Fourteen states increased real per-child spending over this same time period, ranging from about $50 per child to more than $1,000 per child in Arkansas, New Jersey, and New Mexico. In some states, some of the decline in cost per child might be due to economies of scale achieved as a state moved from offering a small-scale pilot program to large-scale implementation for a significant percentage of the population. Reductions in state spending, however, usually accompanied one or more of the following three changes: 1) a redistribution of the cost burden to local schools (or in a few cases, perhaps, parents), 2) a reduction in the quantity of services, and 3) a reduction in the quality of education. Most often, decreases in real spending per child occurred without a reduction in standards for teacher qualifications, class size, ratios, or other program characteristics that affect cost. As a result, decreases in real spending per child would be expected to produce downward pressure on salaries and benefits and/or reductions in spending on professional development, supplies and materials, and other more discretionary program resources.

Per-child spending among the states ranged from more than $10,000 to less than $2,000 in 2006–2007. The national average expenditure by states in 2006–2007 was $3,642 per child, with 16 states above and 22 states below that figure. New Jersey had the highest per-child spending, topping $10,000 per child. New Jersey's high cost per child reflects the high share of the costs borne by the state, a full-day schedule for most children, small class sizes, high standards for teacher qualifications, and a relatively high cost of living. Oregon, Connecticut, and Minnesota followed, all spending more than $7,000 per child. Oregon and Minnesota followed the Head Start model (with an expensive array of services beyond the classroom), and these two states essentially pay for all of the costs. Connecticut's pre-K program is predominately full day, full year, and the state has a high cost of living. At the other extreme, Maine and South Carolina both spent less than $2,000 per child. In states that spent less, much of the burden of paying for quantity and quality of services falls to the local education agencies. Local education agencies also vary greatly in their ability and willingness to pay for pre-K, however, setting the stage for tremendous potential inequalities at the local level in states that provide low levels of funding.

It is difficult to judge the "right" level of state funding per child for a quality preschool education and whether a state is adequately funding its program. States vary in whether they offer a half-day or a full-day program, and many states leave the schedule up to local discretion. As a result, how thinly state funding is stretched depends on local decisions about length of day, and frequently, data are unavailable about how many children are served with each type of schedule. States also vary in the capacity of their local schools to share in the costs of pre-K and what it costs to provide a given amount and quality of preschool education.

One basis for comparison is provided by state expenditures on K–12 education. Most states spent more per child on K–12 education than on preschool education. Often, this is because state pre-K provides only a half-day program, but this still indicates that a state invested less in a year of preschool education than in a year of later education. Eight of the thirty-eight states funding pre-K programs, however, spent more per child on pre-K than on K–12 programs, including New Jersey, Oregon, and Connecticut—the three states with the highest per child state spending. The remaining 30 states spent an average of $2,400 per child more on K–12 than on preschool during the 2006–2007 school year, and this difference ranges from as little as $129 per child in Georgia to as much as $10,376 per child in Vermont.

Comparing spending with the estimated cost per child of a "quality" pre-K program is another basis for assessing the adequacy of state expenditure. As a rough approximation, we used national estimates by Gault, Mitchell, Williams, Dey, and Sorokina (2007) of the costs of 3-hour and 6-hour per day quality pre-K employing teachers with 4-year degrees with an aide in each classroom of 20 children. We adjusted these national figures for differences in costs of labor across the states (Taylor & Fowler, 2006) to derive an estimate for each state of the expenditure required to fund quality full- and half-day pre-K programs. Of course, these expenditure figures are appropriately compared with public expenditures on state pre-K from all sources—federal, state, and local. Unfortunately, it is far from easy to identify all government expenditures for state pre-K programs.

Local and Other Funding for State Pre-K

Although states provide most of the funding for state pre-K programs, local and federal dollars also play an important role. Most often this is because pre-K is funded similarly to K–12, and local education agencies are required, or at least expected, to contribute a share. In some states such as Colorado, this expenditure share is mandated by a statewide school funding formula. In other states, a school funding formula sets the state share, but local spending depends on local decisions. Some states determine their expenditures for pre-K outside the regular school funding process, and some of these states require a specific local match in order to receive state pre-K funds. Federal funds are spent on state pre-K when either the state or local government pays for pre-K with federal funds over which they have discretion. Half of the states with pre-K reported some type of funding in addition to state funds, and 13 reported that they required some kind of local match. This does not mean that no local resources were contributed in any of the other 19 pre-K states, just that the amount of local spending was not reported by these states.

Considerable uncertainty surrounds the amount of nonstate funds because of the extent of local discretion and because local schools, in particular, may support pre-K with administration, services for children with special needs, facilities, maintenance, transportation, and other resources that do not appear in the expenditure reports or budgets for pre-K. In addition, when children attend programs in which the state pays for part of the day and parents may pay for hours beyond those paid for by the state, there is the potential for some parents to de facto pay to raise quality during the state pre-K hours, as well. This has the potential to create inequities in access to quality, particularly in states such as Florida where the per-child expenditure is quite low. As some states appear to be better than others at tracking spending from local sources, the data we have collected on per-child spending from all sources are far from perfect. These data demonstrate that, at least in some states, there is a substantial difference between state expenditure and total expenditures per child in state pre-K programs. For example, the state share in Iowa was $2,966 per child, but total spending from all sources in Iowa was $8,966 per child. Nebraska spent $2,273 per child in state funds, but total spending per child was $6,888.

With spending from all reported sources included, the national average for per-child spending was $4,134. This is likely to be a substantial underestimate given the number of states that could not report spending by local education agencies. In five states (Iowa, Nebraska, Oklahoma, Maryland, and Maine), the additional expenditure was at least twice the state's per-child expenditure on pre-K.

When we compare the more inclusive expenditure figure with the estimated cost of a quality program (either half day or full day, if that is required), we find that 19 states can be said to have adequately funded programs. For some of the others, it is difficult to judge adequacy because all expenditures may not have been reported, and these unreported local expenditures could make up the difference. Florida and Georgia, however, are particularly worrisome because in these states, most children in state pre-K attend private programs that are entirely dependent on state funding, except for what parents pay for additional hours. This raises questions about whether private providers can afford to deliver an effective education and how much educational inequality may result from uneven access to public school pre-K (where in-kind local subsidies of facilities and administration may be provided) and unequal ability to pay supplements to private providers.

CONCLUSIONS

The growth of state pre-K has changed the preschool education landscape, particularly for 4-year-olds. Enrollment in state pre-K at age 4 is approaching 25% of the population nationally, and it exceeds one third in 10 states. Those in preschool special education (another 6% at age 4) might be added to the previously stated figures, although these two systems remain remarkably separate. Moreover, this landscape varies tremendously from state to state. In Oklahoma, school begins at age 4 for nearly all children. A number of other states, including some of the largest (Florida, Georgia, New York, and Texas), are well on the way to offering pre-K to all 4-year-olds, especially when other public programs are counted. In addition, what constitutes "school" at age 4 can be quite different from what it is at kindergarten. Even more growth in overall enrollment and greater differences among the states can be expected in the future based on recent trends. For example, Illinois committed to serve all children at ages 3 and 4, whereas Iowa joined the list of states committed to universal pre-K at age 4. Yet, a dozen states continue to have no state pre-K.

Moving beyond enrollment, the differences among states continue to be at least as important as the overall trends. States vary in their governance structures and approaches to collaboration across public programs and with the private sector. They vary in their program standards, ancillary services, and monitoring and accountability practices. Given all of this variation in policies, it is hardly surprising that there is a great deal of variation in how and how much state pre-K programs are funded. All of this variation raises concerns that access to effective early education will be highly unequal across and within states. Moreover, some of the largest states serving relatively large percentages of their population raise the greatest concerns—Florida, Georgia, and Texas (a low spender with no limits on class size or staff–child ratio).

The tremendous variation among states also provides fertile ground for research on policy and on the consequences of different policies for program administration, classroom practices, and children's learning and development. Description will be the easy part of this agenda, although the problems of recruiting representative samples should not be underestimated. It will be more difficult to conduct research that provides an adequate basis for causal attribution (Rothstein, 2007). As such research moves beyond description, the challenge will be to develop creative approaches that are valid and to persuade policy makers to participate in randomized trials (Angrist, 2004). Both will be difficult, but the opportunities provided by policy making in the educational frontier that is state pre-K should make success highly rewarding.

REFERENCES

Angrist, J.D. (2004). American education research changes tack. *Oxford Economic Review, 20*(2), 198–212.

Barnett, W.S. (1998). Long-term effects on cognitive development and school success. In W.S. Barnett & S.S. Boocock (Eds.), *Early care and education for children in poverty: Promises, programs, and long-term results* (pp. 11–44). Albany: State University of New York Press.

Barnett, W.S., & Belfield, C. (2006). Early childhood development and social mobility. *The Future of Children, 16*(2), 73–98.

Barnett, W.S., Hustedt, J.T., Friedman, A.H., Boyd, J.S., & Ainsworth, P. (2007). *The state of preschool 2007: State preschool yearbook.* New Brunswick: Rutgers, State University of New Jersey, National Institute for Early Education Research.

Barnett, W.S., Hustedt, J.T., Hawkinson, L.E., & Robin, K.B. (2006). *The state of preschool 2006: State preschool yearbook.* New Brunswick: Rutgers, State University of New Jersey, National Institute for Early Education Research.

Barnett, W.S., & Masse, L.N. (2007). Comparative benefit-cost analysis of the Abecedarian program and its policy implications. *Economics of Education Review, 26*(1), 113–125.

Barnett, W.S., & Yarosz, D.J. (2007). *Who goes to preschool and why does it matter? Preschool Policy Brief No. 15.* New Brunswick: Rutgers, State University of New Jersey, National Institute for Early Education Research.

Barnett, W.S., Yarosz, D.J., Thomas, J., Jung, K., & Blanco, D. (2007). Two-way and monolingual English immersion in preschool education: An experimental comparison. *Early Childhood Research Quarterly, 22,* 277–293.

Belfield, C. (2008). Unpublished analyses of data from the 2005 National Household Education Survey.

Bowman, B.T., Donovan, M.S., & Burns, M.S. (Eds.). (2001). *Eager to learn: Educating our preschoolers.* Washington, DC: National Academies Press.

Bryant, D., Clifford, R.M., Saluja, G., Pianta, R., Early, D., Barbarin, O., et al. (2002). *Diversity and directions in state prekindergarten programs.* Chapel Hill: University of North Carolina, FPG Child Development Institute, NCEDL.

Buysse, V., Wesley, P.W., & Keyes, L. (1998). Implementing early childhood inclusion: Barrier and support factors. *Early Childhood Research Quarterly, 13*(1), 169–184.

Collins, R., & Ribeiro, R. (2004). *Toward an early care and education agenda for Hispanic children.* Retrieved April 14, 2005, from http://ecrp.uiuc.edu/v6n2/collins.html

Dowsett, C.J., Huston, A.C., Imes, A.E., & Gennetian, L. (2008). Structural and process features in three types of child care for children from high and low income families. *Early Childhood Research Quarterly, 23,* 69–93.

Early, D.M., Maxwell, K.M., Burchinal, M., Alva, S., Bender, R.H., et al. (2007). Teachers' education, classroom quality, and young children's academic skills: Results from seven studies of preschool programs. *Child Development, 78*(2), 558–580.

Finn, J.D. (2002). Class-size reduction in grades K–3. In A. Molnar (Ed.), *School reform proposals: The research evidence* (pp. 27–48). Greenwich, CT: Information Age Publishing.

Frede, E.C. (1998). Preschool program quality in programs for children in poverty. In W.S. Barnett & S.S. Boocock (Eds.), *Early care and education for children in poverty: Promises, programs, and long-term results* (pp. 77–98). Albany: State University of New York Press.

Frede, E.C., & Barnett, W.S. (1992). Developmentally appropriate public school preschool: A study of implementation of the High/Scope curriculum and its effects on disadvantaged children's skills at first grade. *Early Childhood Research Quarterly, 7,* 483–499.

Fukkink, R.G., & Lout, A. (2007). Does training matter? A meta-analysis and review of caregiver training studies. *Early Childhood Research Quarterly, 22,* 294–311.

Gallagher, J.J., Clifford, R.M., & Maxwell, K. (2004). *Getting from here to there: To an ideal early preschool system.* Retrieved April 23, 2008, from http://ecrp.uiuc.edu/v6n1/clifford.html

Gault, B., Mitchell, A., Williams, E., Dey, J., & Sorokina, O. (2007). *Meaningful investments in pre-K: Estimating the per-child costs of quality programs.* Washington, DC: Institute for Women's Policy Research.

Gilliam, W.S. (2005). *Prekindergarteners left behind: Expulsion rates in state prekindergarten programs* (FCD Policy Brief Series No. 3). New York: Foundation for Child Development.

Gilliam, W.S., & Marchesseault, C.M. (2004). *From capitols to classrooms, policy to practice: State-funded prekindergarten at the classroom level.* New Haven, CT: Yale University.

Gilliam, W.S., & Zigler, E. (2001). A critical meta-analysis of all evaluations of state-funded preschool from 1977 to 1998: Implications for policy, service delivery and program evaluation. *Early Childhood Research Quarterly, 15,* 441–473.

Good, R.H., & Kaminski, R.A. (Eds.). (2002). *Dynamic Indicators of Basic Early Literacy Skills* (6th ed.). Eugene, OR: Institute for Development of Educational Achievement. Also available online: http://dibels.uoregon.edu

Gormley, W.T., Gayer, T., Phillips, D., & Dawson, B. (2005). The effects of universal pre-k on cognitive development. *Developmental Psychology, 41,* 872–884.

Guralnick, M.J. (Ed.). (2001). *Early childhood inclusion: Focus on change.* Baltimore: Paul H. Brookes Publishing Co.

Harbin, G., Rous, B., & Mclean, M. (2005). Issues in designing state accountability systems. *Journal of Early Intervention, 27*(3), 137–164.

Howes, C., Burchinal, M., Pianta, R., Bryant, D., Early, D.M., & Clifford, R. (2008). Ready to learn? Children's pre-academic achievement in pre-kindergarten programs. *Early Childhood Research Quarterly, 23,* 27–50.

Individuals with Disabilities Education Improvement Act (IDEA) of 2004, PL 108-446, 20 U.S.C. §§ 1400 *et seq.*

Kelley, P.J., & Camilli, G. (2007). *The impact of teacher education on outcomes in center-based early childhood education programs: A meta-analysis.* New Brunswick: Rutgers, State University of New Jersey, National Institute for Early Education Research.

LoCasale-Crouch, J., Konold, T., Pianta, R., Howes, C., Burchinal, M., Bryant, D., Clifford, R., Early, D., & Barbarin, O. (2007). Observed classroom quality profiles in state-funded pre-kindergarten programs and associations with teacher, program, and classroom characteristics. *Early Childhood Research Quarterly, 22,* 3–17.

Meisels, S.J., & Atkins-Burnett, S. (2000). The elements of early childhood assessment. In J.P. Shonkoff & S.J. Meisels (Eds.), *Handbook of early childhood intervention* (pp. 231–257). New York: Cambridge University Press.

Meisels, S.J., Jablon, J., Marsden, D.B., Dichtelmiller, M.L., & Dorfman, A. (1994). *The Work Sampling System.* Ann Arbor, MI: Rebus.

Mitchell, A.W. (2001). *Education for all children: The role of states and the federal government in promoting prekindergarten and kindergarten.* New York: Foundation for Child Development.

National Association for the Education of Young Children. (2005). *NAEYC program standards and accreditation criteria.* Washington, DC: Author.

National Education Goals Panel. (1991). *The goal 1 technical planning subgroup report on school readiness.* Washington, DC: Author.

National Institute of Child Health and Human Development Early Child Care Research Network. (1999). Child outcomes when child care center classes meet recommended standards for quality. *American Journal of Public Health, 89,* 1072–1077.

Odden, A.R. (1991). *Education policy implementation.* Albany: State University of New York Press.

Odom, S.L. (Ed.). (2002). *Widening the circle: Including children with disabilities in preschool programs.* New York: Teachers College Press.

Odom, S.L., Vitztum, J., Wolery, R., Lieber, J., Sandall, S., Hanson, M., et al. (2004). Preschool inclusion in the United States: A review of research from an ecological systems perspective. *Journal of Research in Special Educational Needs, 4*(1), 17–49.

Rothstein, J. (2007). *Do value-added models add value? Tracking, fixed effects, and causal inference.* Princeton, NJ: Princeton University.

Schweinhart, L.J., McNair, S., Barnes, H., & Larner, M. (1993). Observing young children in action to assess their development: The High/Scope Child Observation Record study. *Educational and Psychological Measurement, 53,* 445–455.

Schweinhart, L.J., Montie, J., Xiang, Z., Barnett, W.S., Belfield, C.R., & Nores, M. (2005). *Lifetime effects: The High/Scope Perry Preschool Study through age 40.* Ypsilanti, MI: High/Scope Press.

Shonkoff, J.P., & Phillips, D.A. (Eds.). (2000). *From neurons to neighborhoods: The science of early childhood development.* Washington, DC: National Academies Press.

Stahmer, A.C. (2007). The basic structure of community early intervention programs for children with Autism: Provider descriptions. *Journal of Autism and Developmental Disorders, 37,* 1344–1354.

Tabors, P.O., Paez, M.M., & Lopez, L.M. (2003). Dual language abilities of bilingual four-year olds: Initial findings from the early childhood study of language and literacy development of Spanish-speaking children. *NABE Journal of Research and Practice, 1,* 70–91.

Taylor, L., & Fowler, W. (2006). *A comparable wage approach to geographic cost adjustment.* Washington, DC: U.S. Department of Education, Institute of Education Sciences.

Temple, J., & Reynolds, A. (2007). Benefits and costs of investments in preschool education: Evidence from the child–parent centers and related programs. *Economics of Education Review, 26,* 126–144.

Weick, K.E. (1976). Educational organizations as loosely coupled systems. *Administrative Science Quarterly, 21,* 1–19.

Wong, V.C., Cook, T.D., Barnett, W.S., & Jung, K. (2008). An effectiveness-based evaluation of five state pre-kindergarten programs. *Journal of Policy Analysis and Management, 27*(1), 122–154.

Chapter 2

Assessing the School Readiness Needs of a State

Thomas Schultz

Since the early 2000s, public awareness has been growing about the significance of children's early learning years and a concomitant growth in state efforts to improve learning opportunities for young children. These developments are, in part, a result of an expanded awareness of school achievement shortfalls and differential outcomes for subgroups of children. State and federal education reform initiatives, culminating in the No Child Left Behind (NCLB) Act of 2001 (PL 107-110), have linked progressively powerful incentives and sanctions with the explicit performance goals for improving overall achievement and reducing achievement gaps. Implementing these reforms has generated a huge expansion of data on student achievement for all children enrolled in Grades 3–8 and an expanded set of metrics on which to compare the performance of local schools, including disaggregation of test scores by race; disability status; and language spoken, including children who are English language learners (ELLs). This chapter describes and analyzes a sampling of current state efforts to assess young children and the programs and settings in which they are prepared for schooling. To set the stage for this review, the policy context for early childhood programs and funding is discussed as well as how disparate federal and state agencies are proceeding to implement varied approaches to standards-based assessments of programs and children.

Our deepening awareness of the shape and significance of school performance problems has motivated educators and policy makers to understand the root causes of educational performance problems and inequities. These leaders are also searching for new strategies and solutions, including prevention and early intervention through early childhood programs, to foster successful school performance for all children.

Several strands of policy-related research have led educators and policy makers to these conclusions. For example, overwhelming evidence shows that substantial achievement gaps exist between subgroups of children at the time they enter kindergarten and earlier, and these differences are strongly correlated with long-term trends in school performance (Hart & Risley, 1995; Lee & Burkam, 2002; Loeb, Bridges, Fuller, Rumberger, & Bassok, 2005; Rouse, Brooks-Gunn, & Mclanahan, 2005). Brain research shows the complexity, interconnectedness, and significance of early childhood development. We have increasing evidence on the positive effects and cost–benefit returns on investment in high-quality early childhood programs. High-quality learning opportunities, beginning as early as possible and sustained over time, increase the odds that children will succeed in school and become productive citizens (Barnett, 1998; Campbell, Ramey, Pungello, Sparling, & Miller-Johnson, 2002; Gormley & Gayer, 2003; Loeb, Fuller, Kagan, & Carrol, 2004; NICHD Early Child Care Research Network, 2005; Reynolds & Temple, 1998; Schweinhart et al., 2004; Shonkoff & Phillips, 2000).

STATE LEADERSHIP APPROACHES

Unfortunately, most of the centers and settings where young children are cared for and educated are not providing high-quality levels of teaching, learning, and developmental supports, typically due to inadequate resources and a work force with low levels of formal training and compensation and high rates of turnover (Burchinal et al., 1995; Herzenberg, Price, & Bradley, 2005; Pianta et al., 2005). This evidence has led states to introduce a variety of leadership initiatives to improve early learning opportunities for all children. States have adopted one or more of the following approaches. Each of these forms of state leadership and/or investment has sharpened efforts to collect a variety of forms of assessment data on the performance of early childhood programs and young children's learning and development.

Building Overall Systems of Services for All Young Children

These approaches to improving early learning opportunities for young children include organizing new units of state government to coordinate a variety of categorical programs for young children, developing new public–private investment strategies, and sponsoring comprehensive planning efforts at the state and community levels (Bruner, Wright, Gebhard, & Hibbard, 2004; Coffman, Wright, & Bruner, 2006). A related "big picture" perspective is spurring a few states to attempt to connect early childhood, elementary, secondary, and higher education into a more seamless preschool to age 21 (P–21) continuum (Krueger, 2006). These efforts increasingly include focusing more effectively on linking early childhood programs and primary schooling.

Developing and Funding Specific Early Childhood Programs

Most states have focused on efforts to provide high-quality, voluntary prekindergarten (pre-K) programs for all young children. In 2006–2007, 38 states sponsored programs for more than 1,026,000 children at a total cost of more than $3.7 billion. Since 2004, these investments increased pre-K funding by $1.6 billion and swelled enrollments by more than 346,000 children (Barnett, Hustedt, Friedman, Boyd, & Ainsworth, 2007; PreK Now, 2006, 2007).

State agencies are responsible for managing a variety of funding sources to a diverse set of local agencies and institutions including school districts, for-profit organizations, and nonprofit organizations for providing oversight and technical assistance to improve quality and outcomes in local early childhood agencies.

EARLY CHILDHOOD STANDARDS AND ASSESSMENTS: A PLETHORA OF POLICY INITIATIVES

State and federal program offices are managing separate and varied approaches to standards and assessments for children's learning and program quality. Table 2.1 highlights different policy standards and assessments established for four major funding sources for early childhood services: the Head Start and the Child Care and Development Block Grant programs through the U.S. Department of Health and Human Services, Part B of the Individuals with Disabilities Education Improvement Act (IDEA) of 2004 (PL 108-446), through the U.S. Department of Education, and state-funded pre-K programs. Collectively, these programs provide more than $15.7 billion in funding to support services to more than four million preschool children ages 3–5 years. This overview reveals a complex and varied series of policy mandates and accountability systems operating in tandem. Table 2.1 also provides information on the number of states that are implementing various types of standards and assessments in their early childhood programs.

Table 2.1.   School readiness standards and assessments at a glance

	Child care	Head Start	Early childhood special education	State pre-K
Agency	U.S. Department of Health and Human Services	U.S. Department of Health and Human Services	U.S. Department of Education	State agencies (Education and others)
Funding/ enrollment	$5.0 billion (2008) 1.74 million (36% 3- to 5-year-olds) (2004)	$6.9 billion (2007) 908,000	$374 million 680,000 (2006)	$5.2 billion (2008) 1,080,000 (2006)
Program quality standards	State licensing standards (50 states) Quality Rating and Improvement System (QRIS) (More than 12 states)	Program performance standards (federal)	IDEA regulations State program standards	State program standards (39 states)
Program quality assessments	Licensing visits (Mandatory) QRIS assessments (Voluntary)	Program Review Systems Monitoring (PRISM) reviews (federal)	State program monitoring	Program monitoring (30 states)
Standards for children's learning	Early learning guidelines (49 states)	Head Start child outcomes framework (federal)	Three functional goals (federal)	Early learning guidelines (49 states)
Child assessments	No current requirements	National reporting system (federal)	States report percentage of children in four categories on three goals	Pre-K assessments (12 states) Kindergarten assessments (16 states)
Program evaluation/ research	Child Care Policy Research Consortium	Head Start Impact Study Family and Child Experiences Survey	Office of Special Education Programs evaluations	More than 25 state evaluations

An overview of childhood accountability and assessment efforts reveals an array of different forms of child and program assessments, multiple sources of policy mandates in the areas of learning and quality standards, and a series of accountability systems operating in tandem, based largely on the structures of state and federal programs or funding streams. Yet, in spite of the volume and scale of varied assessment mandates, there are numerous shortfalls in our capacity to answer key questions from policy makers, public education leaders, and other key audiences with an interest in the performance of early childhood programs. Overall data on individual providers or local communities is not accessible in one place at a state or national level. Current reporting efforts are not designed to provide information on the numbers of children who are attending multiple programs or benefiting from a combination of separate funding sources in a single program. We lack clear information on the costs of services and how funding sources are combined and used based on the lack of a common system of accounting for costs and varying approaches to defining and documenting in-kind services. It is difficult to interpret feedback of different assessments from an individual agency or a set of providers in a given community or school attendance area because program quality assessments are geared to different systems of standards. Program quality assessments fail to document and account for the influence of children's rates of attendance and participation in instruction and other program services. There is limited capacity to report on the progress and levels of learning for ELLs, in particular to appropriately reflect their learning process in both their home language and in the acquisition of English.

In short, the programs have diverse approaches to design and to accountability and exist in a highly dynamic context. Since 2003, the field has seen new federal and state child outcome frameworks and new child assessment initiatives in states, Head Start, and early childhood special education. "Accountability" is a moving target with the proliferation of new child learning standards and assessments. Policy makers expect early childhood programs to demonstrate their worth over and over again and in new and different ways.

These newer child-focused standards and assessments complement long-standing policy standards and assessment and monitoring systems geared to aspects of program quality, program inputs, and management practices. This means that federal and state program offices as well as local provider agencies are currently engaged in their initial experiences in explaining and interpreting child outcome standards and the potential uses and misuses of newly expanded child assessment data sets. By contrast, federal, state, and local managers have more extensive experience and greater shared understanding of how program quality standards are applied in the context of various forms of licensing and monitoring reviews and enforcement decisions. Assessment strategies related to program quality standards have longer track records and a more robust base of cumulative data and support systems that have been implemented and fine tuned over the course of many years.

Indeed, new approaches to assessing program quality are also being generated from within the early childhood field. Researchers and program managers are creating new tools and strategies to answer questions about how programs are performing in relation to quality standards. The Quality Rating and Improvement System (QRIS) strategy is a leading example of this type of innovation. State-managed QRIS systems provide a series of tiered program quality standards ranging from a minimum level to a high/exemplary level. QRIS efforts also provide technical assistance and resources to help programs attain higher levels of performance. Provider agencies or centers can publicize the level of QRIS-certified quality that they attain, and many states provide higher rates of funding or access to additional sources of funding to high-quality providers. With public QRIS ratings families can make child care choices based on information about the quality of particular settings. At the same time, the nation's largest early childhood professional organization, the National Association for the Education of Young Children (NAEYC, 2005), has restructured its voluntary Program Accreditation system.

This fragmentation is a daily fact of life for state and local managers and practitioners. Early childhood educators must negotiate a complicated maze of policies and directives as they work to understand and implement many new initiatives related to standards and assessments and the program improvement efforts they inform. This policy labyrinth creates many complications:

- *Local early childhood agencies.* Many school districts and other local agencies receive funding from several state and federal sources and, therefore, struggle to respond to multiple assessments, standards, reporting requirements, and monitoring reviews. Program managers are understandably concerned about the rewards and sanctions of these varied accountability initiatives as well as their costs and burdens. Teachers may be required to administer several different (and often changing) assessments to their children. They must try to align their instructional practices to multiple sets of state and federal standards (Macmillan & Neugebauer, 2006).

- *State agencies.* States are responsible for managing varied assessment systems and program improvement approaches, typically, those associated with federal child care and early childhood special education as well as state-funded pre-K programs. States must ensure compliance with multiple sets of standards and typically work with multiple forms of data on the performance of children and programs (Schumacher, Irish, & Lombardi, 2003).

- *Early childhood teachers.* In addition to generating feedback to higher level managers and policy makers, an overarching purpose of standards-based assessments is to influence the perceptions, thinking, and practice of teachers as they work with children. Frameworks of learning goals can shape priorities for teachers and enhance their effectiveness to the extent that they are internalized. However, this goal is exceedingly difficult to achieve when teachers are expected to understand multiple sets of voluminous standards.

- *Policy leaders.* Audiences for data on the status of young children and the performance of early childhood programs face the challenge of interpreting multiple forms of feedback based on differing standards and varied assessment tools. Overall data on individual providers or local communities is not accessible in one place at a state or national level. It is difficult to interpret feedback of different assessments from an individual agency because they may be geared to different systems of standards.

- *Elementary school teachers and principals.* A final problem is the gap between pre-K and K–Grade 3 standards, assessments, data, and related instructional and professional development efforts. The vast majority of young children move from disparate forms of early childhood education into a common and universal public education system. Linkages between programs for preschoolers and the public education system have begun to improve but remain limited and sporadic, despite decades of research showing the benefits to children of continuity in pre-K–Grade 3 learning (Bogard & Takanishi, 2005; Pianta & Kraft-Sayre, 2003; Reynolds, Ou, Topitzes, 2004; Shore, 1998). In many cases, early childhood programs collect valuable data on children's accomplishments, characteristics, and the sequence of their early learning experiences, but available technology that could help transmit these records to kindergarten and primary-grade teachers is not used. The communities where educators can view children's progress across the pre-K–Grade 3 continuum are few and far between. Similarly, most localities do not coordinate preschool and elementary curricula and professional development.

VARIETIES OF STATE READINESS ASSESSMENT INITIATIVES

The following case studies of State Readiness Assessment Initiatives illustrate examples of efforts to assess the progress and accomplishments of young children as well as program quality. State efforts differ in the scope of data collection, types of assessment tools, and how assessment data are reported and utilized.

Assessing Children

The ways in which several states assess preschool children are discussed next.

Maryland

At the time this book was published, the Maryland State Department of Education (MSDE) was entering its sixth year of reporting on a statewide assessment of all young children (Grafwallner, 2006). More than 2,000 kindergarten teachers administer a modified, shortened version of the Work Sampling System (WSS; Meisels et al., 2001) observational assessment to more than 54,000 children during the month of November.

Reporting on a statewide basis highlights trends over time in the overall levels of "readiness" of children and is documented by teacher ratings on 30 indicators across seven domains of learning and development. For example, the 2006–2007 assessments show that 67% of all children scored in the "full readiness" category (defined on the basis of a state-developed benchmarking system), up from 49% of all children in 2001–2002. Assessment data are also reported for various subgroups of children. This information reveals, for example, that the achievement "gap" has narrowed since 2001 for low-income and African American children but has not been reduced for children classified as limited English speaking (also known as English language learners or ELLs) or those in special education. Reports are also provided for children who attend five different types of early care and education programs (child care centers, family child care, Head Start, pre-K, and nonpublic nursery schools) as well as home-based/informal care arrangements. Other reports are provided for each local school district, allowing counties and cities to compare results for their children with overall state averages and trends. Reporting is not broken out on the basis of specific local early childhood agencies, centers, or classrooms, however.

Maryland assessment data are reviewed by state legislative committees as part of a bipartisan effort to implement results-based decision making. For example, the previous governor and the general assembly provided $1.8 million to expand a state Early Childhood Mental Health Consultation Project to address the social-emotional needs of preschoolers based, in part, on the kindergarten assessment data. School districts use the information to develop programmatic initiatives and instructional strategies. Kindergarten teachers are also encouraged to use the WSS assessment on an ongoing basis to monitor the progress of children and in report cards to parents. The MSDE invests close to $1 million in ongoing funding for professional development to prepare teachers to reliably administer the assessment. See Chapter 5 for further description of the Maryland system.

Florida

Florida, like Maryland, is implementing a system of individual assessment of students entering kindergarten. All school districts will administer subsets of the Early Childhood Observation System (ECHOS; Pearson, 2005) and the Dynamic Indicators of Basic Early Literacy Skills (DIBELS; Good & Kaminski, 2002) to students entering kindergarten, reporting a "kindergarten readiness rate" for each public and private pre-K provider. Legislation mandates a progressive sequence of consequences for the lowest performing 15% of provider agencies (based on average readiness rates of children). First the lowest performing providers are given technical assistance. If there is no improvement, new curricula are required. If there is still no improvement in outcomes, funds are denied to the provider agencies.

One strength of the Maryland and Florida systems includes assessing students when they enter kindergarten to minimize pressure on teacher assessors to inflate results. Each state uses a broad-based observational tool highlighting the significance of multiple domains. A positive byproduct of the system is that it is sharpening kindergarten teachers' early awareness of children's abilities and differences; also, having data on all children is useful to early childhood system planning/advocacy and K–12 educators.

The limitations of the two systems include the one-time assessment. A readiness index metric does not reflect differences in children's skills at entry to pre-K or how much progress is made by children during pre-K or kindergarten. And it does not provide feedback on children's progress in preschool or kindergarten. Furthermore, reporting on children's readiness without the context of program quality/learning opportunities does not allow for program improvement. Furthermore, there is concern that outcomes-based consequences could lead programs to selectively recruit children with higher levels of skills.

Assessing Program Quality

This section describes how several states assess program quality.

Pennsylvania

Pennsylvania's Keystone STARS (Standards, Training/professional development, Assistance, Resources, Support) is a statewide effort to improve the quality of early learning programs through an integrated system of program quality standards, professional development, assessments, financial incentives, and public recognition. Since its inception in 2002, voluntary participation in Keystone STARS has expanded to encompass more than 4,300 local early childhood agencies serving more than 153,000 children. This represents 68% of all state-regulated child care centers.

The state's program quality standards encompass staff qualifications and professional development, early learning programs, partnerships with family and community, and leadership and management. Four levels of quality are recognized through the system. The use of a standardized rating tool (e.g., Early Childhood Environmental Rating Scale–Revised [ECERS-R; Harms, Clifford, & Cryer, 2005]) is a key element in the Keystone STARS assessment. Programs are rated on a scale of 1–4, with 4 being the highest. Agencies seeking to qualify for a STAR 2 rating must administer the standardized tool in all classrooms and develop improvement plans to address any subscale scores below a 3.0 (on a scale that runs from 1.0–7.0). External assessors are used with applicants for STAR 3 and STAR 4 ratings. They rate a sample of one third of an agency's classrooms against criteria that incorporate a minimum overall average rating for the agency as a whole (4.25 for STAR 3 and 5.25 for STAR 4) as well as minimum scores and subscale scores for each sampled classroom.

Pennsylvania invests more than $46 million to support Keystone STARS, including more than $22.5 million in funding to participating provider agencies. Based on their level of quality attainment, providers receive STAR merit awards, incentive funding for educating and retaining managers and staff members, and STARS supports to assist agencies in making improvements and moving to higher levels in the rating system.

The Keystone STARS program incorporates references to Head Start's performance standards and program monitoring effort, as well as recognizing voluntary accreditation systems such as those of the NAEYC, the National Association of Family Child Care, and other organizations. Based on a careful crosswalk and comparison of quality standards across these systems, local agencies that attain NAEYC accreditation can qualify for a Star 4 rating if they complete an abbreviated review on a limited set of criteria. The state is considering how Keystone STARS can benefit public schools as well as preschool programs licensed by the department of education. As Keystone STARS evolves, the state also reexamines quality criteria and other elements of the system. For example, an enhancement of criteria in the area of early childhood education requires agencies seeking a STAR 3 or higher rating to utilize a curriculum that is aligned to the state's early learning guidelines.

New Jersey

New Jersey's Department of Education collects and reports several types of data on the quality of services in provider agencies funded through their Abbott Preschool Program, which serves 43,000 children at a budget of more than $450 million. Three standardized tools are used for rating classroom quality. The ECERS-R provides an overview of the quality of classrooms and the capacity to compare scores with results from national research projects as well as to track trends over time by using data from past state evaluation studies. The Support for Early Literacy Assessment (SELA; Smith, Davidson, Weisenfeld, & Katsaros, 2001), a state-developed rating tool, focuses on specific instructional practices supporting children's early language and literacy skills. The Preschool Classroom Mathematics Inventory (PCMI; Frede, Dessewffy, Hornbeck, & Worth, 2001), a state-developed tool, focuses on the quality of materials and instructional practices to support mathematics learning.

A team of early childhood faculty from higher education institutions administers the rating tools in more than 300 classrooms each year. The classrooms that are chosen comprise a random sample in each school district that receives Abbott funding. Data are used by the state in planning professional development efforts. Reports show improvement over time in the average ratings on all three tools on a statewide basis. In addition, state staff members review the results for individual school districts and use the information in developing plans for local technical assistance and professional development efforts. The state also requires master teachers in each local school district to assess the quality of every classroom. This information is used in planning training for individual teachers as well as in evaluating the contracts for funding private child care providers and Head Start agencies. Contracted classrooms must meet or exceed a minimum score in order to continue to be eligible for funding.

In addition, each local program conducts an annual self-assessment using the Self-Assessment Validation System (SAVS; New Jersey Department of Education, 2007), a state-developed tool with a 45-item rating scale based on state program implementation guidelines. State staff members conduct validation to roughly one third of all school districts annually to verify the documentation and validity of the self-assessment data. This information is also linked to program improvement and professional development efforts.

The higher education faculty members also assess a representative sample of children at kindergarten entry for reporting on the state pre-K program as a whole. There is also ongoing external assessment of representative samples of children at kindergarten entry (assessing oral language, early literacy, and mathematics), which also looks at the state pre-K program as a whole.

Teachers use the state-developed Early Learning Assessment System three times a year to assess oral language and literacy skills of all preschool children for use in instructional planning. The assessment will be expanded to include mathematics; results are not reported to the state.

The strengths of the Pennsylvania and New Jersey systems include providing multiple forms of feedback on program quality and children's learning, including ongoing, credible child and program assessment data on state pre-K programs as a whole. Both build local capacity to understand and use a combination of classroom and child assessment data. The corresponding limitation is the capacity to answer questions on children's progress/readiness levels for local school districts or smaller community-based provider agencies and it requires considerable state investment to support ongoing program improvement and external assessment efforts.

Assessing Both Children and Program Quality

Michigan

Michigan has invested in a series of program evaluations of its Michigan School Readiness Program (MSRP), which, at the time this book was published, was funded at nearly $85 million per year and was serving more than 21,500 children. Beginning in 1995, a state-initiated longitudinal evaluation study documented the quality of services in a sample of six local programs and assessed 338 participating children and a comparison group of 258 children with similar background characteristics who did not have a preschool program experience. The evaluation team assessed program quality in sample classrooms via the High/Scope Program Quality Assessment, a standardized rating tool including a total of 10 elements ranging from parent involvement, instructional staff, and administration to curriculum and learning environment. Children were assessed in preschool with the High/Scope Child Observation Record, a broad-based observational tool, and from kindergarten through Grade 4 via the School Readiness Rating Scale and the Michigan Educational Assessment Program. The evaluation also reviewed data on grade retention, referrals to special education services, and school attendance. The study revealed positive and sustained effects on children's learning from kindergarten through fourth grade and lower rates of grade retention. This same database was also used to study other policy questions, such as analyzing the quality and outcomes of full-day versus part-day preschool programs.

Michigan also participated in an evaluation of preschool programs in five states. By assessing an overall sample of more than 5,000 young children, the study produced reports on each of the five state programs and also documented patterns of outcomes across states. This study utilized a series of standardized, direct assessment tools to examine vocabulary, early mathematics, print concepts and phonological awareness, and a regression discontinuity design.[1] The study found significant positive affects of the MSRP on children's academic skills at entrance to kindergarten. Although this evaluation did not assess the quality of program services, it provided corroboration of the benefits of Michigan's program with a new sample of children, a more rigorous evaluation design, and a battery of direct assessment tools.

State officials credit these evaluation studies with creating evidence on the overall effectiveness and positive effect of the MSRP that helped convince state legislators to maintain funding for the program during an era of fiscal stringency in which virtually all state programs and agencies were subjected to budget cuts. In addition, the initial data from the longitudinal study contributed to validating the state's program quality standards and use of the Program Quality Assessment (PQA) as the state's assessment tool for program quality.

Ohio

Ohio has developed a multifaceted accountability approach for its new Early Learning Initiative (ELI) program that was established in 2005 to provide early education for children at risk of school failure and meet the child care needs of working families. The program involves 101 local provider agencies serving up to 12,000 children and was funded at $126 million in 2006. Ohio's accountability/program improvement approach uses a combination of measures of program quality and outcomes.

Three forms of data on program quality are used to document the performance of local provider agencies. External observers assess the quality of a sample of classrooms in each local agency using the Early Language and Literacy Classroom Observation Toolkit, Research Edition (ELLCO; Smith & Dickinson, 2002), a standardized tool that focuses on literacy and language teaching practices and learning oppor-

---

[1]The regression discontinuity design (RDD) is an approach that addresses the problem of selection bias by comparing two groups of children who enroll voluntarily in state pre-k: those just entering pre-k provide the control group, and those who have finished the pre-k and have just entered kindergarten are the treatment group. The RDD methodology relies on a stringent, specified birth date cutoff for pre-k eligibility to define the treatment and control groups among the children in the study. This birth date is unlikely to be associated with other child or family characteristics that would affect their learning.

tunities. Local agencies conduct an ongoing program self-assessment using a tool based on the state program guidelines. State staff members meet with local program managers to verify evidence of improvement, review scores, and provide professional development and technical assistance support. Local provider agencies report a variety of performance data such as teacher credentials, health screening, transition planning, parent education, and curriculum alignment. State staff members verify the accuracy of these reports by on-site visits.

Outcome measures include documenting children's health status, examining kindergarten retention and special education placement rates, and assessing children's literacy and language skills using Get It, Got It, Go! (n.d.), which includes a brief screening tool (Early Childhood Research Institute on Measuring Growth and Development, 1998) that examines vocabulary, rhyming, and alliteration. The state recommends that teachers use this tool frequently to monitor children's progress. Assessment scores are reported to the state in the fall and the spring. To date, Get It, Got It, Go! results are shared with local agencies in discussions with state staff members but provider-level results are not reported to the public. The state is developing a reporting system to disaggregate data by type of school district and provider agency and children's race, English language proficiency, and disability status.

State staff members review data from all of the previous assessment and reporting efforts to identify priority areas for improvement. Data has been used in developing statewide professional development courses and shared with higher education institutions to be used to enhance teacher education programs. Local agencies use the information to develop program improvement plans. Individual teachers can meet with an early literacy and language mentor coach to receive specific assistance in areas where he or she would like to improve.

Future plans include expanding the ELI accountability and assessment efforts to state preschool and early childhood special education programs and research and development work to establish performance benchmarks for the child and program assessment tools. Additional efforts will be directed to connect ELI data with the state's Education Management Information System for elementary and secondary education student data. This system reports the state's kindergarten entrance assessment, which is determined by the Kindergarten Readiness Assessment-Literacy (KRA-L; Ohio Department of Education) tool.

New Mexico

The New Mexico Pre-K Program, initiated in 2005 and funded at $13.5 million, is implementing a new state-developed child assessment initiative based on the state's Early Learning Outcomes. The assessment is primarily designed for use by teachers, but it will also generate data for state oversight and program improvement efforts.

A Pre-K Assessment Task Force guided the development of an observational child assessment tool incorporating 33 indicators in seven domains of learning and development. Teachers rate all children on all indicators three times per year. In addition, teachers use a portfolio-based tool to provide more detailed narrative descriptions of children's performance on a smaller set of five to seven indicators. The state sponsors 3-day training sessions to improve teachers' skills in observing children and to enhance the consistency of ratings on the assessment tool. A second training effort helps teachers use assessment data in curriculum planning.

Planning instruction, reporting to parents, and sharing with schools when children make the transition to kindergarten are the primary purposes of the state's assessment tool. Each local program, however, will also report their assessments to the state. The data about the progress of all children over the course of the fall, mid-year, and spring ratings is aggregated and reported to the legislature. State program managers are also analyzing the data to examine patterns of performance in different types of provider agencies (e.g., school districts, Head Start grantees, private child care providers). They also use the data to set priorities for state training and technical assistance efforts. The state reports overall scores back to each local program and can examine whether patterns of performance for children in different provider agencies are similar to trends for the state program as a whole. The state also provides feedback to local programs on the quality of their portfolio assessment documentation and consistency of ratings. To date, however, assessment information on specific local agencies is not reported to the media, nor has the state established any benchmarks for expected rates of progress or levels of performance on the child assessment tool.

In addition to reviewing child assessment information, state staff members visit each local program twice each year to provide monitoring and technical assistance on the state program quality standards. The state also convenes quarterly meetings of all local programs to clarify expectations and provide assistance in improving program quality and management.

Arkansas

The state's departments of human services and education conduct program quality assessments of all provider agencies in conjunction with a major expansion of Arkansas's Better Chance for School Success (ABC) pre-K program. State staff members conduct on-site reviews of each local program to examine their compliance with the state's program quality standards, including criteria such as staff qualifications, licensing of the facility, and curriculum implementation. In addition, consultants assess program quality by utilizing the ECERS-R in each ABC-funded provider agency at least once per year. All newly funded classrooms and centers are assessed as are one third of all previously funded settings. Each classroom must achieve an overall level of 5.0 or better on the ECERS-R's 7-point scale. Reviewers discuss their ratings with each teacher as well as the local program coordinator to provide specific feedback on each indicator and any needed improvements. Providers scoring below the minimum level receive technical assistance and are reevaluated; any program not achieving an acceptable score after a third round of assistance will lose their funding for that center.

A preschool child assessment initiative calls for all ABC-funded provider agencies to administer the WSS (Meisels et al., 2001) observational tool to all preschool children three times per year. Assessment information is reported to the Arkansas Department of Human Services Division of Child Care and Early Childhood Education. The data can be aggregated at the classroom level, by provider agency, or for the entire state ABC program. To date, the data is primarily used to report to the legislature for the state program as a whole and to show children's increasing levels of proficiency in seven domains of learning and development.

The Qualls Early Learning Inventory (Qualls, Hoover, Dunbar, & Frisbie, 2003), an observational tool aligned with the state's Kindergarten Readiness Indicators, is administered to all children at the beginning of the year and is used by teachers to plan instruction and report to parents.

These states (Michigan, Ohio, New Mexico, and Arkansas) illustrate varied approaches to collecting, reporting, and using standards-based assessments of children's early learning and program quality. They differ in their approaches, assessment tools, and reporting methods. Most notably, Michigan has engaged in several evaluation studies of representative samples of MSRP children and classrooms. This approach provides highly credible data on the overall performance of MSRP programs and children, and even allows comparison of results from the MSRP to outcomes from early education programs in other states. However, it does not generate information on the quality or outcomes of individual communities, local agencies, or classrooms; whereas, Ohio, New Mexico, and Arkansas are collecting ongoing data on all children and all local agencies in their early education programs based on teacher-administered child assessments and program quality assessments administered by state agency staff members or consultants.

STATE SCHOOL READINESS ASSESSMENTS: WHAT IS AT STAKE?

This review of the state of state school readiness assessments began with a scan of a policy landscape characterized by fragmentation and innovation. There are diverse approaches to early childhood standards, assessments, and program improvement, based on the multiple sources of funding for early education services. Moreover, many local early childhood agencies and teachers are striving to understand and implement several new assessment-related mandates and systems—all at the same time. Within this policy context, states are launching, managing, and fine-tuning a variety of assessment efforts. They include new standards-based efforts to assess children's learning and development and the quality of program services and classroom environments. These assessments are generating expanded data and new forms of feedback on the performance of children and programs on a statewide basis, for specific types of state programs, local communities, individual local agencies, and classrooms. States are also devising new mechanisms to use assessment data to improve early education programs, including professional development, technical assistance, and use of financial incentives.

Designing large-scale assessments of young children and accountability strategies for diverse early education programs are complex, challenging, costly and even controversial tasks for state and federal agencies (National Early Childhood Accountability Task Force, 2007; National Research Council, 2008). Devising a technically unassailable accountability system or attaining consensus among all key stakeholders and audiences may appear elusive—if not impossible—goals.

Yet what underscores early childhood accountability efforts is a fundamental, enduring concern for the well-being and futures of young children, a concern shared by the early childhood profession and policy leaders. This era of innovation in how our nation assesses young children and early childhood programs reflects a commitment by the early childhood community to develop more accurate and credible tools to demonstrate the value of programs for young children. It also reflects a commitment to using assessment data as a resource to guide and motivate efforts to help teachers become even more effective in preparing young children for success in school and in life. In a similar fashion, the persistent refinement of state readiness assessments reflects the fact that "accountability" is a moving target. That is, policy makers expect early childhood programs—as well as all forms of public investment—to demonstrate their worth over and over again, and in new and different ways.

REFERENCES

Barnett, W.S. (1998). *Long-term outcomes of early childhood programs on cognitive and school outcomes.* Retrieved October 1, 2008, from http://www.futureof children.org/usr_doc/vol5no3ART2.pdf

Barnett, W.S., Hustedt, J.T., Friedman, A.H., Boyd, J.S., & Ainsworth, P. (2007). *The state of preschool 2007: State preschool yearbook.* New Brunswick: Rutgers, State University of New Jersey, National Institute for Early Education Research.

Bogard, K., & Takanishi, R. (2005). PK-3: An aligned and coordinated approach to education for children 3–8 years old. *Social Policy Report, 19*(3), 3–23.

Bruner, C., Wright, M.S., Gebhard, B., & Hibbard, S. (2004) *Building an early learning system: The ABCs of planning and governance structures.* Des Moines, IA: SECPTAN.

Burchinal, M., Yazejian, N., Clifford, R., Culkin, M., Howes, C., Byler, P., Kagan, S., Rustici, J., Bryant, D., Mocan, H., Morris, J., Peisner-Feingold, E., Phillipsen, L., & Zelazo, J. (1995). *Cost, quality, and child outcomes in child care centers: Public report* (2nd ed.). Denver: Department of Economics, University of Colorado.

Campbell, F.A., Ramey, C., Pungello, E.P., Sparling, J., & Miller-Johnson, S. (2002). Early childhood education: Young adult outcomes from the Abecedarian Project. *Applied Developmental Science, 6*(1), 42–57.

Coffman, J., Wright, M.S., & Bruner, C. (2006). *Beyond parallel play: Emerging state and community planning roles in building early learning systems.* Des Moines, IA: SECPTAN.

Early Childhood Research Institute on Measuring Growth and Development. (1998). *Research and development of individual growth and development indicators for children between birth and age eight* (Tech. Rep. No. 4), Minneapolis, MN: Center for Early Education and Development, University of Minnesota.

Frede, E., Dessewffy, M., Hornbeck, A., & Worth, A. (2001). *Preschool Classroom Mathematics Inventory.* Unpublished instrument.

Get It, Got It, Go! (n.d.). Retrieved March 10, 2009, from http://ggg.umn.edu

Good, R.H., & Kaminski, R.A. (Eds.). (2002). *Dynamic Indicators of Basic Early Literacy Skills* (6th ed.). Eugene, OR: Institute for Development of Educational Achievement. Also available online: http://dibels.uoregon.edu

Gormley, W.T., & Gayer, T. (2003). *Promoting school readiness in Oklahoma: An evaluation of Tulsa's pre-k program.* Washington, DC: Public Policy Institute, Georgetown University.

Grafwallner, R. (2006). *Maryland model for school readiness (MMSR) kindergarten assessment: A large-scale early childhood assessment project to establish a statewide instructional accountability system.* Unpublished paper for the National Early Childhood Accountability Task Force.

Harms, T., Clifford, R., & Cryer, D. (2005). *The Early Childhood Environment Rating Scale–Revised.* Chapel Hill, NC: University of North Carolina.

Hart, B., & Risley, T.R. (1995). *Meaningful differences in the everyday experience of young American children.* Baltimore: Paul H. Brookes Publishing Co.

Herzenberg, S., Price, M., & Bradley, D. (2005). *Losing ground in early childhood education.* Washington, DC: Economic Policy Institute.

Individuals with Disabilities Education Improvement Act (IDEA) of 2004, PL 108-446, 20 U.S.C. §§ 1400 *et seq.*

Krueger, C. (2006). *P-16 collaboration in the states: ECS state notes.* Denver: Education Commission of the States.

Lee, V.E., & Burkam, D.T. (2002). *Inequality at the starting gate: Social background differences in achievement as children begin school.* Washington, DC: Economic Policy Institute.

Loeb, S., Bridges, M., Fuller, B., Rumberger, R., & Bassok, D. (2005). *How much is too much? The influence of preschool centers on children's social and cognitive development* (NBER Working Paper No. 11812). Cambridge, MA: National Bureau of Economic Research.

Loeb, S., Fuller, B., Kagan, S.L., & Carrol, B. (2004). Child care in poor communities: Early learning effects of type, quality and stability. *Child Development, 75*(1), 47–65.

Macmillan, L., & Neugebauer, R. (2006). *Rush to assessment: The role private early childhood service providers play in assessment child and program outcomes.* Unpublished paper prepared for the National Early Childhood Accountability Task Force.

Meisels, S.J., Jablon, J., Marsden, D.B., Dichtelmiller, M.L., & Dorfman, A., (2001). *The Work Sampling System* (4th ed.). Ann Arbor, MI: Rebus Inc.

National Association for the Education of Young Children. (2005). *NAEYC early childhood program standards.* Washington, DC. Author.

National Early Childhood Accountability Task Force. (2007). *Taking stock: Assessing and improving early childhood learning and program quality.* Philadelphia: Author.

National Research Council. (2008). Early childhood assessment: Why, what, and how. Committee on Developmental Outcomes and Assessments for Young Children, in C.E. Snow and S.B. Van Hemel (Eds.), *Board on Children, Youth and Families, Board on Testing and Assessment, Division of Behavioral and Social Sciences and Education.* Washington, DC: The National Academies Press.

New Jersey Department of Education. (2007). *Self-Assessment Validation System (SAVS) for Abbott Preschool Programs–Revised,* 2007–2008. Retrieved March 10, 2009, from http://www.nj.gov/education/ece/abbott/savs.pdf

NICHD Early Child Care Research Network. (2005). Early care and children's development in the primary grades: Follow-up results from the NICHD Study of Early Child Care. *American Educational Research Journal, 42*(3), 537–570.

No Child Left Behind Act (NCLB) of 2001, PL 107-110, 115 Stat. 1425, 20 U.S.C. §§ 6301 *et seq.*

Pearson, N.C.S. (2005). *The Observational Assessment System for Pre-Kindergarten through Grade 2.* New York: Harcourt.

Pianta, R.C., Howes, C., Burchinal, M., Bryant, D., Clifford, D., Early, D., & Barbarin, O. (2005). Features of pre-kindergarten programs, classrooms, and teachers: Do they predict observed classroom quality and child–teacher interactions? *Applied Developmental Science, 9*(3), 144–159.

Pianta, R.C., & Kraft-Sayre, M. (2003). *Successful kindergarten transition: Your guide to connecting children, families, and schools*. Baltimore: Paul H. Brookes Publishing Co.

PreK Now. (2006). *Votes count: Legislative action on pre-k, fiscal year 2007*. Washington, DC: Author.

PreK Now. (2007). *Leadership matters: Governors' pre-k proposals, fiscal year 2008*. Washington, DC: Author.

Qualls, A.L., Hoover, H.D., Dunbar, S.B., & Frisbie, D.A. (2003). *Qualls Early Learning Inventory*. Rolling Meadows, IL: Riverside Publishing Company.

Reynolds, A.J., Ou, S., & Topitzes, J.D. (2004). Paths of effects of early childhood intervention on educational attainment and delinquency: A confirmatory analysis of the Chicago child–parent centers. *Child Development, 75*(5), 1299–1388.

Reynolds, A.J., & Temple, J.A. (1998). Extended early childhood intervention and school achievement: Age 13 findings from the Chicago Longitudinal Study. *Child Development, 69*(1), 231–246.

Rouse, C.E., Brooks-Gunn, J., & Mclanahan, S. (Eds.) (2005). *Closing racial and ethnic gaps. School readiness: The future of children, 15*. Retrieved October, 2008, from http:// www.futureofchildren.org

Schumacher, R., Irish, K., & Lombardi, J. (2003). *Meeting great expectations: Integrating early education program standards in child care*. Washington, DC: Center for Law and Social Policy.

Schweinhart, L.J., Montie, J., Xiang, Z., Barnett, W.S., Belfield, C.R., & Nores, M. (2004). *Lifetime effects: The High/Scope Perry Preschool study through age 40*. Ypsilanti, MI: High/Scope Press.

Shonkoff, J.P., & Phillips, D.A. (Eds.). (2000). *From neurons to neighborhoods: The science of early childhood development*. Washington, DC: National Academies Press.

Shore, R. (1998). *Ready schools: A report of the Goal 1 Ready School Resource Group*. Washington, DC: National Education Goals Panel.

Smith, M.W., & Dickinson, D.D. (with Sangeorge, A., & Anastasopoulos, L.). (2002). *Early Language and Literacy Classroom Observation (ELLCO) Toolkit* (Research ed.). Baltimore: Paul H. Brookes Publishing Co.

Smith, S., Davidson, S., Weisenfeld, G., & Katsaros, S. (2001). *Supports for Early Literacy Assessment (SELA)*. New York: New York University.

Chapter 3

Models for Financing State-Supported Prekindergarten Programs

Anne W. Mitchell

An enduring set of questions has been asked since the first national study of publicly supported preschool care and education, The Public School Early Childhood Study, was conducted by Bank Street College of Education and Wellesley College in the early 1980s: How much do states spend overall per year? Per child? Where does the money come from? The Children's Defense Fund (1999) reported state prekindergarten (pre-K) data in the 1990s, including annual funding; an update on state budget appropriations for pre-K was done in 1998 (Adams & Sandfort, 1994; Mitchell, 1998; Mitchell, Seligson, & Marx, 1989; Mitchell, Stoney, & Dichter, 2001). The annual *Preschool Yearbooks* from the National Institute for Early Education Research (NIEER) have paid particular attention to some of these finance questions, and NIEER is the best source for data on state spending (Barnett, Hustedt, Friedman, Boyd, & Ainsworth, 2007).

This chapter focuses primarily on the latter question of how state preschool programs are funded, rather than the more common issues of spending per state or per child. After a brief discussion of the growth over time of the total investment being made in preschool by the states, the chapter turns to the revenue sources used by the states to fund preschool, some questions and challenges about these different revenue-generating methods, and the outlook for preschool finance strategies in the next decade.

HOW MUCH DO STATES SPEND OVERALL ON PRESCHOOL?

The amount of state funding appropriated for all types of preschool programs has grown dramatically over time. Before 1970, the best estimate is that the total investment was a little less than $25 million among seven states with programs (i.e., California, District of Columbia, New Jersey, New York, Pennsylvania, Washington, West Virginia; Mitchell et al., 1989). By 1988, there were 28 states involved, spending $190 million annually. By now, there are more than 40 states spending close to $4 billion annually (Barnett et al., 2007). This increase in overall investment—from $190 million to more than $4 billion in 20 years—is well beyond inflation, which would have brought the total to roughly $475 million in that time frame. Two points are worth noting—the investment in preschool by states has grown dramatically and state investment in early education has been going on for quite a while.

HOW DO STATES FUND PRESCHOOL?

It is widely known that there are only a few sources of revenue available to a state. Government can generate revenue from what is earned, what is spent, what is owned, and what is used. That is, *taxes* come in the form of income taxes, sales taxes, property taxes, and excise taxes. Revenue can also be generated by *fees,* such as those charged for a driver's license or highway toll. Finally, states can generate revenue through *lotteries* and other gambling proceeds. In addition, there are a few types of federal funds that states can direct (e.g., Temporary Assistance for Needy Families [TANF]). Of course, school districts can choose to fund preschool using federal Title I funds, which has been an option since the passage of the Elementary and Secondary Education Act of 1965 (PL 89-10).

General Revenue

The vast majority of states fund preschool with general revenue. Preschool is in the state budget, either as a separate line item, a line item in the education budget, or embedded within the state education aid formulas. In most states, the preschool budget line is distributed through a grant/contract method. Grants/contracts are between the state and various eligible entities such as school districts, Head Start, child care, and so forth. Or, grants are made directly to school districts that can then contract with other entities.

Only a handful of states distribute preschool funding through the regular education aid formulas. Maine, Oklahoma, Texas, Vermont, West Virginia, and Wisconsin have done this for some time, and Nebraska began doing so in 2006 for districts that had previously received preschool grants.

In November 2007, Nebraska voters approved 54% to 46% a constitutional amendment to allow "perpetual school funds" to be used for early childhood education. The amendment creates an early childhood education endowment fund and moves $40 million into the fund. Interest and income from the fund can be used to support early education. The amendment requires that $20 million in private funds be added to the endowment by July 1, 2011, or the $40 million reverts to the use of the common schools. *Early childhood education* is defined as "programs operated by or distributed through the common [public] schools promoting development and learning for children from birth to kindergarten-entrance age." [1] Assuming a reasonable annual rate of return, the $60 million fund ought to generate at least $4–$5 million annually. As of 2008, Nebraska was spending approximately $2 million on its early childhood grants program and had created the first state endowment fund for early education.

In addition to funding preschool, several states make significant general fund appropriations to early care and education services for children. Two states are notable in this regard: North Carolina's Smart Start initiative ($200 million in general revenue) and Rhode Island's Starting RIght initiative. Rhode Island's general revenue contribution ($66 million) is about three times larger than the federal revenue the state receives for child care (Mitchell, 2005b). Only two states (Georgia and Missouri) fund preschool entirely from a dedicated funding source.

Lotteries

Although lotteries may seem like a modern invention, government-sponsored lotteries—and opposition to them on moral grounds—have been with us since the founding of our nation. All of the original 13

---

[1]Proposed constitutional amendments appearing on the 2006 general election ballot (p. 5). Retrieved January 26, 2007, from http://www.sos.state.ne.us/elec/pdf/const_amd_gen_elect2006.pdf

colonies held lotteries to raise revenue for public purposes. Lotteries were used to raise funds to build universities including Harvard, The College of William and Mary, Yale, Columbia, Dartmouth, and Princeton, as well as libraries and even churches. The social reform movement of the early 1800s eventually put an end to government-sponsored lotteries (and most other forms of gambling). There were no legal lotteries in the United States from 1894, when Congress outlawed them, until 1964, when New Hampshire started the current trend (Dunstan, 1997).

Now lotteries are a popular way to fund education and almost every state has a lottery; only eight states did not at the time of this book's publication.[2] Lottery revenue is usually divided into portions of approximately 50% for prizes, 15% for operations, and 35% for education or other worthy purposes. Georgia has consistently used lottery proceeds to fund preschool since 1993; the Georgia lottery provides approximately $275 million annually for preschool. Florida had funded one of its previous preschool programs partly with lottery dollars until 2002, when the voters approved a constitutional amendment establishing voluntary pre-K for all 4-year-olds. Florida uses general revenue for the constitutionally mandated preschool program called Voluntary Prekindergarten (VPK). The annual appropriation for 2005–2006 was $387 million (Florida Department of Education, 2005). In 2000, Alabama attempted to pass a lottery for preschool, but failed.

In 2003, the Oklahoma legislature approved a two-part ballot measure to establish an education lottery and enact a constitutional amendment to ensure that all proceeds benefit preschool education through higher education. The measure included supplement, not supplant, language. Voters approved the measure on the November 2004 ballot. The lottery began in 2005; 30% of lottery proceeds are placed into the Oklahoma Lottery Education Trust Fund.

Tennessee voters approved a lottery for pre-K through 12th-grade education that began in 2004. No lottery funds were initially appropriated for pre-K, which continued to receive general revenue support. In 2005, Governor Bredesen proposed adding $24 million from lottery funds to the $10 million in general revenue that already supported pre-K, and the General Assembly agreed.

The North Carolina legislature approved a lottery in 2005, with all proceeds to go to education; specifically, initiatives to reduce class size in the early grades and pre-K programs receive about half of the proceeds, and the remainder is allocated for school construction (40%) and college scholarships (10%). Lottery tickets went on sale in April 2006.

---

[2]North American Association of State and Provincial Lotteries. Retrieved January 26, 2007, from http://www.naspl.org

North Carolina appropriated $49 million in general revenue for the More at Four preschool program in 2004–2005 (before the lottery). For 2005–2006, the appropriation rose to $66 million (North Carolina Governor's Office of School Readiness/More at Four Pre-Kindergarten Program, 2006). For 2006–2007, the first year with lottery proceeds, the More at Four appropriation reached $86 million (C. Cobb, personal communication, February 1, 2007).

Gambling-Related Funds (Gambling Proceeds)

Missouri uses a portion of riverboat gambling fees collected by the state to fund its preschool program. Missouri policy makers are quite clear that these are *not* "gambling proceeds" but rather fees (levied on gamblers) that are collected by the state. The allocation for preschool was $21 million in 2000 but has declined in recent years to $12 million in 2006–2007 (Barnett et al., 2007).

Sales Tax

Two states use a dedicated part of the state sales tax to fund preschool. In 1984, South Carolina established preschool for 4-year-olds who were at risk (called 4-K) as part of an education improvement bill and funded it with a 1-cent increase in sales tax. Preschool funding was $22 million in 2006 (Barnett et al., 2007). Arkansas's preschool program was also initiated as part of an education reform package supported by an education trust fund paid for by a dedicated sales tax. Voters in Washington State rejected a measure on the November 2004 ballot that would have authorized a 1-cent increase in sales tax to establish an education trust fund for preschool, improvements in K–12 education and higher education access (Mitchell, 2005a).

"Sin" Taxes

Arkansas has had a preschool program since 1991. When the funding for preschool was threatened several years ago, the legislature enacted a 3% surtax on beer to supplement the general revenue supporting preschool. The beer tax was set to expire in June 2005 and was extended through 2007. In 2005, the tax generated $11 million for preschool—approximately 15% of total preschool funding in Arkansas (Stone, 2006).

In 1998, California voters enacted a tax on tobacco products (Proposition 10) to support early childhood development for children birth to age 5. The tobacco tax raises about $590 million annually now, down from about $723 million in its first year (Mitchell et al., 2001). First Five commissions in each county disburse most of the funds, which are being used to support universal preschool in several counties. In 2004, the Los Angeles County Commission (First Five LA) allocated $600 million over 5 years to create a master plan for universal preschool and launched a public benefit corporation called Los Angeles Universal Preschool (LA-UP) to carry it out (Los Angeles Universal Preschool, 2005).

Arizona has the newest tobacco products tax for early childhood. In November 2006, Arizona voters approved the Early Childhood Development and Health Initiative (Proposition 203) by a margin of 53% to 47%. The initiative is expected to raise as much as $150 million a year from a tax of 4 cents per cigarette (80 cents/pack), 8 cents per cigar, and 9 cents per ounce of other tobacco products. The objectives for which funds can be spent include increasing quality and access to early childhood development and health programs and services, as well as family support, professional development, coordination, and public information (Alliance for Early Childhood Finance, 2007).

The law sets up a state board and regional partnership councils. The state board was appointed and met during January 2007 for the first time. The state board designates regions and appoints the regional councils and will approve regional funding plans. For the first 2 years, the state board was to direct the funds until fiscal year (FY) 2008–2009, when regional councils would be operational. The campaign to pass the initiative was called First Things First and that is likely how the board will brand this initiative going forward.

Tobacco Settlement Funds

Several states, such as Kentucky and Kansas, have used a portion of the state's share of the national tobacco settlement to fund early care and education. When these payments to states began in 2000, Kentucky allotted 25% of its first settlement payment, or $56 million over 2 years, to launch its Early Childhood Development Authority. The state continues to partially support preschool with these funds. Kansas directs about $800,000 of its tobacco settlement into the $12 million Prekindergarten At-Risk program budget. Louisiana also uses tobacco settlement funds for part of its preschool budget. In 2004, these funds were approximately $1.5 million of the total preschool budget of $58 million (General Accounting Office, 2004; Government Accountability Office, 2007; Stone, 2006).

Income Taxes

California had an initiative on the ballot in June 2006 called Preschool for All (for 4-year-olds). The proposed funding source was an income tax surcharge on the wealthiest .6% of Californians. The tax rate increase would have been 1.7% on taxable income of more than $800,000 for married couples and $400,000 for individuals and was expected to raise $2.3 billion.

Income tax is a good choice for a revenue source because incomes tend to increase over time, so the tax nets more over time as compared with other popular sources such as sin taxes, which are meant to decline because the state is simultaneously trying to reduce the "sinful" behaviors. Income taxes are perceived as fairer than other types of taxes. And in the California case, the group being taxed is less than 1% of the population and viewed as able to pay. The proposition failed for a number of reasons but not because of the proposed revenue source (Alliance for Early Childhood Finance, 2007; Institute of Governmental Studies, 2006).

Local Taxation (Property and Sales)

Although state revenue generation for preschool is the main focus of this chapter, several interesting finance models are emerging in counties and cities that support early childhood education, specifically preschool. Localities, not states, generally tax real property, and a few generate funds specifically for early care and education through property taxes. One approach is to increase the property tax millage rate and earmark the increase for early care and education. Seattle has done this in its Families and Education Levy. This tax has been renewed by the voters three times, beginning in 1990, then in 1997, and most recently in 2004. The 2004 levy focused on school readiness, academic achievement, and increased graduation rate. The school readiness section created new Early Learning Networks in two low-income neighborhoods. Networks provide preschool for 350 4-year-olds, a home visiting program for toddlers, wage supplements for child care staff, kindergarten transition teams, and quality support for child care programs serving children under 3 years old. For 2006, the levy budget was $14.7 million; about 18% ($2.6 million) supports early learning activities (City of Seattle, 2006; Mitchell, 2005a).

In 2002, voters in Portland, Oregon, approved (53% to 47%) a measure to create a Children's Investment Fund with a 5-year property tax levy. It raises about $8.5 million a year to finance a variety of children's programs including child-abuse prevention, after-school and mentoring programs, and early childhood education programs. About 40% of the funds ($3.7 million) go for early childhood projects (Children's Investment Fund, n.d.; Mitchell, 2005a).

Another strategy is to earmark a percentage of existing local property tax dollars for children's services. Since 1991, San Francisco has set a baseline budget for children's services and then earmarked a part of the property tax for children's services (2.5¢/$100 of tax collected) above the baseline. In March 2004, San Francisco voters went further and approved a measure (70% to 30%) to increase the city's spending on public education for the next 11 years, beginning at $10 million in FY2005–2006 and reaching $60 million by 2009. One third of the annual funds support preschool programs (Mitchell, 2005a; Mitchell et al., 2001).

Local sales tax is another way to generate revenue for early childhood education. In 1990, voters in Aspen, Colorado, approved a provision to add .45% to the local sales tax and dedicated this portion for affordable housing and child care. In 1999, 66% of voters approved extending the tax through 2010. The tax produces about $500,000 annually to support child care resource and referral, improvement grants to nonprofits, and tuition assistance to families. Twenty percent of tax revenues go directly into a trust fund. Several counties in Colorado have attempted similar propositions without success (Mitchell et al., 2001).

In 2006, Denver voters approved a .12% sales tax increase (12 cents on a $100 purchase) to increase access to and improve the quality of preschool services. It passed with a slim margin and is expected to raise about $12 million annually. Any child living in Denver can get tuition assistance to attend preschool; the amount depends on the quality of the preschool and the family's income. Any program in or within a certain distance from Denver that chooses to participate in the quality improvement system is eligible. The preschool program is to be managed by an independent nonprofit agency (Alliance for Early Childhood Finance, 2007; Denver Preschool Program, n.d.). Local revenue generation can create significant annual investments for early care and education.

Federal Funds: Temporary Assistance for Needy Families

Finally, nine states (Alabama, Idaho, Kansas, Louisiana, Massachusetts, New Mexico, North Dakota, Ohio, and Pennsylvania) have at one point used surplus Temporary Assistance for Needy Families (TANF) funds to support their preschool programs in whole or in part because federal TANF funds that are not spent for assistance may be used for other purposes at a state's discretion. The availability of this source is definitely declining, given new TANF provisions for higher work participation, longer work hours, rising caseloads, and other budget pressures. Ohio is using TANF service funds, not surplus funds, for its Early Learning Initiative, and the children served have to be eligible for TANF. Other federal sources do support preschool (e.g., funds for preschool special education from the Individuals with Disabilities Education Improvement Act [IDEA] of 2004 [PL 108-446]). In addition, school districts have always been permitted to use Title I funds for preschool and may blend these with their state's preschool funding. Many states offer preschool in cooperation with Head Start programs, so federal Head Start funds are part of the finance mix at the state level.

Conclusions on State Funding

State investment in preschool has been going on for several decades, with greater intensity since the 1980s. It is fair to say that publicly funded preschool is now widespread, given that nearly all states are involved, and publicly supported early childhood education for children younger than 4 years old is making some progress as states and communities take steps to build comprehensive early childhood systems for children birth to 5.

An early care and education system is an integrated set of policies, services, and supports for all children birth to 5. From a finance reform perspective, system building can involve redirecting existing investments as well as making new investments. Many states and communities are engaged in building early childhood systems, some with help from national organizations such as the Build Initiative, Smart Start's National Technical Assistance Center, the National Governors' Association, and others. This work is also fueled by the federal Maternal and Child Health Bureau's planning and implementation grants to develop State Early Childhood Comprehensive Systems.

System-building takes many forms. Some states (e.g., Georgia, Massachusetts, Washington) have reorganized state-level governance and administration to support a birth to 5 system, bringing together child care, preschool, Head Start, regulation, and quality initiatives into one agency. Other systems, such as North Carolina's Smart Start, link communities to a statewide public–private system. Illinois established an Early Learning Council to plan a comprehensive system for children birth to 5 and is the only state where preschool funding includes a set-aside for programs for infants and toddlers. Rhode Island created Starting RIght, their early care and education system, which includes quality initiatives, comprehensive services networks similar to Head Start, and health benefits for family child care providers and center staff (Mitchell, 2005b). Pennsylvania established a cross-agency Early Learning Team and a set of regional organizations called Keys to Quality to lead the effort (Mitchell, 2007).

FUNDING ISSUES AND CHALLENGES

General revenue is the most common way that states fund preschool. The key questions to ask about any revenue source are as follows. Does it generate sufficient funds per child enrolled to support a quality program? Is it stable and politically secure? Does it increase over time?

The *adequacy* of state funds per child is an issue regardless of the revenue source. According to the *NIEER 2005 Preschool Yearbook*, the range is huge—from $721 per child in Maryland to $9,305 per child in New Jersey. Between $8,000 and $9,000 per child is an adequate amount to support quality preschool, not $1,000 per child. Receiving local matches is another issue in per-child spending. Many states require local matches for preschool (NIEER, 2007; e.g., Alabama 50%, Arkansas 40%, Iowa 20%, Nebraska 50%, North Carolina, Tennessee, Virginia). In addition, all of those states that use the regular education aid formula for preschool also require local matches. These states may be caught in a bind because the schools have more funding sources for the match but usually less space for the program, whereas community programs have space but no funds for the match.

Generalizability is another funding issue. Some of the revenue sources used by some states can be adapted or adopted by other states. Clearly, every state has a general revenue budget, and it is up to the state's leadership as to whether early education is in that budget. Some of the revenue sources are no longer available. Tobacco settlement funds are already committed. State lotteries are in place nearly everywhere and are already dedicated to funding certain worthy causes. Early childhood education could be a good argument in favor of lotteries in the eight states (Alabama, Alaska, Arkansas, Hawaii, Mississippi, Nevada, Utah, Wyoming) that do not have them yet, but it is probably politically difficult in the rest of the states to change the purpose of lottery proceeds.

Dedicated revenue sources can be perceived as the only revenue needed to address the programs that they are funding. The argument goes something like this: "We dedicated the lottery, the sales tax, or whatever to preschool, so that is taken care of. There is no need for other funds." For example, Colorado is considering reducing the allocation for the Colorado Preschool Program in Denver because Denver passed the preschool initiative!

Some dedicated revenue sources are by their nature declining. Sin taxes, especially tobacco taxes, are likely to decline because government is simultaneously mounting campaigns to reduce smoking, often using the same funds (e.g., California). That is one reason the Preschool for All Initiative in California was so interesting. It used an income tax surcharge because income is an ever-increasing revenue source.

General revenue is probably the most secure funding source. Some would say the education section of the state budget is the best place to be, even though there are pros and cons. Early childhood education is in the education budget two ways—as a grant program usually administered by the education agency (dozens of states) or in the education aid formula (six to seven states). The pros of being in the education budget as a line item are that education is politically stable, is funded with general revenue, and is the largest item in any state budget (so preschool is a small part of a larger secure item). The pros of being in the education aid formula are similar—stability (aid formulas are not revisited that often, so once preschool is in, it is probably there to stay). The cons of the education aid formula, and of being in the education budget in general, are that directing funds beyond public schools will be difficult. The public school culture is strong, and although schools may contract for food or busing, they do not routinely contract for education. Furthermore, the early education effort may get confused with contentious public school issues such as vouchers and charter schools.

Finally, state innovation in governing early care and education is giving us new revenue issues to consider. States are unifying and elevating early childhood education by creating offices and departments under a range of titles—early learning (Washington), early education and care (Massachusetts), early care and learning (Georgia), child development and early learning (Pennsylvania)—that bring together child care, pre-K, and early intervention. For the most part, these agencies have their own budgets and their own claim on general revenue. We will have to see whether they are better revenue generators for early childhood than education budgets or dedicated sources.

REFERENCES

Adams, G., & Sandfort, J. (1994). *First steps, promising futures.* Washington, DC: Children's Defense Fund.

Alliance for Early Childhood Finance. (2007). *What's new! Recent reports and resources on early care and education finance.* Retrieved April 10, 2007, from http://www.earlychildhoodfinance.org/What%27sNew/WhatsNewMarch 2007.doc

Barnett, W.S., Hustedt, J.T., Friedman, A.H., Boyd, J.S., & Ainsworth, P. (2007). *The state of preschool 2007: State preschool yearbook.* New Brunswick: Rutgers,

State University of New Jersey, National Institute for Early Education Research.

Children's Defense Fund. (1999). *Seeds of success: State prekindergarten initiatives 1998–99.* Washington, DC: Author.

Children's Investment Fund. (n.d.). *History of the Children's Investment Fund.* Retrieved January 26, 2007, from http://www.childrensinvestmentfund.org/whatwedo/overview/history

City of Seattle, Office for Education. (2006). *Families and education levy executive summary mid-year report: July 2006.* Retrieved January 26, 2007, from http://www.seattle.gov/neighborhoods/education/Exec%20Summary%20Mid-Year%20Report%20July06.pdf

Denver Preschool Program. (n.d.). *Frequently Asked Questions.* Retrieved January 27, 2007, from http://www.preschoolmatters.org

Dunstan, R. (1997). *Gambling in California.* Retrieved on January 26, 2007, from http://www.library.ca.gov/CRB/97/03/crb97003.html#toc

Elementary and Secondary Education Act of 1965, PL 89-10, 20 U.S.C. §§ 241 *et seq.*

Florida Department of Education. (2005). *Press release: Education budget sets record levels.* Retrieved January 26, 2007, from http://www.fldoe.org/news/2005/2005_05_26-2.asp

General Accounting Office. (2004). *Tobacco settlement: States' allocations of fiscal year 2003 and expected fiscal year 2004 payments.* Washington, DC: Author.

Government Accountability Office. (2007). *Tobacco settlement: States' allocations of payments from tobacco companies for fiscal years 2000 through 2005.* Retrieved April 10, 2007, from http://www.gao.gov/new.items/d04518.pdf

Individuals with Disabilities Education Improvement Act (IDEA) of 2004, PL 108-446, 20 U.S.C. §§ 1400 *et seq.*

Institute of Governmental Studies. (2006). *Hot topic: Proposition 82 universal preschool.* Retrieved April 10, 2007, from http://www.igs.berkeley.edu/library/htUniversalPreschool.html

Los Angeles Universal Preschool. (2005). *Los Angeles universal preschool report to the Los Angeles County Children and Families First–Proposition 10 Commission.* Retrieved April 10, 2007, from http://www.laup.net/downloads/policymakers/Report_to_First_5_LA.pdf

Mitchell, A.W. (1998). *Prekindergarten programs funded by the states: Essential elements for policymakers.* New York: Families and Work Institute.

Mitchell, A.W. (2005a). *Initiative and referendum: What can we learn from the Washington State experience?* Retrieved April 10, 2007, from http://www.earlychildhoodfinance.org/handouts/4WashingtonStateIssueBrief.doc

Mitchell, A.W. (2005b). *Success stories: State investment in early care and education in Illinois, North Carolina and Rhode Island.* Raleigh, NC: Smart Start's National Technical Assistance Center. Available at http://www.earlychildhoodfinance.org/Publications/SuccessStoriesPDFDraft2.pdf

Mitchell, A.W. (2007). *What are the benefits and challenges of the emerging models for governance of early care and education services/systems in the states?* Retrieved April 10, 2007, from http://www.earlychildhoodfinance.org/Meetings&Calls/ConfCall%2012507/ConferenceCallGovernanceResourceBrief.doc

Mitchell, A.W., Seligson, M., & Marx, F. (1989). *Early childhood programs and the public schools: Between promise and practice.* Westport, CT: Auburn House/Greenwood Press.

Mitchell, A., Stoney, L., & Dichter, H. (2001). *Financing child care in the United States: An expanded catalog of current strategies.* Kansas City, MO: The Ewing Marion Kauffman Foundation. Available at http://www.kauffman.org/pdf/childcare2001.pdf

National Institute for Early Education Research (NIEER). (2005). *The state of preschool: 2005 state preschool yearbook.* New Brunswick, NJ: Rutgers University.

National Institute for Early Education Research (NIEER). (2006). *The state of preschool: 2006 state preschool yearbook.* New Brunswick, NJ: Rutgers University.

North Carolina Governor's Office of School Readiness/More at Four Pre-Kindergarten Program. (2006). *More at Four Prekindergarten Program progress report to the North Carolina general assembly.* Retrieved April 10, 2007, from http://www.governor.state.nc.us/Office/Education/_pdf/MAFFeb2006 LegislativeReport.pdf

Stone, D. (2006). *Funding the future: States' approaches to pre-k finance.* Washington, DC: PreK Now.

Chapter 4

Comparing Universal and Targeted Prekindergarten Programs

Aryn M. Dotterer, Margaret Burchinal, Donna M. Bryant, Diane M. Early, and Robert C. Pianta

C oncerns about school readiness, especially as it pertains to children from low-income families, have resulted in massive funding of state prekindergarten (pre-K) programs. Expansion of pre-K can be seen in both enrollment and funding of programs. According to the *2007 State of Preschool Yearbook* (Barnett, Hustedt, Friedman, & Boyd, 2007), 38 states funded pre-K during the 2005–2006 school year, whereas 12 states did not (Alaska, Hawaii, Idaho, Indiana,

We are grateful for the help of the many children, parents, teachers, administrators, and field staff who were a part of this study. This study is supported under the Educational Research and Development Center Program, PR/Award Number R307A60004, as administered by the Institute of Education Sciences, U.S. Department of Education; the National Center for Early Development and Learning (NCEDL). Preparation of this manuscript was supported by The National Institute for Early Education Research; U.S. Department of Education (R305A060021), and Postdoctoral Research Training Fellowship in Education Sciences, Department of Education (R305B060021). The opinions and assertions contained herein are the private opinions of the authors and are not to be construed as official or reflecting the views of the U.S. Government.

Mississippi, Montana, New Hampshire, North Dakota, Rhode Island, South Dakota, Utah, and Wyoming), although Hawaii and Rhode Island had just taken first steps toward an initiative at the time this book went to press (Doctors, 2008). Enrollment of 4-year-olds in state-funded pre-K increased from 14% in 2002 to 20% in 2006 (Barnett et al., 2006). Funding of pre-K programs has also increased. States spent $2.8 billion on pre-K programs in 2004–2005 (King, 2006), typically for early childhood education classrooms for children ages 3–5. States, however, vary considerably in their spending. (See Chapter 1 for more information on the statistics of pre-K.)

Although the importance of early learning is widely agreed on, much debate regarding who should be served exists. One of the most pressing issues in pre-K education that policy makers are faced with is whether pre-K should be available to all children, regardless of background (*universal*), or whether it should be *targeted* to children who are at risk. This chapter reviews these two models of pre-K—universal and targeted, used in the United States—highlighting the arguments for each program. The chapter then provides data from research comparing these two program types on classroom characteristics and child outcomes.

Universal programs provide classroom experiences that are available to all 4-year-old children, regardless of income or background. Parents voluntarily enroll their children. Universal programs are typically funded completely with state pre-K dollars or may be funded through a blending of funding streams across various sources. Each state has individual legislation that sets its mandates for the program. States must ensure full funding of programs and expansion of pre-K services to all geographical regions with families interested in participating in order to meet the goal of universality. Florida, Georgia, New York, and Oklahoma offer universal pre-K, and several states, including Massachusetts and West Virginia, are moving toward universal access.

Targeted pre-K is an alternative to universal pre-K. As with universal pre-K, funding usually comes from state pre-K dollars; however, targeted programs serve only children with particular characteristics or risk factors associated with school failure. States differ on what constitutes a "risk factor" and which or how many characteristics are necessary for program eligibility. Like universal programs, parents voluntarily enroll their children.

THE CASE FOR UNIVERSAL PRE-K

The universal pre-K movement is growing in response to national school readiness and educational goals. Proponents of universal pre-K, such as Steve Barnett (Barnett & Fuller, 2006), argue that lack of school readiness and low achievement are not just problems of the poor and that all children can benefit from a high-quality preschool education. A linear relationship between family income and social and academic skills of kindergartners shows that children from middle-income families tend to be far behind children from high-income families in these areas just as children from low-income families tend to be far behind children from both middle- and high-income families (Barnett, Brown, & Shore, 2004). Barnett and colleagues argued that there is no clear cutoff in which the school readiness gap dramatically narrows and that there is a lot of room for most children to improve their school readiness skills through preschool education. Some suggest that children who are disadvantaged may benefit more from universal programs because the classrooms are more likely to include a heterogeneous mix of children. Research shows that the proportion of children who are poor in the classroom is negatively related to quality (Pianta et al., 2005) and child outcomes (Schechter & Bye, 2007).

The political acceptance of universal programs, and the concomitant willingness to fund them, is likely to be higher if middle-class families can also benefit. Proponents of universal pre-K also argue that this program type is more likely to be adequately funded and with adequate funding, high-quality programs can be ensured. Many programs that serve children and families who are disadvantaged are underfunded, but if the general population also has a stake in universal pre-K, then funding and quality can be ensured.

The positive effects of one universal pre-K program on children's cognitive development were documented in a study of Oklahoma's universal pre-K program. Gormley and colleagues (Gormley, Gayer, Phillips, & Dawson, 2005) used a regression discontinuity design that reduced the threat of selection bias to compare pre-K and non–pre-K children at kindergarten entry. The regression discontinuity design makes use of the birth date cutoff for school entry to compare two groups of children who both enter the program (thereby avoiding the selection bias problem) a year apart, but who differ in age by only 1 day; the children who missed the cutoff attended pre-K the following year. The researchers concluded that attendance in Oklahoma's universal pre-K program increased children's cognitive development by 3.00 points for Woodcock-Johnson letter–word identification using the Woodcock-Johnson III Tests of Achievement (Woodcock, McGrew, & Mather, 2001), 1.86 points for spelling, and 1.94 points for applied problems. Further support for universal pre-K comes from an evaluation of Georgia's program. Henry and colleagues (Henry, Henderson, Ponder, Mashburn, & Rickman, 2003) found that although children who entered the Georgia pre-K program began the year behind children in private preschool on language and cognitive skills, they caught up with the children who attended private programs by the time they entered kindergarten.

THE CASE FOR TARGETED PRE-K

Historically, policy makers have supported targeted pre-K programs because they may compensate for the disadvantages associated with poverty that contribute to poor school-related and developmental outcomes. Early intervention programs such as the Perry Preschool High/Scope Study and the Carolina Abecedarian Study demonstrated the long-term benefits of early childhood programs on the cognitive development of children from low-income families (Campbell, Ramey, Pungello, Sparling, & Miller-Johnson, 2002; Schweinhart, Barnes, & Weikart, 1993; see Chapter 5 for more detailed descriptions of these programs). These programs, however, are intensive, expensive, and often combine early education with home visiting and/or health care services. Many of the large-scale, targeted pre-K programs have not been closely modeled after these exemplary programs. As a result, these programs fail to demonstrate the same large or lasting effects as the intensive early education programs.

One of the chief arguments in favor of targeted pre-K is that it provides early classroom learning experiences for children who are in the most need. Therefore, targeted pre-K can be more efficient and lower in cost. A program that is lower in cost and provides services to children from low-income families may be more likely to receive public support.

Head Start, which began in 1965, is an example of a federally funded targeted early education program for children from low-income households. A Head Start evaluation found small to moderate statistically significant positive effects for 3- and 4-year-old children on prereading, prewriting, vocabulary, and parent reports of children's literacy skills (U.S. Department of Health and Human Services, 2005).

The effects of Head Start were compared with the Georgia universal pre-K program (Henry, Gordon, & Rickman, 2006). In this quasi-experimental study, children who attended Georgia's pre-K program but were eligible for Head Start were compared with a matched sample of children who attended Head Start. Although children in these two program types began pre-K with similar scores on measures of cognitive and school readiness skills, by the end of the school year, children in the universal pre-K program outperformed their Head Start counterparts on the tests of cognitive and school readiness skills (Henry et al., 2006). The researchers also compared Head Start and Georgia's pre-K program on classroom quality measured with the Early Childhood

Environmental Ratings Scale–Revised (ECERS-R; Harms, Clifford, & Cryer, 1998) and found that the two programs did not significantly differ in terms of quality. These findings suggest that universal programs may promote better child outcomes but do not resolve the issue due to the confounding of program type (universal or targeted) with auspice (pre-K or Head Start). A comparison of universal and targeted state-funded pre-K would help resolve that issue.

COMPARING UNIVERSAL AND TARGETED PRE-K

Although the two models appear to be quite different in terms of who is served, implementation of those models by states likely blurs some distinctions. Although universal programs purport greater economic and ethnic diversity in access, there is no guarantee that children will experience that diversity within classrooms. Like universal public education, the ethnic and economic composition of classrooms in universal pre-K programs will likely reflect community characteristics. Similarly, targeted programs have a variety of mechanisms for providing services. They can create classrooms of children who all meet eligibility, blend revenue sources to create classrooms in which some children meet the eligibility criteria for the targeted pre-K services and others do not, or purchase slots in existing programs that meet quality criteria. The programs with these slots often include children from diverse economic and ethnic backgrounds. Thus, the child in the targeted program can be the only child from a low-income family in a classroom, and the child in the universal program can attend a classroom in which all children are from low-income families.

Despite the debate about who is served, there is a lack of empirical evidence comparing the two types of programs. We utilized data from two studies conducted by the National Center for Early Development and Learning: the Multi-State Study of Pre-Kindergarten (Multi-State) and the State-Wide Early Education Programs Study (SWEEP) (Early et al., 2005) to compare universal with targeted pre-K programs on classroom characteristics and child outcomes among children from low-income families.

The Multi-State Study assessed 40 centers/schools in six states (California, Georgia, Illinois, Kentucky, New York, and Ohio) in 2001–2002, with 78% of centers/schools agreeing to participate. SWEEP assessed roughly 100 centers/schools in five additional states (New Jersey, Massachusetts, Texas, Wisconsin, and Washington) in 2003–2004, with 77% agreeing to participate. In both studies, one classroom per site was selected at random for participation and observation ($N = 716$), with 94% of the teachers agreeing to participate. Eight states had targeted programs, two states had universal programs, and one state had both a targeted and a universal program. Classrooms in that state were classified according to which program type they belonged. Overall, there were 547 classes in the targeted group (76%) and 169 classes in the universal group (24%).

The classroom characteristics and indicators of quality were compared between each program type. Structural features included hours per day that children were in Pre-K, years of education of the lead teacher, and the child–teacher ratio; process quality included Early Childhood Environment Rating Scale-Revised (ECERS-R; Harms, Clifford, & Cryer, 1998) and The Classroom Assessment Scoring System (CLASS; La Paro, Pianta, & Stuhlman, 2004; Pianta, LaParo, & Hamre, 2008). Analyses were weighted so that the 100 classrooms per state in SWEEP contributed as much as the 40 classrooms per state in the Multi-State Study.

As expected, universal pre-K classrooms had a significantly lower proportion of children from low-income families in the class compared with targeted classrooms. Being in a universal program, however, did not ensure that children attended economically diverse classrooms, and being in a targeted program did not guarantee that children were in classrooms that were exclusively composed of children from low-income families. The distribution of the proportion of children from low-income families in the universal programs indicated that the classrooms tended to be relatively diverse economically (see Figure 4.1). Of the 169 class-

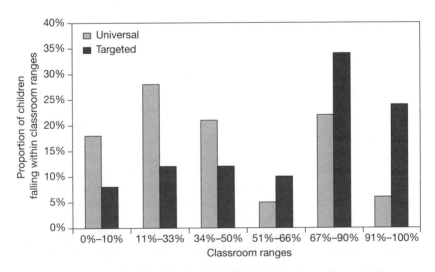

Figure 4.1.   Percentage of children from low-income families in classrooms by program type.

Table 4.1. Comparison of classroom characteristics across program type

Classroom characteristic	Mean (SD)		F	Effect size U–T
	Universal (n = 165–168)	Targeted (n = 320–340)		
Descriptive variables				
Percent of class reported as *poor*	41 (30)	64 (31)	89.63[b] T > U	1.05
Percent of class reported as *Caucasian*	50 (39)	38 (37)	6.37[a] U > T	.28
Hours per day	5.01 (2.19)	4.60 (2.58)	16.38[b] U > T	.46
Teacher education	16.64 (1.53)	15.73 (1.79)	18.43[b] U > T	.48
Child–teacher ratio	9.67 (3.66)	6.92 (2.98)	87.79[b] U > T	1.05
Observed classroom quality				
Early Childhood Environmental Ratings Scale–Revised (ECERS)[1]				
Language/interaction	4.34 (1.14)	4.84 (1.16)	8.62[a] T > U	.33
Provision for learning	3.37 (.81)	3.88 (1.01)	12.13[b] T > U	.38
Classroom Assessment Scoring System (CLASS)[2]				
Emotional climate	5.50 (.62)	5.58 (.70)	0.66	–
Instructional climate	1.78 (.70)	2.15 (.86)	8.21[a] T > U	.33

[a]$p < .001$
[b]$p < .0001$
Key: U, universal; T, targeted
[1]Harms, T., Clifford, R.M., & Cryer, D. (1998).
[2]Pianta, La Paro, & Hamre (2008).

rooms in universal programs, 25% of the classes contained 17% or fewer children from low-income families, 50% of the classes contained 38% or fewer children from low-income families, and 75% of the classes contained 67% or fewer children from low-income families. Similarly, being in a targeted program did not necessarily mean that children were in classrooms composed mostly of children from low-income families.

We also found significant differences in several other classroom characteristics (see Table 4.1). Compared with universal programs, targeted programs had shorter classes, teachers with fewer years of education, and smaller child–teacher ratios. Finally, targeted programs had a lower proportion of Caucasian children per class than universal programs. Program types also differed statistically on observed classroom quality. Targeted programs had higher quality than universal programs on the ECERS–R Teaching/Interactions, ECERS–R Provisions for Learning, and Classroom Assessment Scoring System (CLASS) Instructional Climate (Pianta, La Paro, & Hamre, 2008).

Next, we examined the extent to which gains in early learning skills among children from low-income families differed as a function of program type. We used a multimethod approach to assess early learning skills, using standardized assessments, teacher reports, and directly assessing children's knowledge of letters and numbers, which are thought to be key indicators of emergent literacy and numeracy. Widely used standardized measures administered to children participating in the assessments included the Peabody Picture Vocabulary Test–Third edition (PPVT-III; Dunn & Dunn, 1997) as a measure of receptive language, the Oral & Written Language Scale (OWLS; Oral Expression Scale, Carrow-Woolfolk, 1995) as a measure of expressive language, the Woodcock-Johnson III Tests of Achievement: Rhyming Subscale (Woodcock, McGrew, & Mather, 2001) as a measure of rhyming, and the Woodcock-Johnson III Tests of Achievement: Applied Problems Subtest (Woodcock et al., 2001) as a measure of math skills (see Clifford et al., 2005, for details on these measures). Children were also asked to identify letters and numbers as indicators of emergent literacy and numeracy (National Center for Early Development and Learning, 2001). In the literacy assessment, children were shown a set of mixed capital and lowercase letters and asked to identify as many letters as they could. The highest possible score is 26. In the numeracy assessment, children were shown a sheet of numbers (1–10 printed in random order) and asked to identify as many numbers as they could. Finally, teachers rated the child's language and literacy skills in pre-K using the Academic Rating Scale (West, Denton, & Germino-Hausken, 2000).

Gain scores were computed by subtracting the fall achievement score from the spring score. This method accounts for potential selection bias based on the belief that family and child factors that could bias results had an equal effect on the fall and spring scores (see NICHD Early Child Care Research Network [ECCRN] & Duncan, 2003). Nesting of children in the pre-K classroom was represented in the analysis using hierarchical linear models through estimating two variance terms—variability related to the pre-K classroom and of residual error.

The children differed significantly across the two program types on very few of the child outcomes (see Table 4.2). Without considering the descriptive characteristics and observed quality of the classroom (i.e., the use of statistical controls), children in the universal program learned more letters than children in targeted programs, but these differences were not observed when classroom characteristics were con-

Table 4.2. Child achievement outcomes as a function of pre-K program type among children from low-income families

	Mean (SD)		F No covariates	F Class covariate	Effect size U–T
	Universal (n = 197–207)	Targeted (n = 521–652)			
Language skills					
Receptive language	3.00 (9.75)	3.71 (8.87)	2.46	1.82	–
Expressive language	3.73 (8.33)	2.64 (8.32)	3.60	4.66[a] U > T	.18
Literacy skills					
Naming letters	6.93 (6.70)	5.41 (6.01)	7.04[a] U > T	1.84	.19
Teacher rating ARC	0.65 (0.89)	0.73 (0.76)	1.32	4.26[a] T > U	.24
Woodcock-Johnson rhyming	1.34 (2.59)	1.22 (2.77)	0.20	1.00	–
Math skills					
Woodcock-Johnson applied problems	2.97 (10.29)	1.57 (9.97)	2.19	1.89	–
Naming numbers	2.81 (3.07)	2.30 (2.76)	3.24	1.36	–

[a]$p < .05$
Key: U = universal; T = targeted

sidered. Children in universal programs gained more in expressive language skills than children in targeted programs when we adjusted for classroom characteristics but not when we ignored them. Children in the targeted program gained more in teacher's rating of language and literacy skills when we included classroom covariates but not when we ignored them.

CONCLUSIONS

As many states are moving toward state-funded pre-K programs, policy makers are faced with decisions about whether to support a program that is accessible to all children or one that targets children who are at risk. The issues centered around this debate focus on cost, quality, and public support. To address the lack of empirical evidence on this topic, we used data from an 11-state preschool evaluation. Our findings are a first attempt to provide empirical evidence comparing state-funded universal and targeted pre-K programs to assist in making this decision.

Overall, our evaluation suggests that variability *within* both the universal and targeted programs is far greater than *between* the two types of programs. Inconsistent differences emerged regarding classroom characteristics. Although universal programs had longer classes, teachers with more years of education, a greater proportion of Caucasian children per class, and a lower proportion of children who were poor, observed classroom quality was higher in targeted programs. Neither universal nor targeted programs were consistently related to larger child gains during the pre-K experience.

Failure to observe large differences may be due to the lack of clear distinctions in the degree of economic and racial diversity observed in the two types of programs. Not surprisingly, targeted programs tended to have proportionately more children from low-income families, but both types of pre-K programs included classes that only served children from low-income families and some that served almost no children from low-income families. It is likely that targeted programs that place children who are at risk in existing programs, provided that they meet state pre-K criteria, account for the economic diversity of children in targeted programs. Similarly, it is likely that programs in economically segregated areas result in economically segregated classrooms in universal programs. If the argument for universal care is based on improving child outcomes through creating economically diverse classrooms, then perhaps a clear focus on economic diversity may be a better way to promote child outcomes rather than focusing on universal care. Further evidence supporting this goal can be found in a study by Schecter and Bye (2007). They found that children from low-income families in economically integrated preschool classrooms had greater gains in receptive language during the pre-K year compared with children from low-income families in classrooms composed mostly of other students from low incomes. Some public schools are also making efforts to increase economic diversity within classrooms, and as pre-K becomes part of the public school system, this trend may also take place at the pre-K level.

Many other issues (e.g., financing) will determine whether states decide to offer universal or targeted programs. Evidence from our study provides a small piece of information that may be useful to policy makers as they make decisions related to public pre-K, but further investigation is warranted.

REFERENCES

Barnett, W.S., Brown, K., & Shore, R. (2004). "The universal vs. targeted debate: Should the United States have preschool for all?" *Preschool Policy Matters* 6, 1.

Barnett, W.S., & Fuller, B. (2006). *Universal or targeted preschool?* Washington, DC: Education Sector.

Barnett, W.S., Hustedt, J.T., Friedman, A.H., Boyd, J.S., & Ainsworth, P. (2007). *The state of preschool: 2007 state preschool year book.* New Brunswick, NJ: National Institute for Early Education Research (NIEER).

Campbell, F.A., Ramey, C.T., Pungello, E., Sparling, J., & Miller-Johnson, S. (2002). Early childhood education: Young adult outcomes from the Abecedarian Project. *Applied Developmental Science, 6*, 42–57.

Carrow-Woolfolk, E. (1995). *Oral and Written Language Scales (OWLS).* Circle Pines, MN: American Guidance Service.

Clifford, R.M., Barbarin, O., Chang, F., Early, D., Bryant, D., Howes, C., Burchinal, M., & Pianta, R. (2005). What is pre-kindergarten? Characteristics of public prekindergarten programs. *Applied Developmental Science, 9*(3), 126–143.

Doctors, J.V. (2008). *Votes count: Legislative action on fiscal year 2009.* Retrieved March 10, 2009, from http://www.pewcenteronthestates.org/uploadedFiles/LegislativeReport_Sept2008.pdf

Dunn L.M., & Dunn, L.M. (1997). *Peabody Picture Vocabulary Test–Third Edition (PPVT-III).* Circle Pines, MN: American Guidance Service.

Early, D., Barbarin, O., Bryant, D., Burchinal, M., Chang, F., Clifford, R., Crawford, G., Weaver, W., Howes, C., Ritchie, S., Kraft-Sayre, M., Pianta, R., & Barnett, W. (2005). *Pre-kindergarten in eleven states: NCEDL's Multi-State Study of Pre-Kindergarten and Study of State-Wide Early Education Programs (SWEEP).* Chapel Hill, NC: National Center for Early Development and Learning.

Gormley, W.T., Gayer, T., Phillips, D., & Dawson, B. (2005). The effects of universal pre-K on cognitive development. *Developmental Psychology, 41*, 872–884.

Harms, T., Clifford, R.M., & Cryer, D. (1998). *Early Childhood Environment Rating Scale–Revised (ECERS-R).* New York: Teachers College Press.

Henry, G.L., Henderson, B., Ponder, A., Mashburn, R., & Rickman, D. (2003). *Report of the findings of the Early Childhood Study: 2001–2002.* Retrieved November 10, 2006, from http://www.gsu.edu/~wwwsps/publications/2003/earlychildhood.htm

Henry, G.T., Gordon, C.S., & Rickman, D.K. (2006). Early education policy alternatives: Comparing quality and outcomes of Head Start and state prekindergarten. *Educational Evaluation and Policy Analysis, 28*, 77–99.

King, J. (2006). *Closing the achievement gap through expanded access to quality early education in grades PK–3.* Washington, DC: New America Foundation.

La Paro, K., Pianta, R.C., & Stuhlman, M. (2004). Classroom Assessment Scoring System (CLASS): Findings from the pre-K year. *The Elementary School Journal, 10*, 409–426.

National Center for Early Development and Learning. (2001). *Identifying letters.* Frank Porter Graham Child Development Institute, University of North Carolina at Chapel Hill.

NICHD Early Child Care Research Network. (2005). Early child care and children's development in the primary grades: Follow-up results from the NICHD study of early child care. *American Educational Research Journal, 42*(3), 537–570.

NICHD Early Child Care Research Network & Duncan, G.J. (2003). Modeling the impacts of child care quality on children's preschool cognitive development. *Child Development, 74*, 1454–1475.

Peisner-Feinberg, E., & Burchinal, M. (1997). Concurrent relations between child care quality and child outcomes: The study of cost, quality, and outcomes in child care centers. *Merrill-Palmer Quarterly, 43*, 451–477.

Pianta, R., Howes, C., Burchinal, M., Bryant, D., Clifford, R., Early, D., & Barbarin, O. (2005). Features of pre-kindergarten programs, classrooms, and teachers: Do they predict observed classroom quality and child–teacher interactions. *Applied Developmental Science, 9,* 144–159.

Pianta, R.C., La Paro, K.M., & Hamre, B. (2008). *Classroom Assessment Scoring System.* Baltimore: Paul H. Brookes Publishing Co.

Schechter, C., & Bye, B. (2007). Preliminary evidence for the impact of mixed-income preschools on low-income children's language growth. *Early Childhood Research Quarterly, 22,* 137–146.

Schweinhart, L.J., Barnes, H.V., & Weikart, D.P. (1993). *Significant benefits: Vol 10. The High/Scope Perry Preschool Study through age 27.* Ypsilanti, MI: The High/Scope Press.

U.S. Department of Health and Human Services, Administration for Children and Families. (2005, May). *Head Start impact study: First year findings.* Washington, DC: Author.

Vandell, D.L. (2004). Early child care: The known and the unknown. *Merrill-Palmer Quarterly, 50,* 387–414.

West, J., Denton, K., & Germino-Hausken, E. (2000). *America's kindergartners: NCES 2000-070.* Washington, DC: National Center for Educational Statistics.

Woodcock, R.W., McGrew, K.S., & Mather, N. (2001). *Woodcock-Johnson III Tests of Achievement.* Itasca, IL: Riverside.

Implementation
at the State Level

Chapter 5

Research Evidence About Program Dosage and Student Achievement

Effective Public Prekindergarten Programs
in Maryland and Louisiana

*Craig T. Ramey, Sharon Landesman Ramey,
and Billy R. Stokes*

High-quality prekindergarten (pre-K) programs have been promoted as an effective means to produce gains in young children's learning and as a cost-effective strategy to help end the intergenerational cycle of poverty (e.g., C.T. Ramey, Ramey, & Lanzi, 2006; Heckman, 2008). The most frequently cited scientific findings as the foundation for providing public pre-K programs come from three independent lines of scientific inquiry: 1) the Abecedarian Project and its 11 replication studies (c.f. C.T. Ramey & Ramey, 2006); 2) the Chicago Child–Parent Centers, which included natural variations and replications (Reynolds, 2002; Reynolds, Temple, Roberson, & Mann, 2002); and the single Perry Preschool Project (Schweinhart et al., 2005).

HISTORICAL SCIENTIFIC CONTEXT
FOR EARLY CHILDHOOD EDUCATIONAL PROGRAMS

These scientific studies were launched in the 1960s and 1970s, and thus are able to provide scientific evidence about the long-term effects of the preschool educational program on the children's lives. Each of these projects also has been subjected to multiple economic analyses to yield estimates of return on investments, which have been important in the political decision-making process in many states and school districts that have developed plans for providing pre-K as a means to improve the skills of children who are at risk of poor academic achievement during the elementary school years.

This section selectively highlights key findings from these three projects, all of which helped to inform the two states (Louisiana and Maryland) where we have conducted new research to measure the effect of large-scale, public pre-K programs on children's outcomes. These new state and school district programs built directly on the earlier research findings, yet they differ in many important ways from the original research and demonstration projects. This overview of the earlier research helps to provide a context for understanding the new programs and for interpreting their findings.

The Abecedarian Project and Its Replication Studies

The Abecedarian Project[1] was a randomized controlled trial (RCT) launched in 1972, when it enrolled the first of four successive cohorts that comprise the final study sample of 111 children. The central guiding question for the Abecedarian Project was the following: "Can the developmental trajectories—especially as indexed by children's intellectual development and school readiness—of children living in extreme poverty be improved by providing high-quality, theory-driven education during the first 5 years of life?"

The Abecedarian Project's RCT design permitted rigorous testing of the efficacy of the preschool educational program itself. The project enrolled families with high scores on a Risk Index, a composite of 13

---

[1]We describe the Abecedarian Project in greater detail here than the Chicago Child–Parent Centers or the Perry Preschool Program for two reasons. First, Craig Ramey conceptualized, developed, and then launched this project and its replications as the principal investigator, so we know these projects through more than 35 years of firsthand experience. Second, the Abecedarian Project's design features and approaches to measurement directly contributed to the two new large-scale projects that we present in this chapter.

risk conditions, such as extreme levels of poverty (well below the 50% level of the federal poverty index), low education of mothers and fathers (averaging less than a 10th-grade education), parental unemployment, single parenting, and poor school performance of older siblings. At the time of a child's birth, families and children were assigned to one of two treatment conditions: an educational treatment group and a control group. The educational treatment group was scheduled to receive 1) an intensive, year-round, full-day program that used a specially developed curriculum (Learningames; Sparling & Lewis, 2000) and provided ongoing professional development for staff, monitoring of program quality, and individualizing the curriculum on a weekly basis, starting at the age of 6 weeks and continuing until children entered public kindergarten 5 years later; 2) high-quality pediatric care, following all recommendations from the American Academy of Pediatrics for well-child care as well as treating illnesses and injuries; and 3) ongoing, high-quality, and personally responsive social services for the family to address a wide range of issues, such as housing, employment, mental health and substance abuse issues, and domestic violence. The control group in the Abecedarian Project also received many supports and services and thus is not an untreated group of children and families. The control group received the same type and level of health care and social services as those in the educational treatment group. The health care and social services provided to families were documented for both groups during the entire first 5 years of the children's lives. This design feature has been an extremely valuable one in discerning whether the benefits of the educational program provided to children resulted in their improved outcomes versus the provision of universally needed health care and social services to families living in challenging and, oftentimes, dire circumstances. This research ethic of not having an untreated control group was adhered to in all of the replication studies of the original Abecedarian Project as well—for both important humanitarian purposes and for increasing the scientific specificity about the factors that influence the course of children's lives.

The Abecedarian Project's findings have been reported in detail in many peer-reviewed scientific articles, including scientific journal articles that summarize the long-term findings (e.g., Campbell et al., 2002; C.T. Ramey et al., 2000), as well as in popular books, such as Hillary Clinton's *It Takes a Village and Other Lessons Children Teach Us* (1996) and Ronald Kotulak's *Inside the Brain: Revolutionary Discoveries of How the Mind Works* (1996), and television specials (e.g., by Walter Cronkite, Diane Sawyer, and National Geographic's *Brilliant Minds*). Table 5.1 provides an overview of the major findings regarding the impact of the high-quality educational program that was provided for the first

Table 5.1. Summary of key findings on the effects of preschool education from the Abecedarian Project from 18 months—21 years old

Preschool education increases . . .	Preschool education decreases . . .
↑ Intelligence (IQ)	↓ Grade repetition
↑ Positive mother-child interactions	↓ Special Education placement
↑ Reading and math skills	↓ Teen pregnancies
↑ Academic locus-of-control	↓ Teen depressive symptoms
↑ Social competence	↓ Smoking and drug use
↑ Years of school	
↑ Attendance at college, especially 4-year college/university	
↑ Full-time employment in early adulthood	

All benefits are statistically significant and reported in peer-reviewed journal articles.

Preschool education was not associated with any negative outcomes. (e.g., poor mother–child attachment, disruptive behavior, lowered self-esteem)

Other benefits: Mothers were more likely to continue their own education and be employed.

5 years of children's lives. The arrows that point upward indicate significant gains, whereas those that point downward reflect decreased levels of the indicated outcome. All of these findings have been previously published and are documented by statistically rigorous analyses. (The Abecedarian Project has been archived and is publicly available as a national resource at the University of Michigan.)

The Abecedarian findings support a highly consistent pattern of performance for those children who received the intensive, high-quality educational intervention—these children consistently performed better than did the children in the comparison group on all major outcomes, starting at 18 months of age and continuing through 21 years of age. In other words, these benefits did not fluctuate (such as children reading at higher levels at some ages but not other ages), but rather a stable pattern of long-term positive outcomes in multiple domains emerged. The final data collection is being completed for the 30-year follow-up of these children. At age 21, 99% of the children still living participated in the follow-up assessment, and at no age was there less than 90% participation (Campbell et al., 2002); thus, the Abecedarian findings are unlikely to be biased by selective attrition (that is, lack of data on some children in one of the groups).

The findings relevant to successful school transition are that the children in the control group, who did not receive the systematic preschool program, performed at significantly lower levels (well below national averages) on all indicators of academic progress, including receiving lower scores on individually administered, standardized tests of reading achievement and math achievement. They also showed higher rates of grade retention (repeating a grade), and placement in special education compared with those in the educational treatment group. The children in the control group exhibited more signs of depression, higher levels of smoking and drug abuse as young adults, and lower levels of college attendance and full-time employment (Campbell et al., 2002).

Replications of the Abecedarian Project

The first Abecedarian Project replication was launched 5 years later, in the same location, and with the same enrollment criteria, the same preschool setting and teaching staff, and the same study design. Its purpose was to determine whether the early benefits detected in the Abecedarian Project would be upheld in a new and independent sample of children born into similar life circumstances. The replication also added a second type of treatment group to determine whether an intensive 5-year home visiting program using the educational curriculum would yield benefits. In fact, despite the positive reception by families and home visitors to this new treatment approach, there were no major or lasting benefits for the children associated with the home visiting program. This project, The Carolina Approach to Responsive Education, or Project CARE, found almost identical benefits for children in the center-based Educational Treatment Group as those found in the Abecedarian Project (C.T. Ramey & Ramey, 2004b; Wasik, Ramey, Bryant, & Sparling, 1990). These children also have been followed into adulthood and showed similar long-term positive outcomes (Campbell et al., 2008).

The Abecedarian Project was replicated with two other groups, each differing in their risk conditions from the original Abecedarian Project and Project CARE. The Infant Health and Development Program (IHDP, 1990) enrolled children at birth on the basis of prematurity and low birth weight (LBW). IHDP was conducted in eight sites and enrolled 985 infants. The IHDP control group received free health and social services, whereas the educational treatment group received an intensive educational program modeled after the Abecedarian program, using the *Partners for Learning* curriculum (Sparling, Lewis, & Ramey, 1995), in addition to free health and social services. In IHDP, children began participating in the center-based educational program when they were 12 months of age. Prior to that, they received an intensive home visiting program that took into account their special needs as premature infants who were LBW. The center-based program and home visiting activities continued until children were 3 years of age.

In IHDP, children came from a wide range of socioeconomic, ethnic, and racial groups, whereas 100% of the Abecedarian and Project

CARE families lived in poverty and 99% were African American. Key findings from IHDP at age 18 affirm lasting cognitive and language gains, with greater benefits for children from lower income and less-educated families and children who participated at higher levels, as indexed by days of attendance at the preschool center and home visits (Blair, Ramey, & Hardin, 1995; McCormick et al., 2006; C.T. Ramey et al., 1992).

Finally, we conducted two replication studies using an RCT design in Romania in the children's *leagans* (institutional care settings, often labeled incorrectly as *orphanages* by outsiders) in response to requests and funding from philanthropic international relief organizations. These two replication studies involved translating the Abecedarian curriculum into Romanian; making cultural and practical changes as needed; training local staff to provide the program; and setting up rooms to provide the educational program with the comparable staffing ratios used in the Abecedarian Project, Project CARE, and the eight IHDP sites. In Romania, there was a 1:4 teacher–child ratio in the 1- to 3-year-old age group. The Romanian replications addressed two scientific questions: "Can children benefit from this form of educational intervention even after they have experienced the extreme deprivation of institutionalization?" and "Will younger children show greater benefits than older children?" In the control condition, additional enrichment materials and staff training were provided, but there was no change in the staffing levels or systematic rearrangement of the children's activities during waking hours to ensure that the enrichment supplies and staff training would result in altered care.

The major findings from providing 12–14 months of educational intervention were that 1) young children, regardless of their age group, benefited in all measured areas of language, general cognition, social-emotional development, and fine motor development from the Abecedarian curriculum and program; and 2) the gains measured indicate typical or healthy developmental growth—approximately 1 year of growth (advance in assessed skills) for 1 year of participation in the educational treatment, but that true catch-up did not occur. That is, the large detected delays in children's development at the start of the project (e.g., 15-month-old children performed, on average, at the level of 7- to 8-month-old infants) were not overcome by 1 year of educationally enriching experiences. In other words, the educational intervention served to prevent further decline and delays in the children's development, which continued to occur for the children in the control group (Sparling et al., 2005).

To summarize, the Abecedarian Project is frequently referred to as one of the "landmark studies," distinguished by demonstrating long-lasting benefits of the preschool educational program and by being replicated with both similar and different groups of children in 10 different cities over a period from the 1970s to the 1990s. In all of these studies, the educational intervention involved full-day, year-round, theory-driven educational programs that had ongoing staff professional development, systematic and direct monitoring (with immediate corrective actions if any deviations from the program's fidelity were detected), and assessment of children at regular intervals. To the extent possible, these features served as guiding principles in the research partnerships we have established in many communities, including our ongoing research in pre-K programs in Montgomery County, Maryland, and the state of Louisiana (c.f. C.T. Ramey, Ramey, & Lanzi, 2006; S.L. Ramey & Ramey, 2007).

Positive Long-Term Effects of Prekindergarten from the Chicago Child–Parent Centers and the Perry Preschool Project

The Chicago Child–Parent Centers provided a naturalistic study (rather than an RCT) with a large sample and operated via federally and locally funded programs, with natural variation in the duration and other program features. Although the educational intervention was not systematically controlled, considerable documentation occurred, and a long-term study was funded later to track high school age and young adult outcomes. The major conclusions are that the center-based educational experience resulted in significant and lasting gains for the children. Furthermore, receiving 2 years of the program sometimes resulted in larger benefits than receiving 1 year. A set of sophisticated data analyses that tested different hypotheses about the primary mechanisms responsible for the positive outcomes resulted in the conclusion that the cognitive and academic-related experiences were the primary pathways responsible for children's improved school performance. Similar to the Abecedarian Project, there were benefits to the children in multiple areas including higher educational attainment, lower school dropout, and lower rates of juvenile arrests (Reynolds et al., 2002).

The Perry Preschool Project is the oldest landmark study, launched in the mid-1960s in Ypsilanti, Michigan. This project included only children living in poverty who already showed significant developmental delays by the age of 3, with all children in the study having tested IQ scores of less than 85 when enrolled. This project provided valuable information about whether children who already displayed intellectual impairment could benefit significantly from a high-quality early educational experience, using a similar comparison group. The Perry Preschool findings included decreased rates of grade retention and special education placement, but did not detect significant gains in children's IQ scores or their performance on standardized tests of academic achievement. This study is frequently cited, however, for the long-term benefits of reduced adult criminal incarceration and increased employment, which are factors that contribute to estimates of high return on investment. (Schweinhart et al., 2005).

We consider these landmark studies—all characterized by their emphasis on improving school readiness and children's educational attainment—important for demonstrating that although the children varied in their initial risk for school failure, lived in different geographical areas, and received different intensive center-based educational programs, they showed significant and long-lasting benefits. The pre-K movement currently underway, however, often seeks to serve a much broader group of children, many with lesser degrees of initial risk for school failure, and often provides a less-intensive educational program, as indexed by hours per day and total days per year. Furthermore, many studies confirm that there is a wide range of quality in these pre-K programs and community centers nationwide, with much of it being poor quality (e.g., NICHD Early Child Care Research Network, 2005).

PRESSING NATIONAL AND SCIENTIFIC QUESTIONS ABOUT PRE-K

In almost all press coverage and policy discussions, questions are raised about whether the positive findings from the landmark studies can truly be realized through the types of large-scale, public and private sector programs that strive to provide high-quality early education to young children. Foremost is the question, "Are public school systems and communities prepared and willing to provide comparably high-quality, educationally driven, and actively monitored programs, including assessment of children's progress?" This question often is framed as one of scalability or scale-up. In other words, can large-scale, sustainable programs be established that will produce comparable or at least demonstrable benefits for enrolled children? Figure 5.1 illustrates the complex web of supports needed from many sectors in order to provide high quality pre-K programs to benefit young children.

In this chapter, we provide new evidence from two large-scale pre-K programs operated with state and local district funding: in Louisiana, the statewide LA4 program that was started in 2001 and scaled up each year so that in 2008–2009, more than 14,000 children were served in LA4; and in Maryland, the Montgomery County Public Schools, which has expanded its pre-K classes consistent with state pre-K standards to serve more than 2,500 4-year-olds in 2006–2007.

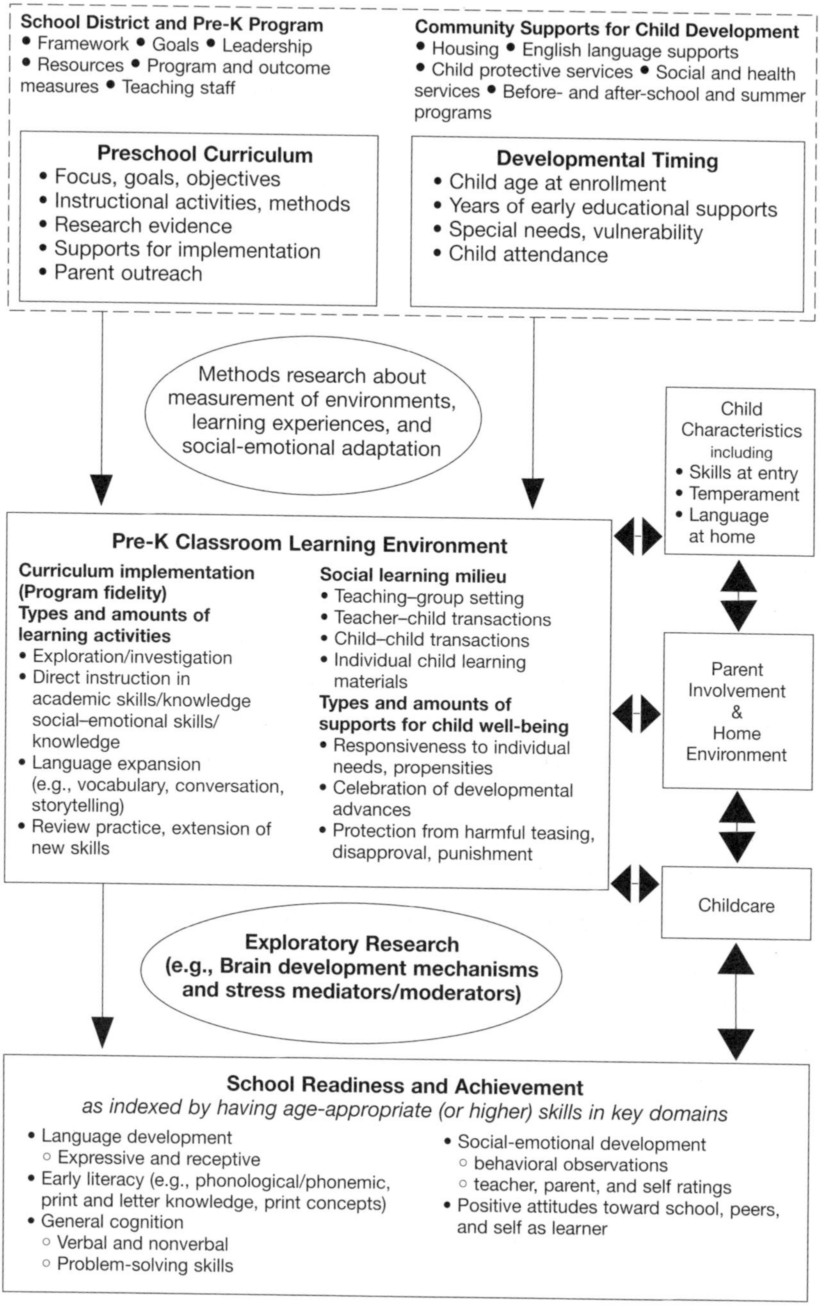

School District and Pre-K Program
- Framework • Goals • Leadership
- Resources • Program and outcome measures • Teaching staff

Community Supports for Child Development
- Housing • English language supports
- Child protective services • Social and health services • Before- and after-school and summer programs

Preschool Curriculum
- Focus, goals, objectives
- Instructional activities, methods
- Research evidence
- Supports for implementation
- Parent outreach

Developmental Timing
- Child age at enrollment
- Years of early educational supports
- Special needs, vulnerability
- Child attendance

Methods research about measurement of environments, learning experiences, and social-emotional adaptation

Child Characteristics
including
- Skills at entry
- Temperament
- Language at home

Pre-K Classroom Learning Environment

Curriculum implementation (Program fidelity)
Types and amounts of learning activities
- Exploration/investigation
- Direct instruction in academic skills/knowledge social–emotional skills/knowledge
- Language expansion (e.g., vocabulary, conversation, storytelling)
- Review practice, extension of new skills

Social learning milieu
- Teaching–group setting
- Teacher–child transactions
- Child–child transactions
- Individual child learning materials

Types and amounts of supports for child well-being
- Responsiveness to individual needs, propensities
- Celebration of developmental advances
- Protection from harmful teasing, disapproval, punishment

Parent Involvement & Home Environment

Childcare

Exploratory Research (e.g., Brain development mechanisms and stress mediators/moderators)

School Readiness and Achievement
as indexed by having age-appropriate (or higher) skills in key domains

- Language development
  ○ Expressive and receptive
- Early literacy (e.g., phonological/phonemic, print and letter knowledge, print concepts)
- General cognition
  ○ Verbal and nonverbal
  ○ Problem-solving skills
- Social-emotional development
  ○ behavioral observations
  ○ teacher, parent, and self ratings
- Positive attitudes toward school, peers, and self as learner

Figure 5.1. The complex framework of sources needed to provide high-quality pre-kindergarten education to all children. (*Source:* Ramey & Ramey, 1992, 1998, 2000).

In both of these large-scale public pre-K programs, we established active research partnerships that permitted prospective study of children's outcomes and monitoring of pre-K program quality. Because these public programs operated in two quite different geographical areas and served diverse types of children, we are able to provide new scientific evidence that the "promise of pre-K programs" is not beyond reach, but one that can yield measurable benefits.

Similarities Between the Louisiana and Maryland Pre-K Programs

Both the Louisiana and Maryland pre-K programs resulted from careful planning, with strong support from superintendents and an intention to build on what was already known about the science of effective early educational programs. Specifically, important similarities between these two major public pre-K programs were the following:

- They were implemented in classrooms in public elementary schools.

- They served 4-year-old-children, with a priority on serving high-risk families (indexed primarily by family income) but included some children who were not living in poverty.

- Each classroom had a certified teacher with a bachelor's or master's degree and specialization in early childhood with a qualified teacher's assistant or paraeducator.

- The teachers received wages and benefits comparable to those of other public school teachers.

- The classroom sizes were restricted to a maximum of 20 students.

- The classrooms had a specified pre-K curriculum with an explicit focus on language and early literacy.

- The programs had designated statewide learning standards and benchmarks for children's progress.

- Professional development was provided for all teachers, typically exceeding 18 hours per year (and sometimes considerably higher).

- Programs had the full range of additional supports available to elementary school classrooms, including specialists in reading, language, special education, and learning English.

- Children's progress was measured at least twice a year by classroom teachers themselves as part of the program to monitor individual children's progress and make adjustments in classroom instructional activities based on children's progress.

- Collaboration and coordination occurred with other needed services and supports, such as health and mental health, child care (wraparound services), and social services.

Differences Between the Louisiana and Maryland Pre-K Programs

The most notable differences in these two large-scale programs concerned program dosage as indexed by the length of the school day and the diversity of the children served. Specifically, the differences that are important to consider when comparing outcomes from these public pre-K programs are the following:

- Louisiana offered the program for a full day and it was identical in length to the elementary school day, approximately 6 hours, whereas Montgomery County Public Schools offered their pre-K for a half day (ranging from 2.5 to 3.25 hours).

- Montgomery County Public Schools prioritized enrollment of children based on screening of families. The risk factors (in order of importance considered) were family income (below poverty or near poverty), immigration status, family spoke a language other than English at home, and single parent status. In contrast, Louisiana did not screen individual families based on risk, but rather funded school districts that applied to offer the LA4 program. In Louisiana, children whose families were below the poverty level received the LA4 program for free, whereas some tuition was charged for families with higher incomes.

- In Maryland, the demography of both the county and the pre-K children served was far more diverse, as indexed by the number of languages children spoke at home, the racial and ethnic groups represented, and immigration status of families. In Louisiana, the population served was almost exclusively African American and Caucasian/non-Hispanic, with extremely low rates of other linguistic or ethnic/racial groups.

- The poverty rates in the locales where the pre-K programs operated differed markedly. In Montgomery County, children living in poverty represented a relatively small minority, considerably below the national level of child poverty. In Louisiana, the rate of child poverty exceeded the national rate, and children living in poverty represented the majority of children enrolled in the public schools.

THE MARYLAND AND LOUISIANA PARTNERSHIP PARADIGM FOR STUDYING EDUCATIONAL INITIATIVES

The paradigm we developed for conducting long-term, practically useful research in Maryland and Louisiana (as well as in other locales) has been one of true partnership. This collaboration has involved initial endorsement and support from leadership at the highest levels, including school district and state superintendents who make public commitments to implementing high-quality pre-K programs—largely as a means to improve children's school readiness and close the achievement gap—and to measuring the degree to which the programs achieve their goals. These partnerships were established specifically with educational scientists (Drs. Craig and Sharon Ramey and Billy Ray Stokes) and their academic institutions (major universities) in a manner that involved extensive initial joint planning, preparing documents that represented the partnership's memorandum of understanding (including the purpose of the long-term partnership as well as the roles and responsibilities of the partners), and then publicly announcing the partnership and making appropriate commitments to long-term research intended to directly benefit the schools and children, as well as to advance scientific understanding of the factors that promote (or decrease) children's school preparedness and later school success.

These partnerships are not projects set up for the purpose of one study only or to answer just a single question. Rather, the partnerships are focused on in-depth study of early childhood education and the operation of effective public systems to support children and families. We have created databases that are shared, openly engaged all partners in planning and reviewing data analyses and their reporting, and shared the findings first with key project participants and school systems and later with professional groups and the public. As developmental and educational scientists, we actively participate in many planning and review sessions about the progress and the future direction of the pre-K programs; comparably, many of the public school leaders and their educational boards engage in reviewing the scientific findings and selecting topics for future research efforts. Each of these partnerships has been active for more than 5 years, with an original intention that they would last approximately 10 years. These partnerships have received funding from multiple sources, depending on the opportunities and the issues that have arisen and that continue to evolve. These partnerships also acknowledge what we refer to as the *dual self-interest principle*—in other words, there are major differences in the missions and evaluative criteria used in public school systems for children and in higher education and scientific communities (C.T. Ramey & Ramey, 1994). To sustain partnerships, they cannot be one sided, serving mostly the needs of the schools but not the scientists, or vice versa. From the start, we openly talked about and recognized these substantial, preexisting differences in values, as well as acknowledging and respecting that there will be differences in how "home" institutions or systems operate. Without a doubt, these partnerships take time and nurturing from many people in both the school and scientific arenas. At the same time, we strongly endorse the value of this so-called new style of educational research partnerships (C.T. Ramey & Ramey, 1994). Our experiences affirm that these public partnerships help to promote high scientific integrity, breadth, continuity, practical usefulness, and policy relevance.

GENERAL CONCEPTUAL FRAMEWORK GUIDING THE RESEARCH IN LOUISIANA AND MARYLAND

The conceptual framework used to inform the research builds on systems theory and scientific evidence about the factors that promote children's learning. Broadly, the Ramey and Ramey framework referred to as Applied Biosocial Contextual Development, or the ABCD model (for an expanded discussion, see C.T. Ramey, Ramey, & Lanzi, 2006), set the stage for the research presented here. In the ABCD framework, we show children's educational achievement as part of a larger context of their health, social-emotional well-being, and family–school relationships. This framework has been valuable in helping to generate and then test particular hypotheses (ideas) about the relationship of pre-K program elements, such as its timing (age when children enrolled and when children leave), its intensity or dosage (how many hours per day and days per year), its curriculum focus (or the effectiveness of a particular curriculum), and amounts and types of professional development to children's outcomes. Also, the ABCD conceptual framework has offered a common picture to the working partnership about the multiple sources of influences on the lives of children, which is helpful when developing, monitoring, measuring, and then refining or improving programs and supports for successful transitions to schools. We often develop a project-specific conceptual framework for each major research endeavor that shows the specific interventions or program supports being tested, particularly when the study involves an RCT.

In this chapter, we selectively highlight two types of findings that our partnerships have judged useful for their local and state considerations, as well as providing relevant data to answer pressing national questions. The first set of findings concerns a key issue of whether 4-year-old children can make meaningful educational gains that represent an acceleration of their rate of development during the course of 1 school year. In other words, does the pre-K education move the children to higher levels of academic readiness for kindergarten? If so, how large are these gains? If these gains are significant, will they result in improvements in children's performance once they enter kindergarten (sufficient data for long-term findings are only available for Louisiana at this time).

The second set of findings concerns differential child outcomes in Louisiana and Maryland and the degree to which they are consistent with a principle of program intensity or dosage. The dosage of the pre-K program in Louisiana was at least twice that in Montgomery County Public Schools and, as we describe next, appears to be the most likely single factor accounting for the differential benefits. Of note, the LA4 program itself had a built-in test of the intensity principle because in its first year of implementation, it operated for only one half of the school year due to the late availability of funds. Because children were studied even in the partial-year (pilot) implementation, estimates of magnitude of benefits can be calculated, and these support the same conclusion that the amount of time children receive the educational pre-K program relates in a linear way to the magnitude of academic benefits.

Can Large Public Pre-K Programs Operated by School Systems Produce Measurable Benefits for Children's Kindergarten Transition?

This section seeks to answer the question of whether large public pre-K programs operated by school systems produce measurable benefits for children's transition into kindergarten. As outlined previously, the LA4 program and the Montgomery County Public Schools pre-K program had standards that uphold many of the agreed-on features to ensure a high-quality program. Within each of these large-scale systems, we gathered classroom environmental indicators on tools such as the Early Childhood Environment Rating Scale–Revised (ECERS-R; Harms, Clifford, & Cryer, 2004), the Early Language and Literacy Classroom Observation (ELLCO; Smith & Dickinson, 2002), and other observational assessments that affirmed that, on average, these programs were providing good to excellent classroom supports. Before testing the major hypothesis about benefits to children, we consider it informative to consider the evidence that the programs were provided as intended. Indicators of program quality can include measures such as classroom ECERS-

R scores in a representative sample of LA4 programs randomly selected for each successive year (five cohorts thus far) the program has operated and fall and spring scores on the ELLCO in the Maryland pre-K programs we studied. In addition, we have other indicators such as children's attendance (very high in both state settings) and direct observations of teacher and paraeducator instructional activities in Maryland.

Environmental indicators of classroom quality in Louisiana, for example, establish that the LA4 classrooms, on average, were among the highest ECERS-R scores reported in the literature, and these scores are at or above the level that the ECERS-R authors state is indicative of a high-quality classroom. Specifically, the mean ECERS-R scores for the LA4 classrooms are 5.7 (7.0 is the highest obtainable) for Cohort 1, 6.0 for Cohort 2, 6.0 for Cohort 3, and 5.9 for Cohort 4. A further indicator of uniformly good to high-quality classrooms in the LA4 program is that the range was very narrow, with virtually no programs scoring below 4.0, and some programs with scores in the high 6s. In the Maryland classrooms, the Early Language and Literacy Classroom Observation (ELLCO; Smith & Dickinson, 2002) scores had average ranges of 90–100, which are consistent with the observation that these were literacy-enriched environments with many supportive language and literacy learning activities.

Key Findings from Louisiana's Statewide LA4 Program

Figures 5.2, 5.3, and 5.4 present findings about children's academic progress on the Developing Skills Checklist (DSC; CTB Macmillan/McGraw-Hill, 1990) in the LA4 program for the pilot year (when children were enrolled in January) and the first four cohorts. The DSC scores are presented in the figure in terms of children's national percentile ranks in the areas of language (Figure 5.2), print (Figure 5.3), and math (Figure 5.4).

General Language Development

As Figure 5.1 shows, LA4 children entered the program scoring at about the 10th percentile in terms of their general language development, and for each of the full-year cohorts, they exited the program at a median score of the 50th national percentile. During the pilot year, however, children entered with slightly higher scores, consistent with evidence that they were acquiring some skills due to maturation and other educationally relevant experiences prior to being enrolled in LA4, and they exited at a median percentile rank of 31. Thus, the pilot year children demonstrated benefits, but to a significantly lesser degree than

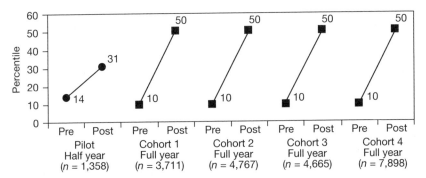

Figure 5.2. National percentile ranks on the Developing Skills Checklist for language as a measure of children's progress in Louisiana's LA4 program.

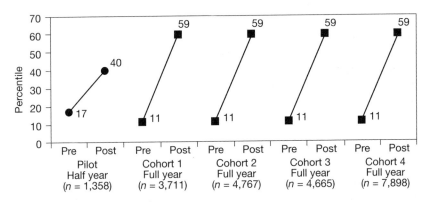

Figure 5.3. National percentile ranks on the Developing Skills Checklist for print as a measure of children's progress in Louisiana's LA4 program.

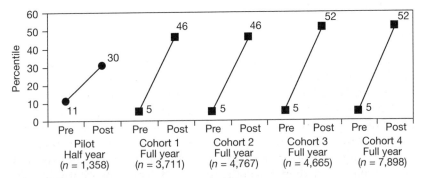

Figure 5.4. National percentile ranks on the Developing Skills Checklist for math as a measure of children's progress in Louisiana's LA4 program.

those receiving the full-year program. During the years of scale-up of the LA4 program, each successive cohort has involved a considerable increase in the number of schools operating LA4 programs and in the total number of children served. In the pilot year, approximately 1,400 children were served, Cohort 1 served about 3,700 children and Cohort 5 served 7,900 children, an almost sixfold increase in less than 5 years. The highly consistent pattern of benefits for each successive cohort indicates that the scale-up in program did not lead to a decline in its positive effects on children. Furthermore, we note that achievement gains of this magnitude are impressive in terms of their educational meaning for schools. Children entering kindergarten with developmental skills at national average are far better prepared to succeed than they would have been if they entered near the 10th percentile (that is, the developmental trajectory they had been on only a year earlier).

Print and Math Skills

In the area of print skills, the pattern of performance of children in the LA4 program is highly similar to that in language. Year after year, the LA4 children entered close to the lowest 10% of children in the nation and exited with scores that placed them above the national 50th percentile. On average, the successive cohorts of LA4 children performed near the 60th percentile rank in the spring of their pre-K year. Once again, the gains were significantly lower for the pilot year children who had only half a year of the LA4 program. Finally, children's math performance indicated that the LA4 children started the pre-K year at about the 5th percentile rank and exited between the 46th and 52nd percentiles, depending on the cohort. Once again, each cohort demonstrated large magnitude gains, with much smaller benefits for children in the pilot half-year program.

Grade Retention

To what extent were the gains in the pre-K year sufficient to improve the performance of the LA4 children when they entered kindergarten programs throughout the state? Early indicators show that the benefits of the LA4 program had a direct effect of the children's early school performance as revealed by their significant decreases in rates of grade repetition (i.e., not advancing to first grade on schedule) and placement in special education. Figure 5.5 summarizes the findings about kindergarten grade retention for the first two cohorts.

In these data analyses, we have considered the topic of differential risk and differential benefits by displaying the data separately for those children whose families differed in income level, as indexed by their

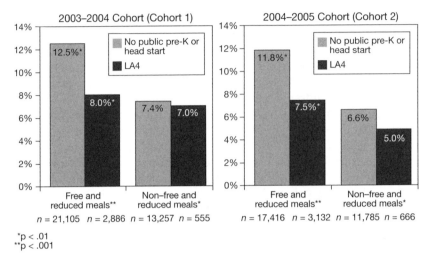

Figure 5.5. Grade-retention percentages of students who received either no public pre-K or Head Start or who were in Louisiana's LA4 program.

eligibility for free and reduced meals. In each year, the vast majority of the LA4 children were eligible for free and reduced meals, although about 20% of the children in Cohorts 1 and 2 were from higher income families. Figure 5.5 indicates two major sets of findings. First, for both cohorts, in the large group of children who did not receive any public pre-K or Head Start, the rates of kindergarten retention were significantly higher for children in the free and reduced meals group than for those from higher income families. For children from the lower family income group, nearly 1 in 8 repeated the kindergarten year (approximately 12%), in contrast to only 1 in 14 children in the higher family income group (approximately 7%). Second, the LA4 program reduced the rates of grade repetition for children in both family groups, although the benefits reached practical significance only for the children in the free and reduced meals group. For these children who are at higher risk, the LA4 program decreased their grade failure rate by more than 35%. More detailed data analyses confirmed that the benefits of the LA4 program on reducing kindergarten repetition occurred for both boys and girls and for African American and Caucasian children.

Another way of considering the effects of the LA4 program for these first two cohorts is that more than 1,700 children likely would have been prevented from unnecessary retention in kindergarten if the LA4 program had been available statewide to those children who received no public pre-K or Head Start. This would have decreased the negative effects on children and their families, the additional cost to the

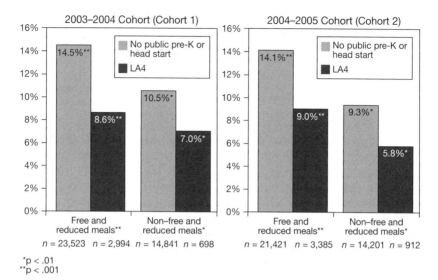

Figure 5.6. Rates of special education placement for Cohorts 1 and 2 of Louisiana's LA4 for children in the free and reduced meals group and those not in the group.

public school system, and the costs related to additional educational planning and administration.

Another important indicator of early school success relates to transfer from the regular education system into the special education system. Figure 5.6 summarizes the rates of special education placement for Cohorts 1 and 2 for children in the free and reduced meals group and those not in the group. For the children who received no public pre-K or Head Start and who were eligible for free and reduced meals, slightly more than 14% were placed in special education by the spring of their kindergarten year. This is a significantly higher rate than for children with higher family incomes, who average just below 10%. The LA4 program resulted in decreases in placement rates for children in both family income groups. Specifically, the special education placement rates were reduced to 8.6% and 9.0% for the LA4 children from the lower family income group in Cohorts 1 and 2, respectively; whereas rates declined to 7.0% and 5.8% for the LA4 children who did not receive free and reduced meals. The magnitude of these reductions is large and practically significant in terms of major cost implications and the tremendous effect on children and families associated with early transfer into the special education system after a child fails to meet expectations during the kindergarten year. Similar to the previous findings about grade repetition, there were significant benefits for both boys and girls and for African American and Caucasian children. Once again, the magnitude of documented benefits was significantly larger for children from the lower versus higher family income group.

Key Findings About Pre-K Education
in a Large, Urban–Suburban School District in Maryland

The historical context for providing pre-K education in Maryland's Montgomery County Public School system is quite different from the LA4 program. Montgomery County is a very large school district serving more than 144,000 students. Montgomery County has long been considered a relatively economically affluent and high-performance school district according to many indicators, such as student achievement scores, high school graduation rates, college attendance rates, and frequent identification of its high schools as among the nation's best. Since the late 1990s, however, there has been a rapid and large shift in the economic, linguistic, and racial diversity of the student population. A particular challenge has been the successful inclusion of students from very low-income, low-educated households; recently immigrated students; and students from multirisk families (e.g., single-parent households, families with substance abuse and domestic violence, highly mobile families). Dr. Jerry Weast, Montgomery County Public Schools superintendent during the time of this project, and the school board developed and implemented a plan to maximize "success for all" that has added pre-K and Head Start classrooms in the public schools as part of its strategy to help prepare children from high-risk circumstances for successful transition to kindergarten. The Head Start and pre-K classrooms are identical in terms of staffing qualifications and the educational curriculum framework and standards. The one difference is that the Head Start classrooms operate for 3.25 hours per day, the minimum required by the federal Head Start program, whereas the pre-K classrooms that serve children from slightly higher income families operate for 2.5 hours per day.

In 2002, Montgomery County Public Schools and Georgetown University partnered to focus on school readiness and the pre-K/Head Start program. During the first 4 years, we conducted research on alternative levels of job-embedded coaching to promote full implementation of an evidence-informed curriculum; evaluation of new teacher-administered assessments for 4-year-olds; evaluation of the Early Reading First program enacted in five elementary schools; and study of the overall effectiveness of the pre-K/Head Start program in promoting children's school readiness. In this chapter, we selectively highlight findings from representative classrooms about children's progress

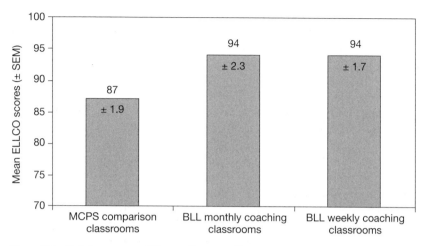

Figure 5.7.   Early Language and Literacy Classroom Observation (ELLCO) scores of Montgomery County, MD, children either in a comparison group or who were receiving monthly or weekly coaching. *(Key:* MCPS = Montgomery County Public School program; BLL = Scholastic's *Building Language for Literacy)*

in emergent literacy skills from the fall to spring, as well as from the RCT conducted in 24 classrooms that demonstrated benefits to both classrooms and children when additional professional development was provided to teachers using an individualized coaching model.

Figure 5.7 summarizes data from the ELLCO, with higher scores indicative of more literacy- and language-enriched environments. Three types of classrooms are represented in this figure: 1) representative classrooms from the Montgomery County Public Schools program; 2) classrooms that received year-long, *monthly* coaching using Scholastic's *Building Language for Literacy* (BLL) curriculum developed by Neuman and Snow (2000); and 3) classrooms that received year-long, *weekly* coaching in BLL implementation. The curriculum coaching provided was a structured intervention with coaches who had master's degrees in reading and who received additional training from Scholastic and Dr. Susan Neuman regarding the BLL curriculum. Dr. Neuman provided ongoing supervision throughout the study. All coaching sessions were documented using a BLL Curriculum Fidelity Checklist and supplemented with systematic field notes about activities that occurred. Coaching lasted for the entire length of the school day. In addition, we provided teachers in the coaching conditions with monthly group professional development sessions. (Attendance was voluntary; teachers were paid the school district's standard professional development stipend for participating.) Attendance was uniformly high for these monthly meetings.

As Figure 5.7 indicates, classrooms in both coaching conditions earned higher mean ELLCO scores than did those in the comparison classrooms. Furthermore, classrooms that received weekly coaching had the highest ELLCO scores. We also note that these ELLCO scores for classrooms in all conditions are consistent with the conclusion that these are enriched language and literacy classrooms. As mentioned earlier, all classrooms had certified teachers with a specialty in early childhood education; the school system provided ongoing professional development for the entire pre-K program; and the school system implemented a variety of monitoring strategies, including teacher-administered, systematic assessment of all children three times per year. In this chapter, all findings presented from Montgomery County Public Schools derive from data collected by trained, independent research associates from Georgetown University's Center on Health and Education.

We assessed children's achievement in early literacy by individually administering the Test of Early Reading Abilities (TERA; Reid, Hresko, & Hammill, 2001) in the fall and spring, along with *Get It! Got It! Go!* (University of Minnesota College of Education and Human Development, 2006) and *Concepts of Print* (from the Developing Skills Checklist (CTB Macmillan/McGraw-Hill, 1990). Figure 5.8 shows the findings regarding the Montgomery County Public Schools children's performance on the TERA. On average, the children in Montgomery County Public Schools started their pre-K year performing near the

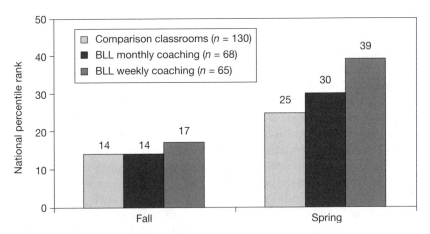

Figure 5.8. Findings regarding the Montgomery County Public Schools children's performance on the Test of Early Reading Abilities (TERA). (*Key:* MCPS = Montgomery County Public Schools program; BLL = Scholastic's *Building Language for Literacy*)

15th national percentile. By spring, those children in the comparison classrooms demonstrated significant gains, to a mean of the 25th percentile (a 10-point gain for this group). In contrast, the children in the two BLL coaching conditions displayed even larger gains—those whose teachers received monthly coaching had a mean score placing them in the 30th national percentile and those whose teachers had weekly coaching placed in the 39th national percentile. These findings indicate that children in all classrooms benefited from this Montgomery County Public Schools program, with far greater gains associated with additional professional development for teachers, primarily through systematic and documented job-embedded coaching.

Comparison of Student Performance in the LA4 and Montgomery County Public School Pre-K/Head Start Classrooms

These two separate, large-scale pre-K programs provide new evidence about the feasibility of scale-up programs that serve a wide range of children who are at risk, are informed by current scientific evidence about what comprises quality programs, and have made a commitment to actively monitoring their effectiveness. The findings to date provide a naturalistic opportunity for considering variations in the magnitude of detected student benefits. Length of the school day, or the overall intensity (dosage) of the pre-K program children received, is the major difference in these two programs. In Louisiana, the dosage issue also was addressed while implementing the LA4 program because the pilot year provided only a half-year or half-dose to the children. Figure 5.9 combines the findings using national percentiles as the common metric (although the children were assessed with the different tools as described earlier).

Surprisingly, children served in the LA4 program, in a state with one of the nation's lowest levels of family income and educational attainment among adult citizens, were only slightly lower in their initial emergent literacy skills than were children in the Montgomery County Public Schools program who were at risk and from low-income families. In both pre-K programs, children showed large gains, although the magnitude of the gains was nearly double from the full-day and full-year LA4 program compared with the half-day Montgomery County Public Schools program and the half-year (pilot year) LA4 program.

Because both public pre-K programs were considered to be solid, well staffed, and environmentally enriched, we consider the data to

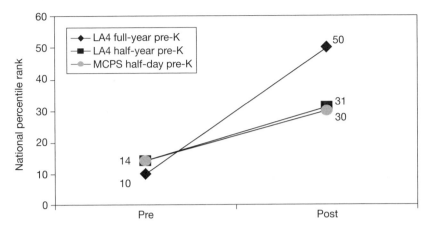

Figure 5.9. National percentile ranks of children from Louisiana and the Montgomery County, MD, pre-K programs in pre- and posttests. In both pre-K programs, children showed large gains, especially from the full-day and full-year LA4 program compared with the half-day Montgomery County Public Schools program and the half-year (pilot year) LA4 program.

provide new and strong support for the principle of program intensity or dosage, through independent validation using a variety of standardized tools (see S.L. Ramey & Ramey, 2006, for an updated summary of the major principles of effective literacy interventions from RCTs). These findings also are highly consistent with the public policy theme of Return on Investment (ROI), with the larger investment in a full-day program yielding significantly higher returns. These returns already transcend the pre-K year and in Louisiana extend to practical cost savings due to lower rates of grade repetition and placement in special education.

These findings are part of ongoing partnerships focused on collecting useful, trustworthy data for practice, policy, and educational science; and we are continuing to study these programs in depth and soon will have longitudinal findings that track multiple aspects of the children's performance into later elementary school grades. At this time, the evidence from these states affirms that quality preschool education can definitely boost the children's academic performance significantly—to levels that place the children at much greater likelihood of succeeding in elementary school than if they had not received such early educational supports. These findings are consistent with the three landmark studies—the Abecedarian Project and its replications, the Chicago Parent-Child Centers, and the Perry Preschool Project.

REFERENCES

Blair, C., Ramey, C.T., & Hardin, M. (1995). Early intervention for low birth weight premature infants: Participation and intellectual development. *American Journal on Mental Retardation, 99*, 542–554.

Campbell, F.A., Ramey, C.T., Pungello, E., Sparling, J., & Miller-Johnson, S. (2002). Early childhood education: Young adult outcomes from the Abecedarian Project. *Applied Developmental Science, 6*, 42–52.

Campbell, F.A., Wasik, B.H., Pungello, E., Burchinal, M., Barbarin, O., Kainz, K., et al. (2008). Young adult outcomes from the Abecedarian and CARE early childhood educational interventions. *Early Childhood Research Quarterly, 23*, 452–466.

Clinton, H.R. (1996). *It takes a village and other lessons children teach us.* New York: Simon & Schuster.

CTB Macmillan/McGraw-Hill (1990). *Developing Skills Checklist (DSC).* Monterey, CA: Author.

Gross, R.T., Spiker, D., & Haynes, C.W. (Eds.). (1997). *Helping low birth weight, premature babies: The Infant Health and Development Program.* Stanford, CA: Stanford University Press.

Harms, T., Clifford, R.M., & Cryer, C. (2004). *Early Childhood Environment Rating Scale–Revised.* New York: Teachers College Press.

Heckman, J.J. (2008). The case for investing in disadvantaged young children. In *Big ideas for children: Investing in our nation's future* (pp. 49–58). Washington, D.C.: First Focus.

The Infant Health and Development Program. (1990). Enhancing the outcomes of low birth weight, premature infants: A multisite randomized trial. *Journal of the American Medical Association, 263*, 3035–3042.

Kotulak, R. (1996). *Inside the brain: Revolutionary discoveries of how the mind works.* Kansas City, MO: Andrews & McMeel.

McCormick, M.C., Brooks-Gunn, J., Buka, S.L., Goldman, J., Yu, J., Bennett, F.C., et al. (2006, March). Early intervention in low birth weight premature infants: Results at 18 years of age for the infant health and development program. *Pediatrics, 117*(3), 771–780.

Neuman, S.B., & Dickinson, D.K. (Eds.). (2006). *Handbook of early literacy research* (2nd ed.). New York: Guilford Press.

Neuman, S.B., & Snow, C. (2000). *Building language for literacy: Research-based early literacy instruction.* New York: Scholastic.

NICHD Early Child Care Research Network. (2005). *Child care and child development: Results from the NICHD Study of Early Child Care and Youth Development.* New York: Plenum Press.

Ramey, C.T., Bryant, D.M., Wasik, B.H., Sparling, J.J., Fendt, K.H., & LaVange, L.M. (1992). Infant Health and Development Program for low birth weight, premature infants: Program elements, family participation, and child intelligence. *Pediatrics, 89*, 454–465.

Ramey, C.T., Campbell, F.A., Burchinal, M., Skinner, M.L., Gardner, D.M., & Ramey, S.L. (2000). Persistent effects of early childhood education on high-risk children and their mothers. *Applied Developmental Science, 4,* 2–14.

Ramey, C.T., & Ramey, S.L. (1994). Which children benefit the most from early intervention? *Pediatrics, 94,* 1064–1066.

Ramey, C.T., & Ramey, S.L. (1998). Early intervention and early experience. *American Psychologist, 53,* 109–120.

Ramey, C.T., & Ramey, S.L. (1999). Beginning school for children at risk. In R.C. Pianta & M.J. Cox (Eds.), *The transition to kindergarten* (pp. 217–251). Baltimore: Paul H. Brookes Publishing Co.

Ramey, C.T., & Ramey, S.L. (2004a). Early educational interventions and intelligence: Implications for Head Start. In E. Zigler & S.J. Styfco (Eds.), *The Head Start debates* (pp. 3–17). Baltimore: Paul H. Brookes Publishing Co.

Ramey, C.T., & Ramey, S.L. (2004b). Early learning and school readiness: Can early intervention make a difference? *Merrill-Palmer Quarterly, 50,* 471–491.

Ramey, C.T., & Ramey, S.L. (2006). Early learning and school readiness: Can early intervention make a difference? In N.F. Watt, C.C. Ayoub, R.H. Bradley, J.E. Puma, & W.A. Lebeouf (Eds.). The crisis in youth mental health: Critical issues and effective programs: Vol. 4. *Early intervention programs and policies* (pp. 291–317). Westport: Praeger Press.

Ramey, C.T., Ramey, S.L., & Lanzi, R.G. (2006). Children's health and education. In I. Sigel & A. Renninger (Eds.), *The handbook of child psychology* (Vol. 4, pp. 864–892). New York: Wiley.

Ramey, S.L. (2005). Human developmental science serving children and families: Contributions of the NICHD Study of Early Child Care. In NICHD Early Child Care Research Network (Ed.), *Child care and child development: Results from the NICHD Study of Early Child Care and Youth Development.* New York: Plenum Press.

Ramey, S.L., & Ramey, C.T. (1992). Early educational intervention with disadvantaged children: To what effect? *Applied and Preventive Psychology, 1,* 131–140.

Ramey, S.L., & Ramey, C.T. (1997). Evaluating educational programs: Strategies to understand and enhance educational effectiveness. In C. Seefeldt & A. Galper (Eds.), *Continuing issues in early childhood education* (2nd ed., pp. 274–292). Upper Saddle River, NJ: Prentice Hall.

Ramey, S.L., & Ramey, C.T. (2000). Early childhood experiences and developmental competence. In J. Waldfogel & S. Danziger (Eds.). *Securing the future: Investing in children from birth to college* (pp. 122–150). New York: Russell Sage Foundation.

Ramey, S.L., & Ramey, C.T. (2006). Early educational interventions: Principles of effective and sustained benefits from targeted early education programs. In S.B. Neuman & D.K. Dickinson (Eds.), *Handbook of early literacy research* (2nd ed., pp. 445–459). New York: Guilford Press.

Ramey, S.L., & Ramey, C.T. (2007). Establishing a science of professional development for early education programs: The knowledge application information systems (KAIS) theory of professional development. In L.M. Justice &

C. Vukelich (Ed.), *Achieving excellence in preschool language and literacy instruction* (pp. 41–63). New York: Guilford Press.

Ramey, S.L., Ramey, C.T., & Lanzi, R.G. (2004). The transition to school: Building on preschool foundations and preparing for lifelong learning. In E. Zigler & S.J. Styfco (Eds.), *The Head Start debates* (pp. 397–413). Baltimore: Paul H. Brookes Publishing Co.

Reid, D.K., Hresko, W.P., & Hammill, D.D. (2001). *Test of Early Reading Ability–Third Edition: Examiner's Manual.* Austin, TX: PRO-ED.

Reynolds, A. (2002). Success in early intervention: The Chicago Child–Parent Centers. Lincoln, NE: University of Nebraska Press.

Reynolds, A.J., Temple, J.A., Roberson, D.L., & Mann, E.A. (2002). Ae 21 cost—benefit analysis of the Title 1 Chicago Child–Parent Centers. *Educational Evaluation and Policy Analysis 4*(24), 267–303.

Schweinhart, L.J., Montie, J., Xiang, Z., Barnett, W.S., Belfield, C.R., & Nores, M. (2005). *Lifetime effects: The High/Scope Perry Preschool Study Through Age 40.* Ypsilanti, MI: High/Scope Press.

Smith, M.W., & Dickinson, D.D. (with Sangeorge, A., & Anastasopoulos, L.). (2002). *Early Language and Literacy Classroom Observation (ELLCO) Toolkit* (Research ed.). Baltimore: Paul H. Brookes Publishing Co.

Sparling, J., Dragomir, C., Ramey, S.L., & Florescu, L. (2005). An educational intervention improves developmental progress of young children in a Romanian orphanage. *Infant Mental Health Journal, 26,* 127–142.

Sparling, J., & Lewis, I. (2000). *Learningames, the Abecedarian curriculum.* Tallahassee, FL: Early Learning Press, Inc.

Sparling, J., Lewis, I., & Ramey, C. (1995). *Partners for Learning.* Lewisville, NC: Kaplan.

University of Minnesota College of Education & Human Development (2006, February 21). *Home of the preschool individual growth and development indicator* (IGDI). Retrieved February 21, 2006, from http://ggg.umn.edu/

Wasik, B.H., Ramey, C.T., Bryant, D.M., & Sparling, J.J. (1990). A longitudinal study of two early intervention strategies: Project CARE. *Child Development, 61,* 1682–1696.

Chapter 6

Georgia's Prekindergarten Program

Bright from the Start

Marsha H. Moore

Georgia's prekindergarten (pre-K) program began in 1992 when it was piloted for 750 children who were considered at risk. The program was established as a result of a campaign promise made by then Governor Zell Miller to establish a state lottery to fund special education projects, one of which was a voluntary pre-K program to provide 4-year-olds with high-quality preschool experiences to help prepare them for kindergarten. In 1995, Georgia's pre-K program was opened to all 4-year-old children, regardless of family income. Each year since its inception, the program has increased the number of children served and has enhanced the quality of the program. In the 2006–2007 school year, this unique program served more than 76,000 4-year-olds.

An evaluation by Georgia State University found that children who attended pre-K had higher academic and social ratings by their kindergarten teachers and better kindergarten attendance than children who did not attend preschool programs (Henderson, Henry, Gordon, & Ponder, 2003). Participation in a high-quality lottery-funded preschool program also helps children develop social and preacademic skills that will help them succeed in kindergarten and throughout their educational career.

On July 1, 2004, Bright from the Start: Georgia Department of Early Care and Learning (Bright from the Start) was created when several state entities, all of which dealt with early childhood care and education, were merged. The department's responsibility is not only to administer various early care and education programs, but also to lead the state's efforts to create a coordinated, streamlined, efficient, and comprehensive system of early care and education for Georgia. Bright from the Start was the first department of its kind in the nation to bring together most of the publicly funded care and education programs that serve young children in Georgia—Georgia's pre-K program, licensure and regulation of child care facilities, administration of federal food programs (the Child and Adult Care Food Program and the Summer Food Service Program), the federal quality set-aside funds from the Child Care and Development Funds (CCDF), early childhood education program quality improvement initiatives, the Even Start Family Literacy Program, Head Start, and coordination of Georgia's child care resource and referral agencies (Georgia General Assembly, 2004).

GEORGIA'S PRE-K PROGRAM

Georgia's pre-K program continues to update policies and standards each year to increase quality services for children and families. The program offers appropriate and developmental environments for 4-year-old children. An appropriate program for 4-year-olds looks and functions differently than kindergarten. Children learn through play and learning centers, which are integral parts of pre-K classrooms. Pre-K programs reflect an understanding of how children learn by emphasizing active learning, implementing daily routines, and using positive behavior management and assessment strategies. The school readiness goals of the pre-K program provide appropriate preschool experiences emphasizing growth in language and literacy, math concepts, science, social studies, arts, physical development, and social-emotional competence. To define the high-quality educational pre-K experience, Georgia identifies four key areas of classroom and program function: Environment, Curriculum, Child Assessment, and Program Evaluation.

ENVIRONMENT

Specific environmental elements are required to provide a developmentally appropriate classroom for the children in Pre-K classes.

Universal and Full Day

Children must be 4 years of age on or before September 1 of the school year and be residents of the state of Georgia to participate in pre-K. Five-year-old children who have not previously attended the pre-K program and who have late birthdays or developmental delays that affect their readiness for school may also enroll at the request of their parents. The program provides a full 6.5-hour instructional day for children, 5 days a week, 180 days a year, following the public school calendar.

Variety of School Settings

Georgia's pre-K operates through a public–private partnership in terms of who provides pre-K services. Georgia pre-K offers high-quality classroom environments in a variety of settings: public and private elementary schools; private child care centers; lab schools at colleges, universities, and technical colleges; Department of Family and Children Services offices; hospitals; military bases; YMCA/YWCAs; and Head Start programs. The variety of programs offered through the public–private partnership provides parents choices for the most appropriate classroom setting for their child.

Daily classroom experiences offer children a wide variety of learning opportunities, including independent play, adult-guided exploration, cooperative projects/tasks, and materials to enhance learning. Pre-K classrooms are richly equipped with materials and supplies in a diverse group of learning areas. Typical learning areas in the pre-K classroom include language and literacy, math and manipulatives, art and creative expression, block play, science, dramatic play, music and movement, and an outdoor play area. Bright from the Start consultants guide and support pre-K providers in equipping each classroom using an exhaustive list of suggested materials for the classroom, photo essay pictorial guides, and experienced on-site technical assistance.

Pre-K Staff

Each pre-K classroom has a lead teacher and an assistant teacher. Qualifications for classroom staff have evolved as Georgia's pre-K program has grown. Currently, pre-K lead teachers must have a minimum of an associate's degree in early childhood education (or a related field).

Lead teacher salaries are based on the teacher's credentials. Lead teachers may hold a bachelor's degree in early childhood or elementary education (or a related field). The highest level of credential belongs to teachers who are certified in Georgia. As of 2008, approximately 80% of Georgia's pre-K lead teachers were state certified or have a 4-year degree. Pre-K classroom staff are offered, and required to attend, ongoing professional development courses annually. Developed in conjunction with leading early childhood education professionals, topics for workshops are determined by demonstrated classroom needs, current research in early childhood education, and changes to pre-K program guidelines. All of these elements combine to create a child-centered program that is responsive to the changing needs of children.

A national survey of public kindergarten teachers (U.S. Department of Education, Institute of Education Sciences, 2008) noted three primary essentials for school readiness: children are physically healthy, rested, and well nourished; they are able to communicate needs, wants, and thoughts verbally; and they are enthusiastic and curious in approaching new activities. Georgia's pre-K program provides children with experiences that foster all these essentials.

CURRICULUM

Georgia's pre-K program has focused on academics from its inception. The curriculum for Georgia's pre-K program is guided by Georgia's Pre-K Content Standards, a complete and thorough set of standards that provide a framework to guide children's learning. Georgia's Pre-K Content Standards were last revised in August 2006.

The revised standards establish appropriate and meaningful performance goals that clearly identify what Georgia's 4-year-olds should know, understand, and be able to do during their pre-K year. The Content Standards have been aligned with the Georgia Early Learning Standards (for children from birth through age 3) and with Georgia's Performance Standards for kindergarten through Grade 12, which provides a seamless set of learning standards for Georgia's children from birth through high school (Georgia Department of Early Care and Learning [DECAL], 2007).

The Content Standards serve as the basis for instructional planning for teachers and provide families with a clear understanding of what their children are being taught. The 2006 edition of the Content Standards have been updated to include correlations with Kindergarten Georgia Performance Standards (K-GPS), strategies to support inclusive classrooms, "Learning in Action" suggestions for classroom practice, professional resources for each curriculum domain, lists of high-quality children's literature for each curriculum domain, and tips to support family involvement in the child's education. The seven learning domains are the following:

1. Language and literacy

2. Math

3. Science

4. Social studies

5. Create

6. Social and emotional health

7. Health and physical development

One performance indicator of language and literacy development would be the following: "Children will develop skills in listening for the purpose of comprehension." Listening to and following the teacher's directive: "Hang up your jacket and come to the group area" is an example of the Learning in Action for that performance indicator.

With the addition of the K-GPS correlations, it is clear how what is taught in pre-K lays the foundation for expectations in kindergarten. Each Pre-K Content Standard has been matched to an appropriate K-GPS (see Table 6.1). In some cases, a Pre-K Content Standard will match several kindergarten standards; however, there is not always a corresponding kindergarten standard for every Pre-K Content Standard. It is important to remember that the Pre-K Content Standards and the Kindergarten Performance Standards reflect what children should know at the end of pre-K or the end of kindergarten—not at the beginning. Seeing how these standards relate is helpful to pre-K teachers, kindergarten teachers, and parents, all of whom have a part in making children successful in the early years.

The section of the Content Standards dealing with strategies to support inclusive classrooms helps individualize instruction to meet the needs of all students in the classroom. Encouraging hands-on and sensory experiences such as touching, holding, exploring, tasting, smelling and manipulating objects is one strategy to support an inclusive learning environment, for example. The "Learning in Action" section of the Content Standards provides examples of appropriate and fun activities to build these skills. One such activity is "Make independent 'time alone' play." Parents are directed to talk with their child afterwards and encourage him to talk about what he did. Another activity is to look through old photos of the child often and point out how much he has grown over time.

Table 6.1. Example of Content Standards (partial) in math for Pre-K matched to Kindergarten Georgia Performance Standards (K-GPS)

Math Development (MD 1): Children will begin to develop an understanding of numbers.

	Performance Indicators	Learning in Action	K-GPS
MD 1a	Counts by rote	Counts in finger plays or rhymes	MKN1a Count a number of objects up to 30
		Sings a counting song	SKCS2a
MD 1b	Arranges sets of objects in one-to-one correspondence	Matches blocks with animals Places a spoon on each plate at the table	MKN1a Count a number of objects up to 30
MD 1c	Counts objects using one-to-one correspondence	Counts manipulatives Counts the number of children present	MKN1a Count a number of objects up to 30
MD 1d	Compares sets of objects using language	Identifies *more than, less than,* or *same* when comparing two groups Explains that all of the long sticks are in one box and all the short sticks are in another box	MKN1e Compare two or more sets of objects (1–10) and identify which set is equal to, more than, or less than the other. MKN2a Use counting strategies to find out how many items are in two sets when they are combined. MKN2b Build number combinations up to 10 and for doubles to 10. MKN2c Use objects, pictures, numbers, or words to create, solve, and explain story problems for two numbers that are each less than 10.

From Georgia Department of Early Care and Learning (DECAL): Bright from the Start (2007). *Georgia's pre-K program content standards* (Rev. ed.; p. 25). Author; adapted by permission.

The professional resources and children's literature for each domain help in planning quality instruction based on current research. Family involvement and support, covered in the Home and Family Connection tips, are important to a child's academic success, so each learning domain now includes ideas for strengthening the connection between home and school.

The Content Standards are used for planning instruction, assessing growth and development, and sharing information with families. These standards are important for a number of reasons:

1. Instruction must be planned to meet each child's individual needs because pre-K children learn and develop at varying rates.

2. Pre-K children learn best with a balance of teacher-directed and child-initiated activities that encourage thinking, reasoning, and communication.

3. Pre-K children need movement, hands-on activities, lots of language practice and interaction, and a supportive environment.

National research shows that pre-K programs with effective teaching practices and challenging and appropriate curricula enhance children's intellectual, physical, and emotional development. Bright from the Start utilizes these standards to help pre-K programs exceed expectations in all program areas.

As the program began to expand, it became readily apparent that additional curricula options were needed to meet the varied requirements of a diverse pre-K population. Providers now choose from the following curriculum options: *Bank Street, Creative Curriculum, High/Scope, High Reach Framework, High Reach Butterflies, Montessori, Scholastic Workshop,* or a locally developed curriculum approved by Bright from the Start. Parents, after learning about each of these curricula, can choose a center that uses the curriculum they feel will best meet the needs of their child. Each pre-K program selects the curriculum from the approved list that they feel best supports their use of the Content Standards in meeting the needs of the program's unique community.

CHILD ASSESSMENT

Since its inception, Georgia's pre-K program has trained and supported teachers in practicing authentic child assessment, which is based in the child's natural classroom environment and occurs over a period of time (as opposed to an on-demand/one-time assessment). In the early 2000s, the program began revising its approach to child assessment by developing and implementing Georgia's Pre-K Assessment (DECAL, 2007) to promote children's learning and development by identifying their strengths and weaknesses in relation to school readiness.

Designing and implementing Georgia's Pre-K Assessment has made Georgia's pre-K program stronger. By implementing the assessment statewide, teachers are provided with a structured, formal way to assess each child's progress toward meeting the readiness benchmarks and Content Standards. Assessment results provide teachers with data that can be used to plan instruction to meet the needs of individual learners.

Georgia's pre-K program holds strongly to the belief that parents are a child's first and most important teachers. In addition to instructional planning that meets the needs of individual children, assessment data provides ongoing opportunities to share information with parents regarding their child's performance and strategies for enhancing growth and development.

Georgia's Pre-K Assessment is designed to provide an emerging picture of a child's readiness for school. It is designed to provide information for parents and teachers to use as a basis for discussion, planning, and designing instructional activities to promote growth and development during the pre-K year. In addition, assessment results should provide a clear picture of an emerging learner for kindergarten teachers. It may not be used for making decisions regarding placement in any program.

Georgia's assessment is holistic, taking into consideration the whole child including cognitive/general knowledge, language/literacy skills, social-emotional skills, health, physical/motor development, and approaches to learning. Multiple sources of data are used to assess a child's readiness for school in all domains.

Results of assessments provide information to teachers and parents for instructional planning and guidance to further enhance children's learning and development. Georgia's Pre-K Assessment includes training and support for teachers and parents because of the critical roles of both in a child's education. In addition to Georgia's Pre-K Assessment, local screening and referral procedures are in place to identify children for health and other services. The well-documented and respected Work Sampling System (WSS; ERIC Digests, 1996) assessment tools were selected to provide the framework and structure for Georgia's Pre-K Assessment.

Why Work Sampling?

Georgia chose WSS as the pre-K assessment tool because it is developmentally appropriate for 4-year-old children. Assessments of pre-K children cannot be accomplished by children taking a pencil-and-paper test but must be done with ongoing observations because of the way 4-year-old children learn and develop school readiness skills. WSS clearly meets the purpose of an assessment for 4-year-old children in that it provides information for screening children to see if they need intervention, for planning instruction to ensure that the needs of all children are being met, for identifying program improvement and staff development needs, and for evaluating the extent to which programs are meeting children's needs.

Results of assessments enhance the communication between parents and teachers. The assessment tool helps the teacher identify areas in which the child is performing as a 4-year-old who is typically developing and where the child is not. Teachers can then use the information to engage and work closer with parents to further enhance their child's development. In Georgia's pre-K program, WSS provides status reports to parents about their child's development and is the basis for scheduled parent–teacher conferences.

Determining what children already know, understand, and can do is necessary in order to adjust curriculum and instruction to meet the needs of individual children. Assessment is a collaborative process that should take place over time and in natural settings. It involves observing, recording, and documenting data about children as they interact with the world around them. Assessment results of young children can be affected by many factors and should be viewed as an emerging picture of a child's learning and development.

Data Collection

Georgia's Pre-K Assessment includes collecting the following data for individual children to provide a holistic picture of emerging learners:

- Immunizations (up to date)

- Eye, ear, dental (completion status / referrals)

- Rate of growth (height / weight)

- Fine and gross motor skills development

- Section 504 medical disabilities (referral / Section 504 supports plan in place or in progress)

- Referrals for suspected behavior disorders

- Request for suspensions / results of request

- Individualized education program / referrals for speech–language therapy

- Approaches to learning

- Social-emotional development

- Language/communication skills

- Emerging literacy skills

- General knowledge/cognition

A progress report was developed specifically to meet the needs of Georgia's families and classrooms. The progress report includes information on child progress on developmental goals as well as information related to school absences; tardiness/early departure information; ear, eye, and dental screening information; and issues involving referral for special services. Pre-K classroom staff complete the progress report twice per school year (or more often if needed for technical assistance) to provide specific feedback and information on each child's progress. The progress report contains information in each of the seven learning domains found in Georgia's Content Standards and in WSS: language and literacy, math, science, social studies, creative, social and emotional, and health and physical development.

PROGRAM EVALUATION

Georgia's pre-K Program Quality Assessment (PQA) was developed to help monitor and assess each pre-K program. The PQA is completed annually by consultants employed by Bright from the Start to monitor compliance with the pre-K program guidelines. The PQA provides a "snapshot" of the pre-K program and helps identify program strengths and areas needing improvement. Site directors and pre-K teachers are recommended to use the PQA regularly for program self-evaluation and improvement.

The PQA is arranged in four sections: Program Administration, Physical Learning Environment, Instruction and Curriculum, and Transition and Family Involvement. A series of items have been created in each section to guide classroom practice. Thirty-four items make up the PQA, and each item is scored based on a series of tiered indicators using one of four scoring options (i.e., *Not Met, Partially Met, Meets, Exceeds*) (see Figure 6.1 for an example). The indicators for each item are divided into four categories that align with the four scoring options. The categories build on one another, meaning that the indicators in the *Not Met* category are basic indicators of quality building through the *Partially Met* and *Meets* indicators to arrive at high-quality indicators in the *Exceeds* category. Bright from the Start uses the PQA to monitor compliance, evaluate program growth, guide technical assistance, and provide data for state school report cards.

Section B: Physical Learning Environment

☐ ☐ **B 1. The classroom is arranged into clearly defined learning areas that are equipped with appropriate learning materials and supplies that enhance children's growth and development.** | Due Date |

Partially Meets	Meets	Exceeds
☐ The room arrangement supports an appropriate instructional environment.	☐ Learning areas are changed to reflect current topics and interests.	☐ Boundaries are established for each learning area.
☐ Materials are accessible to the children.	☐ A protected space is accessible for one or two children to work or play without interruptions.	☐ More than one protected space is accessible in the classroom.
☐ Materials and furniture are in good repair.		
☐ Learning areas are clean and well lit.	☐ Centers are arranged for independent use by the children.	☐ Diversity is reflected in the classroom learning areas and materials.
☐ Quiet and noisy areas are separated.		
☐ The classroom is organized and uncluttered.		

☐ ☐ **B 2. The classroom display reflects the children's interests and activities.** | Due Date |

Partially Meets	Meets	Exceeds
☐ Children's creative efforts are displayed in the classroom.	☐ The majority of the display in the classroom reflects children's unique and individual expression.	☐ The classroom display reflects the current topics and children's interests.
☐ Children's creative efforts are displayed at varying levels.	☐ The children's creative efforts are displayed throughout the classroom.	☐ Pictures of the children and/or families are displayed in the classroom.
☐ Displayed work includes a variety of media.	☐ The items displayed in the classroom are current and are changed regularly.	☐ Children select the location to display their work.
		☐ The classroom display includes charts and/or stories of current activities.

☐ ☐ **B 3. The Language and Literacy area is equipped to provide many opportunities for children to explore, manipulate, investigate and discover.** | Due Date |

Partially Meets	Meets	Exceeds
☐ The reading area is cozy and inviting.	☐ A listening area with books and corresponding tapes is accessible.	☐ Books made by individuals and groups of children in the class are accessible.
☐ Children's appropriate literature is accessible.	☐ The flannel board and flannel board stories are accessible.	☐ Language and literacy props related to the current story or topic of study are accessible.
☐ At least one book per child is displayed in an orderly manner.	☐ A writing area is accessible with a variety of materials that address differing developmental levels.	
☐ Additional books are available for rotation.	☐ Various literature types are accessible.	☐ Additional language props are available.
☐ Language and literacy props are in good repair.	☐ Various cultures, abilities, ages and races are represented in the accessible reading materials.	☐ Materials are accessible to enhance children's understanding of the alphabetic principle.
	☐ Books related to the current topics are accessible in order to expand children's interests and vocabulary.	☐ Language and literacy props are rotated.
	☐ Books are rotated to maintain children's interest.	☐ Books are available for children to check out, take home and return.

Figure 6.1.   Partial Program Quality Assessment (PQA) from Bright from the Start. This section assesses whether the physical learning environment partially meets, meets, or exceeds expectations. (From Georgia Department of Early Care and Learning (DECAL): Bright from the Start (2007). *Georgia's pre-K program content standards* (Rev. ed.). Author; reprinted by permission.

GEORGIA'S DEFINITION OF SCHOOL READINESS

Bright from the Start has adopted a comprehensive definition of school readiness to support its mission and vision. The school readiness definition was created and adopted following an extensive review and evaluation of national research and policy related to school readiness.

The first of the National Education Goals, developed in 1995 by a national goals panel, states, "All children will start school ready to learn" (U.S. Department of Education, Educational Programs that Work, 1995). Georgia formulated a definition of school readiness based on the following underlying principles: School readiness must be defined within the context of families and how they live, within the context of communities and the services they provide, and within the context of schools and their readiness for children.

Four-year-olds are, by nature, curious and enthusiastic learners. They are becoming more aware of themselves and others as well as the world around them. Increasing language and literacy skills provide opportunities to interact with others and help prepare them to learn to read when they are ready. Social and interpersonal skills are emerging, allowing them to form appropriate relationships with the children and adults around them. Their fine and gross motor skills are developing, expanding their ability to interact with the world around them.

Four-year-olds' learning is best characterized as sporadic and explosive. It is highly influenced by how they are feeling, what is happening around them, and what their interests are at the moment. They grow and change rapidly. They are easily distracted and have no personal interest in assessment. Therefore, assessment of 4-year-olds must be ongoing, developmentally appropriate, administered cautiously, and broadly interpreted.

Indicators for each dimension of school readiness include, but are not limited to, the following:

- Possible health barriers that block learning have been detected.

    —Eye, ear, and dental screenings will detect problems related to seeing, hearing, and dental health.

    —Immunizations will be on schedule.

    —Diseases and other health issues will be detected as early as possible.

    —Rate of growth and mobility within an identified range will be determined.

- Suspected physical or mental disabilities have been addressed.

- Suspected physical or mental disabilities will be detected, and referrals will be made as early as possible.

- Enthusiasm, curiosity, and persistence toward learning is demonstrated.

    —Attitudes toward and interest in learning will demonstrate a readiness to learn.

    —Persistence in completing tasks will be evident.

- Feelings of both self and others are recognized.

    —Feelings will be identified and expressed appropriately.

    —Feelings of others will be understood and accepted.

    —An increasing capacity for self-control will be evident.

- Social and interpersonal skills are emerging.

    —Ability to work or play cooperatively with others will be evident.

    —Ability to form appropriate relationships with children and adults will be demonstrated.

    —Emerging conflict resolution skills will be evident.

    —Increasing capacity to follow rules and routines will be evident.

- Communication with others is effective.

    —Listening skills will be evident.

    —Ability to follow simple directions will be evident.

    —Expressing needs and wants will be demonstrated.

    —Using language to interact socially with others will be demonstrated.

    —Ability to describe people, places, things, and events will be evident.

    —Ability to ask and answer age-appropriate questions will be demonstrated.

- Early literacy skills are evident.

    —Association between spoken and written words will be recognized.

    —Understanding of beginning alphabetic knowledge will be demonstrated.

    —Ability to discriminate sounds will be evident.

—Knowledge of basic book and story components will be evident.

—Use of shapes and marks to convey meaning will be demonstrated.

—Writing letters to represent words and syllables will be demonstrated.

- A general knowledge about the world, things, places, events, and people has been acquired.

—Recognition of name will be evident.

—Basic awareness of self, family, and community will be demonstrated.

—Knowledge of simple science concepts will be evident.

—Knowledge of simple math concepts will be evident.

—Ability to count to 10 will be evident.

—Basic understanding of shapes and colors will be demonstrated.

—Ability to sort and classify objects will be evident.

Guided by Georgia's definition of school readiness, each provider participating in Georgia's pre-K program is given the task of meeting the individual needs of the families and children enrolled in their program.

Governor Sonny Perdue created the Alliance of Education Agency Heads to encourage and strengthen collaboration between Georgia's education agencies: the Georgia Department of Education, the Department of Technical and Adult Education, the Board of Regents, the Office of Student Achievement, the Georgia Student Finance Commission, the Georgia Professional Standards Commission, and Bright from the Start. The leaders of these education agencies meet regularly to identify similar goals and to develop collaborative strategies to meet these goals and to develop a seamless educational system that supports children from the moment they enter formal state-funded education to postsecondary. Assigning a student identification number is one example of the alliance's collaboration. Each child entering the formal public education system will be assigned a unique student ID number that will help ensure smooth navigation throughout the educational system.

To further school readiness in Georgia, Bright from the Start is collaborating with the Georgia Department of Education in an initiative designed to improve the communication and collaboration between pre-K and Grades K–3. Georgia applied for and received a planning grant from the National Association of State Boards of Education to begin the process of implementing a PK–3 approach to learning by aligning standards, curriculum, instruction, and assessment for pre-K through the third grade. The PK–3 approach integrates the subject matter focus of K–3 with the child development focus of early childhood education. In addition, a PK–3 approach sustains and maintains pre-K investments in young children. Vertical teams are created through partnerships between early childhood education and primary education systems by connecting teachers, administrators, families, and communities.

Georgia has begun these PK–3 efforts by aligning child assessment. The introduction of Georgia's Pre-K Assessment and WSS provided a starting point for the alignment. The Georgia Department of Education is in the initial stages of developing a new kindergarten assessment called Georgia Kindergarten Inventory of Developing Skills (GKIDS). Bright from the Start is playing an active role in the development of GKIDS to ensure that the alignment between WSS and GKIDS continues.

The success of Georgia's pre-K program has clearly been the catalyst for increasing the focus on school readiness for Georgia's children. For more than a decade, Georgia's leaders have worked diligently to ensure that children and their families receive high-quality early child care and education services. What began as a pilot program for 750 students who were at risk has evolved into a department of state government committed to serving children from birth to age 5 and to supporting early care and education providers, families, and communities.

REFERENCES

ERIC Digests. (1996). *Performance assessment in early care and education: The Work Sampling System*. ERIC Identifier ED382407. Retrieved 2007. Access on website. http://www.ericdigests.org/1996-1/early.htm

Georgia Department of Early Care and Learning (DECAL): Bright from the Start. (2007). *Georgia's pre-K program content standards* (Rev. ed.). Author.

Georgia Department of Education. (2007). *Georgia Kindergarten Inventory of Developing Skills* (GKIDS). Retrieved November 30, 2007, from http://www.gadoe.org/ci_testing.aspx?PageReg=CI_TESTING_GKIDS

Georgia General Assembly. Session 2004: Senate Bill 456. (2004, May). Retrieved Dec. 15, 2008, from Georgia Legislature web site access: http://www.legis.state.ga/legis/2003_04/fulltext/sb456.htm

Henderson, L. Henry, G., Gordon, C., & Ponder, G. (2003). Georgia Pre-K longitudinal study: Final Report 1996–2001. Atlanta, GA: Andrew Young School of Public Policy Studies. Available from http://aysps.gsu.edu/publications/grklsfinalreportmay2003.pdf

U.S. Department of Education, Educational Programs that Work. (1995). *National Goals for Education*. Retrieved November 30, 2007, from http://www. ed.gov/pubs/EPTW/eptwgoal.htm/

U.S. Department of Education, Institute of Education Sciences (2008). *National Center for Educational Statistics, Early Childhood Longitudinal Study-ECC* (ongoing). Retrieved December 10, 2008, from UDDOE web site access: http://nces.ed.gov/surveys/frss/publications/93410/

Chapter 7

North Carolina's More at Four Prekindergarten Program

A Case Study of Funding versus Quality and Other Issues in Large-Scale Implementation

Carolyn T. Cobb

Until 2001–2002, North Carolina remained one of two states in the Southeast that did not have a state-funded prekindergarten (pre-K) for children at risk of school failure. Michael F. Easley ran for governor with two key educational goals: reducing class size in grades K–3 and establishing a pre-K program for 4-year-old children who are at risk. When introducing the legislation to establish the More at Four (MAF) Prekindergarten Program, he said,

> We must build a system of education in North Carolina that gives every child every opportunity to succeed, regardless of geographic location or economic condition. If we are to eliminate the achievement gap and give

Carolyn Cobb retired as Executive Director of the Office of School Readiness, North Carolina Department of Public Instruction, effective March 1, 2007. She currently is working as a consultant and as the North Carolina Ready Schools Initiative Coordinator through the North Carolina Partnership for Children (Smart Start).

all children a chance to succeed, then we must provide high-quality pre-K opportunities to our 4-year-olds who need them the most.

Even though in 2001–2003, the state experienced the largest budget deficits since the Depression, Governor Easley, with broad support from the early childhood community, was able to initiate and even expand MAF.

NATIONAL PERSPECTIVES ON FUNDING AND THE COSTS OF EARLY EDUCATION AND PRE-K

Numerous articles and policy papers discuss the costs of financing pre-K programs—either universal or those targeted to children who are at risk. Almost all discussions focus on the fragmentation and inadequacy of resources. Several policy analysts point out that the costs of early care and education are too low to promote high quality and too high to be affordable to a wide range of families (Brandon, Kagan, & Joesch, 2000; National Association for the Education of Young Children, 2001).

Funding mechanisms are another area of discussion. Mitchell, Stoney, and Dichter (2001) discussed current and innovative financing strategies. Greenberg and Schumacher (2003) discussed the use of and technical issues with the Child Care and Development Fund (CCDF) and Temporary Assistance to Needy Families (TANF), which are federal sources that support pre-K programs. The National Child Care and Information Center (n.d.) cites an array of sources for the early care and education system: Head Start/Early Head Start, CCDF, TANF, Early Intervention for Infant and Toddlers with Disabilities, Preschool Grants for Children with Disabilities, 21st Century Community Learning Center, Even Start, Title I Preschool, Social Services Block Grant, Early Reading First, Child Care, and pre-K in states. Similarly, Stoney and Edwards (2006) delineated new sources of revenue for child care financing and gave examples in which each has been employed (local property taxes; state and local sales taxes; "sin" taxes; state income tax credits, deductions, and exemptions; corporate income taxes; property tax abatements to local industry; various state education and human services funds; state health care funds; higher education funds; crime prevention and criminal justice funds; local government; employers; unions; community-based philanthropy and foundations; public–private partnerships; and various commercial lender and government sector partnerships). Vast (2002) considered how higher education financing models might inform strategies for early care and education.

Calculating the costs of pre-K per se has generated considerable discussion. Barnett, Hustedt, Hawkinson, and Robin (2006) specifically looked at state spending and the variation that can result given other resources. The amount of funding in inflation-adjusted dollars actually decreased between 2001–2002 and 2004–2005, potentially affecting quality of and access to pre-K programs, although this trend appeared to be halted in 2006–2007 (Barnett, Hustedt, Friedman, Boyd, & Ainsworth, 2007). They also noted a lack of parity with K–12 in expenditures per child, as well as the various components of pre-K that contribute to the costs of a quality program. Each year, the National Institute for Early Education Research (NIEER) publishes a yearbook that reports each state's pre-K status, including quality indicators and costs per child (although the methodology for estimating costs generates considerable discussion with state representatives). In the 2007 yearbook (Barnett et al., 2007), $3,642 was the estimated average state contribution per child nationwide. Stebbins and Langford (2006) also estimated costs and components of quality early care and education and attempted to develop a model for estimating costs. Drawing on data from the multistate study of pre-K, Bryant, Clifford, Early, and Little (2005) reported actual costs of pre-K classrooms ranging from $1,000 to more than $5,000, based on local costs as well as the quality components in those programs.

NORTH CAROLINA'S PERSPECTIVE ON COSTS OF PRE-K

Initially, we had no valid cost estimates on pre-K classrooms in North Carolina. Using national estimates and the ongoing work of National Center for Education, Development, and Learning (NCEDL) and its multistate pre-K study, as well as examining parity with the primary grades, we developed estimates of $7,500 per classroom in the earlier years. We raised that to a minimum of $8,000 over time as the cost of living and salaries increased. In the 2002–2003 annual legislative report (Governor's Office of North Carolina, 2003), jointly submitted by the governor's office, the North Carolina Department of Health and Human Services (DHHS), the North Carolina Department of Public Instruction (DPI), and the MAF Task Force, we summed the total expenditures for all major early care and education programs in North Carolina. Table 7.1 shows the estimated sum of expenditures from all key sources for birth to age 5. Note that they are not a great deal more than the funding for even one grade level in K–12.

To try to refine our cost estimates, the MAF office contracted with the evaluators at Frank Porter Graham (FPG) Child Development Institute to use the methodology for the national study for purposively

Table 7.1.   Budgeted funding supporting North Carolina's early care and education system: 2002–2003

	Federal	State	Total Birth to 5-year-olds	4-year-olds
Strategy 1	Smart Start—Total This includes all state funds from Smart Start by core services	–	$198,554,511	$198,554,511	–
Strategy 2	Child care assistance to families—Total This includes Child Care Development Funds (CCDF), Temporary Assistance for Needy Families (TANF), Social Services Block Grant (SSBG), and state funds for child care subsidy	$169,542,104	$49,866,160	$219,408,264	–
Strategy 3	Head Start—Total This includes Head Start, Early Head Start, federal expansion funds, Head Start collaboration project, and professional development funds	$130,749,161	–	$137,644,268	–
Strategy 4	Public school prekindergarten (pre-K)—Total This includes Title I basic grants for preschool, Title I Even Start family literacy and special education preschool grants IDEA 2004 funds Exceptional children	$54,756,241 $39,041,070 $4,215,171 $11,500,000	$34,500,000 – – $34,500,000	$89,256,241 $39,041,070 $4,215,171 $11,500,000 $34,500,000	$39,041,070 $39,041,070 – – –
Strategy 5	More at Four (MAF) pre-K—Total	–	$35,975,802	$35,975,802	$35,975,802
Other system support—Total	This includes T.E.A.C.H. early childhood scholarship program T.E.A.C.H. early childhood scholarship program—MAF Early intervention—Comprehensive[c]	$29,350,000 $350,000 – $29,000,000	$52,413,795 $2,600,000 $813,795 $49,000,000	$81,763,795 $2,950,000 $813,795 $78,000,000	$813,795 – $813,795 –
Total budgeted funding effort for strategies SFY 02–03		$384,397,506	$371,310,268	$762,602,881	$75,830,667

Note 1: Breakdowns of state and federal funds were estimated by applying the state and federal percentages of funds budgeted for all children to the estimated expenditures for children in those age groups. Funding for subsidized child care is not budgeted with specificity to individual ages. The amounts in this section are estimated to be attributable to these ages based on the percentages of total SFY 01–02 subsidized child care funds spent on 5- and 0–5-year-olds.

Note 2: Figures for Strategy 2 only include funds that are spent for direct child care services paid through the subsidized child care reimbursement system at the Division of Child Development (DCD). These figures do not include other DCD funds that are budgeted to support the overall quality and infrastructure of child care in North Carolina. This includes funding that supports the regulation of child care homes and centers across North Carolina and other activities that promote high-quality care in these settings.

Note 3: These figures are estimated SFY 02–03 budget figures. They reflect very closely the SFY 01–02 budget figures. Included in this table are preschools for children who are visually impaired, preschools for the deaf and hard of hearing, early intervention activities within the department of health and human services. Included in this table are preschools for children who are visually impaired, preschools for the deaf and hard of hearing, early intervention DEIE/OESA/DPH, DECs, and early intervention and infant/toddlers grant—DMH.

Note 4: Included in this column are only actual budgeted amounts dedicated to 4-year-olds. Some funds for 4-year-olds will be expended in other areas. We have no way to establish that amount by age level at this time because funds are not budgeted specifically by age.

Note 5: The child and adult food program supports child care centers, family child care homes, after-school programs that target children who are at risk, homeless shelters, and adult selected classrooms in North Carolina. Their report (Yonce, Clifford, Doig, & Nugent, 2006), based on the 2002–2003 school year, yielded an average cost estimate of $7,800 per classroom, which includes cash expenditures as well as in-kind costs. Thus, across the 6 years of MAF operation, the state has funded approximately half the real costs of a high-quality pre-K classroom in North Carolina. The state legislation specifies that other resources of local, state, and federal funds have to be used to help fund MAF. Using other resources is a necessity, given the level of state funding. Although state policy decisions allow for combining some state funds (e.g., subsidy and MAF), clearly the creative solutions to funding pre-K in North Carolina will be found at the local level. In conversations with other states, this challenge appears to be nearly universal.

MORE AT FOUR PRE-K: THE BEGINNING

Although North Carolina began to establish and grow its pre-K program for students at risk of not succeeding in school only since 2001, it has been cited as one of the top quality pre-K programs in the nation, now one of two states meeting 10 out of 10 quality indicators specified by NIEER (Barnett et al., 2007). How did we get there, and can it be maintained?

Legislation was passed for the 2001–2002 fiscal year that established MAF pre-K with $6.5 million to serve up to 1,600 children. The legislation referred to the program as an "academic pre-K" program to focus on literacy, mathematical understanding, and social-emotional development. Subsequent reference to the program by developers described it as an "educational" pre-K program to prevent the inference of a highly structured, direct instruction program to teach specific academic skills. Yet, we did not want to infer that it was simply "child care" without an intentional educational program. In addition, it was clear that goals for the program included reducing the achievement gap in K–12, building a high-quality voluntary program, serving children who are at risk, and building on the existing service delivery system.

Context Matters: Where We Started

If we take the lesson from nonlinear systems theory that "where we start matters" (Reilly, 2000), then it is important to look at the state context in which MAF pre-K was framed. As the director of this program, I felt that I had landed in a brain trust for early childhood in North Carolina. The human resources and programs already in existence made the initial start-up much easier than if I had a blank slate with which to work. Decisions on how to roll out the program were made using the existing infrastructure for early childhood programs.

Governor James Hunt had championed early childhood in the early 1990s through the concept of Smart Start, an initiative that attempts to provide early childhood infrastructure for children birth to age 5 at the local and state level. Started in 1993, Smart Start provides quality enhancement services for child care providers; provides 30% of its funding to subsidy (although they have considerable control over how they define subsidy and use it); promotes family support programs; and tries to bring the community together around early childhood issues, needs, and services. In 1999, the North Carolina Division of Child Development (DCD), DHHS, began its star-rated licensing system for child care and soon moved to tiered subsidy reimbursement based on the rating system.

Other early childhood initiatives included Teacher Education and Compensation Helps (T.E.A.C.H.), which provides scholarships for child care workers who take coursework in early childhood education to advance their credentials (requiring commitments from the worker and their child care provider as well) and provides health insurance—within available funding—to centers who have staff participating in the scholarship program. The FPG Child Development Institute has long provided research and project support to a variety of early childhood programs, family support, inclusion for exceptional children, and other related programs.

In 2000, Dr. Mike Ward, superintendent of DPI, and Governor Hunt convened a Ready for School Goal Team, following the lead of Goal 1 of the National Goals Panel—"all children ready for school" (Ready for School Goal Team, 2000). This team consisted of both educators and early childhood specialists who did not totally trust the public school systems' understanding of the needs of young children. This author served on that team as a member of the DPI and, at that time, as staff to the state board of education's K–2 assessment committee. It took time to build trust between the early childhood and the public school communities. We had to define what school readiness was *not* before we could advance to defining what it *was*. But the work of the team resulted in a multipart definition—probably the first in the nation—of school readiness: the condition of children when they entered school (i.e., children who were ready for school) and the capacity of schools to meet the needs of all children (i.e., schools that were ready for *all* children). In addition, it addressed components of "ready communities" and "ready families" (Ready for School Goal Team, 2000). Clearly, North Carolina has a strong history of early childhood initiatives, leadership, and infrastructure that gave the MAF pre-K a head start in its implementation. The MAF program built on a number of the components of the existing system.

The authorizing legislation called for a statewide MAF Task Force to be chaired by the secretary of DHHS and the superintendent of DPI. MAF was to be a collaborative effort between these two agencies and the governor's office. The task force approved the program guidelines and provided general guidance on issues. Because I needed to move quickly on many issues, I asked that the two chairs approve an executive committee that could work with me to make decisions quickly. The executive committee consisted of the Director of the Division of Child Development—then Peggy Ball; the President of Smart Start—then Karen Ponder; the Special Assistant for the Superintendent—then Priscilla Maynor; the Director of Child Care Services Association (operating T.E.A.C.H)—Sue Russell; and a senior research scientist from FPG—Dr. Richard Clifford. Thus, I had many early childhood leaders working with me as I began this new program.

Quality Defined: A Brief Overview of the Program

It is important to know what we are trying to fund before addressing funding issues. What are the components of the pre-K system that will most likely lead to positive outcomes for children? A committee appointed by the governor's staff had been working on recommended program guidelines even prior to the passage of the legislation. The program standards reflected many components based on the key pre-K programs that provide the research basis for the large-scale implementations of pre-K across the nation (i.e., High Scope/Perry Preschool Program [Schweinhart et al., 2005], Chicago Parent-Child Centers Project [Reynolds, Temple, Robertson, & Mann, 2001], and the Abecedarian Project [Campbell, Ramey, Pungello, Sparling, & Miller-Johnson, 2002]). (See Chapter 5 for more on these four national studies.) These guidelines were approved, with minor changes, by the statewide MAF Task Force. Some of the key elements include

- Class size maximum of 18; teacher–child ratio of 1:9

- A 6- to 6½-hour school day

- A birth–kindergarten (B–K) teaching license for lead teacher (more than 4 years to attain that credential with a minimum of 6 semester hours of schooling per academic year)

- A child development associate (CDA) for teacher assistants, with strong encouragement to attain a 2-year associate's degree in early childhood education

- Comparable salaries and benefits to school teachers for pre-K teachers in child care or Head Start

- Required early learning standards implemented in conjunction with recommended curricula (which must reflect five comprehensive developmental domains: 1) language and communication, 2) health and physical development, 3) cognitive development, 4) social/emotional development, and 5) approaches to learning)

- Developmental assessment/screening within 90 days of entry using an approved screening instrument, including referral for further evaluation if needed

- Ongoing instructional assessment throughout the school year to monitor each child's progress and to inform instruction

- A score of 5.0 on the Early Childhood Environmental Rating Scale–Revised (ECERS-R; Harms, Clifford, & Cryer, 1998) by the second year (originally 4.5, with 5.0 instituted during 2005–2006)

- A 4- or 5-star license issued by the division of child development in private child care or Head Start, with a 3-star accepted if that site agrees to upgrade to at least a 4-star within 3 years. Public school pre-K classes are strongly encouraged to obtain licensing.

Because of the obvious expense required to meet these high standards, the state MAF pre-K office has made modifications to some time lines and standards. The requirement for the B–K license is taking many teachers longer than 4 years. Exceptions to the time line are typically granted when the teacher and the provider are making continued progress toward the goal. Similarly, paying comparable salaries to teachers in private child care is essentially impossible given that the current reimbursement rate per child ($4,050/10-month year in 2006–2007) is approximately half the cost of a high-quality pre-K program. Thus, we developed a lower target salary based on a beginning public school teacher's salary that can include any combination of salary, health coverage, and/or retirement. Even with these challenges, we feel that the standards are among the highest across states for pre-K programs.

Funding More at Four: What and How?

The following text describes what is funded in the state's pre-K initiatives and how the money is distributed.

What Is Funded?

State funds appropriated for MAF primarily cover operating costs for classrooms and one-time start-up funds ($500/slot) for new slots the first year they are awarded. State funds also provide money that goes for scholarship assistance, partial health insurance coverage for some teachers, ECERS-R evaluation assessments in a classroom's second year, professional development, and the external program evaluation. Funds for administrative staffing and related costs are also covered and to date run just over 3% of the total budget.

Flowing Money to the Local Level

When I was hired in November 2001, the governor expected that children would be served within a couple of months. Decisions had not been made, however, about how to allocate the $6.5 million. Because we needed to distribute these funds quickly and there were communities waiting for this program, a "fast track" request for proposal (RFP) was developed with a short turn-around time (approximately 3 weeks as opposed to 8 weeks). That was followed with a "standard track" RFP, which still required a rather short turn-around time but allowed for more planning by community teams. We funded 34 grants that first partial year, with children enrolled as early as January 2002. We eventually served just more than 1,200 children.

Starting with the 2002–2003 fiscal year, we developed a formula for allocating both the number of slots and the amount of funding per slot to counties. The *number* of slots was determined by the percentage of the state free/reduced price lunch total that each county comprised. Each county was offered the number of slots represented by their equivalent free/reduced price lunch percentage. If a county could not use all of the slots offered to it, then those slots were reallocated to other counties who needed more than their percentage calculation indicated. We attempted to use a needs assessment form for a couple of years to help communities determine where "real" need was. But we found that estimated numbers served in a county by various programs (e.g., public school pre-K, Head Start, subsidy) did not often match actual waiting lists. Or, the county would show a need on paper but not be able to find any children who were not being served. We discontinued that practice because data systems were typically unconnected, inaccurate, or unreliable.

Five categories of reimbursement rates for the *amount* per slot were established using the DPI's low wealth formula. DPI established this formula in response to Leandro v. State of North Carolina (1997), a class-action lawsuit on school funding equity, and ranked all 100 North Carolina counties by wealth using a complex formula of economic indicators. Although the average rate per slot in 2001–2002 was about $3,500, the actual amount funded for each county ranged from about $3,200 to $4,200, with poorer counties getting the higher rates.

In subsequent years, we have issued a call for slot requests without regard to any formula and based allocations on those requests. First priority goes to counties that are establishing new pre-K spaces and serving children previously not served anywhere. Second priority includes slots that are supplementing existing pre-K slots, especially if they raise standards in lower quality settings, expand Head Start, and so forth. Accepting MAF slots requires any provider to meet our standards within specified time lines.

Local Committees and Contract Administration

Each county or region that chooses to participate in the MAF program must establish an MAF local advisory committee (MAFLAC). This committee must be chaired by the superintendent of schools and the board chair of the local partnership for children (Smart Start). It must include other early care and education representatives such as Head Start, private child care, school systems, child care resource and referral, parents, and any other key organizations in that community. The MAFLAC selects an entity to be the contract administrator who receives the funding and is responsible for carrying out the program at the local level. The committee is to provide guidance and oversight to the contract administrator. This administrator works with the committee to choose providers who are interested in serving pre-K children who are at risk and can meet MAF standards. Figure 7.1 shows the structure of the funding flow and guidance for this system.

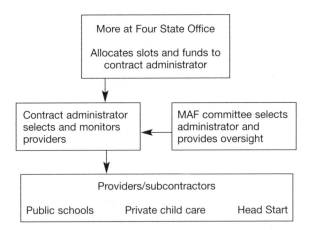

Figure 7.1.   Flow of funds to providers and guidance for North Carolina's More at Four program.

For the 2006–2007 fiscal year, there were 91 contract administrators covering the 100 counties in North Carolina (some serve multicounty regions). The breakdown by type of entity serving as local administrator is school systems: 49 (54%), Smart Start partnerships: 39 (43%), Head Start: 2 (2%), and nonprofit child care centers: 1 (1%).

System of Funding and Reimbursement

Our contract methodology follows a procedure called a *purchases of services* contract. In short, that means that as long as we set the standards and flow dollars to approved providers and they are delivering the services as defined by us, we are "purchasing" those services. Therefore, we can provide dollars on a per-child basis without requiring monthly line-item reimbursement requests. We define *service* as a minimum of 5 attendance days in a month. Accountability for these services is ensured by having preapproved providers who meet the program requirements, ongoing monitoring by the contract administrator as well as MAF-assigned regional program consultants, and providing online data systems for both program and child data. The child data system (MAFKids) includes attendance records that state staff can monitor in real time. For payment purposes, the contractor prints hard copies of the online attendance registers, obtains verification signatures from both provider and contractor, and submits them on a monthly basis for reimbursement. This system means that fewer dollars are spent on administrative costs that would otherwise be required for more intensive monthly line-item accounting and reimbursement.

Funding Infrastructure to Promote Quality

As we developed the MAF program, I realized that it would require a great deal more than the slot operating and start-up funds to support a high-quality program. Over time, a number of components have been put into place to promote quality and to help providers and teaching staff meet the rigorous standards. Some funds in our state budget are allocated to the T.E.A.C.H. program for scholarship assistance for local staff to pursue our required credentials. We also provide funding to help providers pay for health insurance for some MAF teachers. We pay for the required ECERS-R assessments in the second year of the program, as well as repeat assessments should a program not meet the required score on the first assessment. After that, we expect the assessments to be built into the 3-year licensing cycle of the provider. If the provider should not be licensed (i.e., some public schools), then provisions will have to be made to cover that expense as well.

Realizing that we needed to assist local contractors and providers with various implementing challenges, we have gradually developed a program section that includes a section chief with seven regionally assigned program consultants, as well as program consultants for Title I preschool, Even Start, and children with disabilities. Their primary purpose is to provide technical assistance and professional development in a wide array of services and to formally monitor program and fiscal requirements once a year. We have established nine demonstration classrooms that combine MAF funding with funding for preschool children with disabilities (Part B-619 of the Individuals with Disabilities Education Improvement Act [IDEA] of 2004 [PL 108-446]). Although these originally started out as literacy demonstration centers, they have become more broadly focused and are to serve as locations where other teachers can visit to see good practice.

As we encountered other barriers, challenges, and/or weaknesses in our program, we considered ways to assist in removing them. Our program standards require "meaningful family involvement," yet we think this is a weak area for many programs. A family involvement consultant was hired in March 2007 to lead efforts in this area. Similarly, we found that teachers in private child care and Head Start were having the most trouble getting into B–K training programs and moving through the required licensing bureaucracy. The public school systems are allowed to

- Issue lateral entry licenses to teachers with related degrees to begin the formal B–K training

- Provide the mentoring and evaluations required to obtain permanent licensing status

- Provide for student teaching to be accomplished in their regular classroom

Thus, the Office of School Readiness (OSR) became its own licensing entity, with North Carolina Board of Education approval, in which it acted as the licensing authority for *nonpublic* school teachers—providing lateral entry licenses, mentoring, quarterly evaluations, and student teaching options. Two positions have been established in the OSR to operate this program, and funds are allocated to pay for mentors, evaluators, and other related expenses.

Ongoing professional development offerings have increased each year. In 2006–2007, the OSR offered more than 50 workshop sessions across a range of topics, including several of the recommended curricula, early learning standards, literacy, developmental screening, social-emotional development and strategies, science and inquiry-based learn-

Table 7.2. Growth in size and approximate funding of the More at Four pre-K program: 2001–2007

Fiscal year	Funding increase for each year	Number of slots
2001–2002 (pilot)	$6.456 million	1,621
2002–2003	$28 million	7,621
2003–2004	$8.6 million	10,000
2004–2005	$7.9 million	More than 12,000
2005–2006	$16.7 million	15,453
2006–2007	$17 million	18,653

Total funding for 2006–2007: $84,635,709
$4,050 per child state average for allocated operating costs ($75.5 million)

ing (Levels I, II, and III), and outdoor learning environments. Some regional training is also offered by the program consultants. Finally, the OSR partners with the North Carolina Association for the Education of Young Children to sponsor the annual conference. In addition to paying some of the costs for the conference, we develop the pre-K track, offer a preconference session for MAF teachers and administrators, and pay the registration for at least 1,000 MAF teachers/administrators at the local level.

Growth of Funding and Program Location

MAF has grown rapidly each year since its inception. Table 7.2 illustrates the increase in funds each year and the cumulative number of slots. The budget for the 2006–2007 fiscal year was $84,635,709, and the statewide average slot rate was $4,050 per child. (This per child amount rose to $5,000 per child in 2008–2009, with additional funds generated from both lottery and general funds to meet needs.) Figure 7.2 shows the distribution of children across types of settings, suggesting that the legislative requirement that we build on the existing service delivery system has been met. Continued inclusion of private child care, however, has special challenges given the level of funding, which is discussed later in this chapter.

CHALLENGES: POLITICAL, ORGANIZATIONAL, AND FINANCIAL

Although the challenges confronted in beginning and growing this program do not always neatly fit into just one category (e.g., some organizational issues are also political), they can be grouped in ways that

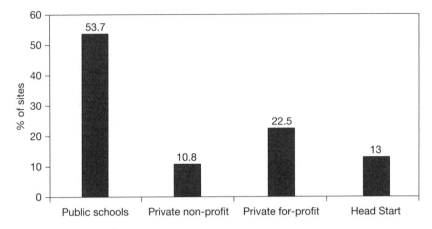

Figure 7.2.   Settings where children are served by percent of sites.

provide a better understanding of what many state pre-K programs might encounter.

Political Challenges

MAF pre-K did encounter some initial "push back" from Head Start and private child care. At my first meeting with Head Start grantee directors, I was confronted with the assertion that MAF would "take all the 4-year-olds" just as kindergarten had taken the 5-year-olds in the 1970s. I urged them to give the program time to roll out and emphasized that we were committed to building on the existing service delivery system. Some of their programs could be a home for MAF slots or classrooms. Over time, that has come to be true. Although some Head Start programs do not wish to participate, a number of them have been willing partners. And many more are expressing interest as Head Start funds have been cut or remain stagnant and the federal office of Head Start has emphasized greater collaboration with state pre-K programs.

North Carolina experienced extreme financial deficits during the 2001–2003 biennium. The governor faced some legislative resistance over new funding when many programs were being cut. The difference in Smart Start (a more general infrastructure program for birth to age 5) and the proposed pre-K program (a targeted, age-specific service program) was often difficult for legislators to understand. Subsequently, Smart Start funding was cut during this biennium, which created "friendly tension" among the early childhood communities. In addition, some local Smart Start partnerships believed that they were the primary state early childhood program and should have received the responsibility and funding to implement the pre-K program. Since 2003, these beliefs appear largely to have dissipated, relationships are strong, and many local partnerships administer the MAF program in their county or region.

Title I funding is a source that should easily blend with state pre-K funding. The Title I staff in the DPI, however, interpreted the federal regulations in ways that allowed only rigid cost allocation. Even conference calls with federal staff, who were cautious about taking any side in the debate, did not easily resolve this issue. The U.S. Department of Education did help clarify that children could, based on meeting both sets of criteria, qualify as both Title I and MAF. In this case, funding could be blended without strict cost allocation.

Finally, although collaboration at the state level often appeared to be extraordinary, collaboration at the local level was not always smooth or positive. Competition between the Smart Start partnerships and school systems, Head Start resistance, private child care resistance or resentment, or other factors occasionally played into difficult relationships. The OSR staff have mediated on occasion. But overall, relationships have been smooth, and those areas where difficulties exist have been gradually resolved or at least accommodated in some way.

Organizational Challenges

Although MAF funding flowed through the DHHS, the actual program was housed in the governor's office and reported to the governor's policy advisor. This allowed a more independent program, as it began, that could work collaboratively with DHHS and DPI, as well as Smart Start.

In 2002–2003, our MAF executive committee established an ongoing, self-appointed governance work group consisting of the members of the executive committee and adding the Head Start collaboration office director and the state interagency coordinating council director. Over a period of 3 years, this group worked to put our turf "on the table," hired an outside facilitator with assistance of a Pew Grant through North Carolina Partnership for Children (NCPC) and MAF funding, and ultimately developed a written plan to establish an office of child development and school readiness that would combine all early childhood education programs ages birth to 5.

This plan was presented to the governor's staff but was not supported at that time. There was not opposition to the concept per se, but Governor Easley was more interested in substantive programs than working with organizational bureaucracy. We acknowledged that this plan would require dealing with bureaucratic turf in several agencies and divisions and likely would be met with resistance by some agencies and/or staff. An interim step to our plan was to recommend that the

OSR be established to combine all public preschool programs (MAF; Title I; preschool disabilities—IDEA 2004 Part B, Section 619; Even Start; and the Head Start state collaboration office). The charge from the governor's office was to "make it so." Although agreement was reached at the highest levels of DHHS and DPI, the decision was not open to endorsement by the various preschool program staff. Resistance occurred from staff not involved in the decision, those who felt they had been the key representatives of early childhood to date, and from the Division for Exceptional Children (DEC), which felt that "giving up" its preschool disabilities staff was harmful to the overall continuity of the exceptional children's programs. Even our arrangement for the preschool disabilities consultants to be co-located in both offices was not deemed acceptable. Although the decision had already been made, the arguments to reverse that decision were intense. Some staff felt that the MAF program overshadowed the contributions of the other preschool funding sources.

The first year of the merger of the public school programs (2005–2006) was difficult for many staff members as we worked out coordination and supervision across agencies (staff were not to be physically transferred across agencies until the following fiscal year). Considerable time was devoted to strategic planning with new staff, building teamwork and relationships, and listening to the concerns and fears of staff. In July 2006, the OSR was formally moved to the DPI, reporting directly to the deputy superintendent. Working through the bureaucracy during this year to establish the OSR, negotiating complex budget and contract procedures in a new agency, and encountering other bureaucratic challenges proved to be an extremely trying time. Strategic planning work continued for the office as a whole, particularly making all preschool components feel equal in the overall state preschool picture. A planning session with an outside facilitator in December 2006 and January 2007 seemed to be a major turning point for the OSR to become a cohesive organizational unit. Also, new staff had joined the OSR who were not involved in the initial transition and who were enthusiastic. I believe that the continued good reputation of OSR staff and services in the field also has contributed to increased organizational effectiveness.

Fiscal Challenges

Clearly, the primary challenge is funding that covers half the cost of a high-quality pre-K program. Although the 2006–2007 MAF allocation was $4,050 per child for a 10-month program, the 2006–2007 base state allocation for students in grades K–3 was $5,110. This figure does not count other state supplements for low-wealth, disadvantaged students' funds, small schools, and so forth (NCDPI, 2007). Local programs are required by legislative mandate and necessity to gain access to other state, federal, or local resources to fund the remainder of the costs, but many of the other resources had been cut or redirected. Smart Start gained $14 million in 2006–2007, but had been cut more than that since the beginning of the MAF program. Head Start was cut by 1%, with overall effects even greater considering annual cost of living increases. Title I preschool dollars are being redirected in many school systems to meet the needs and mandates of the No Child Left Behind Act of 2001 (PL107-110) and improvements for schools and districts that are not making adequate yearly progress.

Transportation, comparable salaries for teachers in non–school settings, and physical space are some of the program needs that require additional funding. Many school systems in North Carolina are growing so rapidly that classes are crowded for K–12, and there is no room for preschool classes. The low-wealth funding formula that was the basis of our county per-child allocations proved to be less appropriate for high-wealth, urban counties. Although a higher rate of reimbursement to poorer counties was consistent with preschool provided by public schools, the urban counties tended to serve MAF children in private child care due to lack of space in the schools. These counties also have the highest market rate for child care, requiring even more funding per child. To begin addressing this issue, we decided to allocate the average $200 per child *increase* in 2006–2007 so that counties serving a higher percentage of the MAF children in private child care received a greater increase than the counties serving children in schools.

Moving MAF funding from general revenue to the new North Carolina Education Lottery in 2006–2007 created new funding issues. The lottery, a controversial issue in North Carolina, finally passed in 2006 by a very slim margin. Statute requires that it be used for four educational purposes: reduction of class size in K–3, MAF, school construction based on a formula allocation, and college scholarships for the needy. Given the existing funding for class size reduction and MAF at that time, half of the anticipated proceeds for the lottery were already committed. Governor Easley has called for a major expansion of MAF for the 2007–2009 biennium—10,000 children each year. The governor proposed an additional $400 per slot increase for 2007–2008, and we included a $3 million "capacity enhancement" fund in the proposed budget to be used for adding or remodeling physical space, transportation, and so forth. Additional professional development and T.E.A.C.H. funds were added as well. The total proposed expansion was $59 million to the MAF budget of $84.6 million. To accomplish this expansion, the governor proposed reducing school construction funding from the lottery, generating considerable opposition from educational leaders and general assembly members. In addition, the proceeds from the lottery have fallen short of projections. The governor's proposed solution to this problem is to increase the percentage of lottery proceeds going to prizes (North Carolina has the lowest percentage among lottery states). Policy makers disagree, however, about the extent to which this strategy will resolve the shortfall. In 2008, the resolution to this issue was still pending.

How do we resolve these fiscal challenges? There are no easy answers short of more funding. The state could reconsider some of its standards. The maximum class size could rise to 20 and still meet national standards. We could require a bachelor of arts degree rather than a teaching license per se and still meet national standards. Advocates as well as OSR staff, however, have been reluctant to pursue those options.

We are increasing consultation with local administrators to consider differentiated funding at the local level (e.g., more funds to private child care and less to Head Start or public schools). These decisions cannot be made at the state level because each local context is unique. Although some policies have been made at the state level to allow for blending of funds, it is clear that the local level is where the greatest creativity can be found in combining funds to provide quality services.

THE FUTURE: ISSUES FOR STATES

Several issues appear to be common across states as they seek ways to fund pre-K programs and maintain quality.

Start Where You Are: Move to a Vision

As any state develops a system of early care and education—or any part of that system—the context will determine what can be done, how much, and when. Obviously, political and organizational relationships will facilitate changes or create barriers. A vision of the desired system (or system of systems) will at least provide a goal toward which incremental (or transformational) change can move. Although common critical components may be desired in any state, what they look like and how they are organized can vary considerably. The guiding principle is always what serves children and families best.

Change Is Not by Popular Vote

Clearly, the change process works best when everyone is part of the decision making and agrees about the direction taken. If governmental bureaucracies are to change to better serve children, then we can never wait for unanimous consent. Key leaders and policy makers must make decisions, albeit with careful thought and input, about the structures that will be most successful in their state and then move forward in deliberate ways and with appropriate timing. Attention to the change process is critical, allowing staff to have input and help shape the structures ultimately put in place. But the decision to move may need to be made in the face of resistance. Ultimately, strong and committed leadership with a clear, long-term vision and integrity will lead to a system that eventually will have support and will better serve children.

Consider Level of Funding versus Quality

Most states are not allocating enough funding to provide for high-quality pre-K programs. Other resources are required, and many of the likely resources are being reduced or redirected. Local creativity and/or a compelling case for greater state funding are essential. The manner of funding bears consideration. Although most states fund on a per-child basis like North Carolina, there may be good reason to fully fund classrooms (e.g., Tennessee) or some combination of classes and students (e.g., Alabama's new funding structure that allocates entire classes but funds per child using a combination of state dollars based on family income plus private fees). Although fewer children may be served in the short term, full funding could include private child care programs as well as Head Start and public schools.

Federal and state policies need to be reconsidered to allow various funding sources to be blended. Of particular importance are Head Start, Title I, Even Start, IDEA 2004 Part B-619, TANF, and the Child Care Developmental Block Grant (CCDBG). Funds should also allow for a comprehensive services provision for pre-K children. Head Start already has an exemplary service model in this area, but more pre-K children and their families should have access to social, mental health, and medical services. Funding must be sufficient to provide physical space and transportation. These capacity issues are central to providing quality services to children wherever they live.

Maintain Quality in Large-Scale Implementation

I always fear that the key components of successful small-scale programs that provide evidence on which large-scale implementations are based will be lost in translation, whether these components refer to early childhood or K–12 programs. The ability to control key classroom variables between teacher and child is severely limited from the state level. The standards and parameters that we establish may provide the essential foundation but may not be sufficient to ensure the necessary teaching processes that will lead to successful child outcomes. (And what, exactly, are the necessary teaching processes?) These elements must be monitored and facilitated by skilled professionals at the local level. The extent to which that is lacking will limit the success of any program and should be a key consideration for states as they implement pre-K programs and other components of the early childhood education system.

Consider Evidence of Long-Term Success

Although strong support exists for pre-K programs across the nation, long-term support may be contingent on long-term outcomes. Showing success (however it is defined) after pre-K or kindergarten is critical. But success by Grade 3 or in later years will be outcomes that political leaders will begin to expect as well. What kind of instruction will most likely lead to those outcomes? To what extent does peer mediation play a role? Are the types of peers (e.g., heterogeneous groups) critical in that process? Should we expect that pre-K alone will be able to produce enduring outcomes across domains in large-scale programs?

Extend Services Around Pre-K

Although more states are moving toward or discussing universal pre-K, it is not likely that most states will be able to fund this type of program in the near future. Arguments for supporting children in a range of settings and with mixed peer groups are strong with universal pre-K. The funding required to implement such a program, however, would likely divert funds away from targeted services to infants and toddlers who are at risk. Regardless of how it is accomplished, states cannot ignore the need to begin even earlier in their efforts to address quality intervention for those children least likely to be successful in school.

Likewise, *schools* must begin a more systematic effort to ensure that they are ready for *all* children. Careful transitions between preschool and kindergarten; appropriate curriculum and instructional practice; alignment across grades from preschool to Grade 3 for standards, curriculum, instruction, and assessment; and involvement of the community and family are critical for schools to ensure all students' success. Nationally, this initiative is referred to as "Ready Schools" or "PK–3". The Foundation for Child Development refers to the PK–3 (or ages 3–8) as the "base camp" for K–12 education (Graves, 2005). North Carolina, through Kellogg Foundation funding to Smart Start and in collaboration with the DPI, is beginning a statewide Ready Schools initiative. The state board of education is in the process of adopting a definition of a Ready School developed by a task force, as well as supporting a recommendation that elementary schools use a Ready Schools assessment instrument as part of the school improvement planning process. They also will endorse the "Power of K" position paper developed by the K–2 section of DPI, which delineates an appropriate and powerful kindergarten program. Any early childhood education system cannot ignore a plan for services to children birth to age 8 and the link between preschool and elementary grades.

CONCLUSION

North Carolina's story has developed in unique ways consistent with the state's history and context. Although there are common components of early care and education that cut across states and best practice, each state must find the strategies and structures that best suit its infrastructure, politics, and service configuration. Sustainable funding, along with maintaining quality, are key common concerns.

This story shows that barriers systematically and jointly addressed can be resolved—or at least alleviated. Moving the OSR to DPI has not proved to be the "disaster" predicted by some in the child care community. In fact, it has strengthened our ability to link early care and education to K–12 education while we continue to build strong linkages to DHHS and child care. Although private child care participation is a continuing challenge, work to leverage dollars and a commitment to diverse service delivery settings has continued to include them in MAF. Smart Start is our largest "other funding source," working closely with and leading MAF in many communities. State policies continue to evolve to allow leveraged funds, although this continues to be a need. Local communities are providing creative solutions for using various funding sources. Collaboration is good at the state level; and although challenges presented themselves at the local level, progress has been made there as well. Head Start involvement is continuing to grow for even greater coordination across programs.

Clearly, the strong leadership across settings and organizations has been integral to the success of MAF as well as early childhood systems' building in general. We have much to accomplish still, but quality pre-K has been established and should continue to grow as part of the educational foundation for children in North Carolina.

REFERENCES

Barnett, W.S., Hustedt, J.T., Hawkinson, L.E., & Robin, K.B. (2006). *The state of preschool: 2006.* Brunswick, NJ: National Institute for Early Education Research, Rutgers University.

Barnett, W.S., Hustedt, J.T., Friedman, A.H., Boyd, J.S., & Ainsworth, P. (2007). *The state of preschool 2007: State preschool yearbook.* New Brunswick: Rutgers, State University of New Jersey, National Institute for Early Education Research.

Brandon, R.N., Kagan, S.L., & Joesch, J.M. (2000). *Design choices: Universal financing for early care and education.* Seattle: Human Services Policy Center, University of Washington.

Bryant, D., Clifford, D., Early, D., & Little, L. (2005, Spring). *Pre-K education in the states.* In Winton, P., & Buysse, V. (Eds.), *Early Development, 9*(1), pp. 6–9.

Campbell, F.A., Ramey, C.T., Pungello, E.P., Sparling, J., & Miller-Johnson, S. (2002). Early childhood education: Young adult outcomes from the Abecedarian Project. *Applied Developmental Science, 6*, 42–57.

Clifford, R., & Bryant, D. (2005, Spring). Pre-K education in the states. *Early Development, 9*(1), 6–9.

Governor's Office of North Carolina. (2003, January). *Report to the North Carolina General Assembly (on the More at Four pre-K program).* Raleigh, NC: Author.

Graves, B. (2005, October). *PreK–3 as public education's base came: Getting there.* New York: Foundation for Child Development.

Greenberg, M., & Schumacher, R. (2003). *Financing universal pre-kindergarten: Possibilities and technical issues for states in using funds under the Child Care and Development Fund and Temporary Assistance for Needy Families Block Grant* (Rev. ed.). Washington, DC: Center for Law and Social Policy.

Harms, T., Clifford, R.M., & Cryer, D. (1998). *Early Childhood Environment Rating Scale–Revised.* New York: Teachers College Press.

Individuals with Disabilities Education Improvement Act (IDEA) of 2004, PL 108-446, 20 U.S.C. §§ 1400 *et seq.*

Leandro v. State of North Carolina, 346 NC 336 (179PA96) (1997).

Mitchell, A., Stoney, L., & Dichter, H. (2001). *Financing child care in the United States: An expanded catalog of current strategies.* Kansas City, MO: Ewing Marion Kauffman Foundation.

National Association for the Education of Young Children. (2001, July). *Financing the early childhood education system.* Washington, DC: Author.

National Child Care and Information Center. (n.d.). Administration for Children and Families, U.S. Department of Health and Human Services. Retrieved January 2, 2006, from http://nccic.acf.hhs.gov/poptopics/ecare funding.html

No Child Left Behind Act of 2001, PL 107-110, 115 Stat. 1425, 20 U.S.C. §§ 6301 *et seq.*

North Carolina Department of Public Instruction. (2007, February). *Highlights of the North Carolina public school budget.* Raleigh, NC: Author.

Ready for School Goal Team. (2000, June). *School readiness in North Carolina: Strategies for defining, measuring, and promoting success for all children.* Raleigh, NC: Public Schools of North Carolina.

Reilly, D.H. (2000). Linear or nonlinear? A metacognitive analysis of educational assumptions and reform efforts. *International Journal of Educational Management, 14*(1), 7–15.

Reynolds, A.J., Temple, J.A., Robertson, D., & Mann, E. (2001). Long-term effects of an early childhood intervention on educational achievement and juvenile arrest. *Journal of the American Medical Association, 285*(18), 2339–2346.

Schweinhart, L.J., Montie, J., Xiang, Z., Barnett, W.S., Belfield, C.R., & Nores, M. (2005). *Lifetime effects: The High/Scope Perry Preschool Study Through Age 40.* Ypsilanti, MI: High/Scope Press.

Stebbins, H., & Langford, B.H. (2006, May). *A guide to calculating the cost of quality early care and education.* Washington, DC: The Finance Project.

Stoney, L., & Edwards, K. (2006). *Child care financing matrix.* Washington, DC: National Child Care and Information Center.

Vast, T. (2002). *Learning between systems: Adapting higher education financing methods to early care and education.* Lumina Foundation.

Yonce, K.G., Clifford, R.M., Doig, S.P., & Nugent, L.M. (2006, November). *North Carolina's More at Four pre-kindergarten program: A cost study.* Chapel Hill: Frank Porter Graham Child Development Institute, University of North Carolina.

Chapter 8

Implementing Large-Scale Prekindergarten Initiatives

Lessons from New York[1]

Moncrieff Cochran

W hy are many states instituting prekindergarten (pre-K) programs for some or all 4-year-olds (and sometimes 3-year-olds)
within their jurisdictions? In most cases, the answer is to help
these children prepare for school—to make them "school ready." On
the face of it, the process involved sounds pretty simple: Find the eligible children, get them to school-like settings, and provide them with
experiences through which they learn what is needed for success in
kindergarten. But the social and economic realities of American family
and community life intrude. Most of these children's parents work outside the home. In order to do so, they rely on support from an array of

[1]Appreciation is expressed to the following colleagues for their assistance with the
research in New York State that forms the basis for many of the ideas expressed in this
chapter: Dr. Kristi Lekies, Dr. Sarah Watamura, Dr. Taryn Morrissey, Cindy Gallagher,
Eleanor Greig Upoli, Dr. Henry Solomon, Maria Benehán, and Fran Schwartz. This research was supported by grants from The Foundation for Child Development, the A.L.
Mailman Foundation, and an anonymous donor.

formal and informal support systems, including regulated child care (child care centers and family child care homes) and informal networks of kith and kin (family, friends, and neighbors). The health and well-being of these support systems is dependent on a more encompassing infrastructure, which includes health- and safety-oriented regulation and support by public agencies, economic subsidies to families and providers, professional preparation and training of caregivers, and policy and program oversight by appropriate state departments.

The various elements that together constitute the environment surrounding the preschool-age child do not operate in isolation from one another. They are connected in systems of interdependence. Child care centers, for instance, depend on the willingness and capacity of families to provide them with children and to pay for that care. Families depend on the staff in those centers to partner with them in nurturing and stimulating their children. Some families may depend on public agencies for financial assistance in meeting the financial costs of child care, and the centers or family based caregivers they use may also depend on those agencies for timely provision of financial subsidies. Within the center, the costs of care vary by age of child. One reason is that state and center rules and regulations often require a smaller adult–child ratio for classrooms caring for infants and toddlers than for those caring for 3- and 4-year-olds, and thus these classrooms must hire more teachers. Because most young parents cannot afford the full cost of infant/toddler care, center directors and their governing boards often lower those costs by charging families with older children somewhat more than the true cost of caring for their children. In this way, the parents of the younger children are dependent on those parents whose children are older, and the center itself is dependent on this arrangement to make infant/toddler care available at all.

State pre-K programs enter into these already existing interdependent systems of support and adaptation when they establish themselves in local communities. Their success at finding eligible children, getting them into appropriate settings, and providing them with experiences that lead to success in kindergarten will depend heavily on the extent to which they are designed to recognize and acknowledge existing systems of family support and utilize those systems to attain their policy goal. This chapter applies this standard to developing and implementing the universal pre-K (UPK) program in New York and draws a set of lessons with more general applicability. A description of the purposes driving the New York policy and its key provisions is followed by in-depth examination of arguably the most significant of those provisions—the requirement that school districts contract a percentage of UPK services to community-based organizations (CBOs) outside the public school system (e.g., child care centers, Head Start programs, family resource centers). Attention then shifts to a number of other issues central to the large-scale, statewide implementation of pre-K: whether to make the program available to all 4-year-olds (universal) or limit it to those living in low-income circumstances (targeted), whether to serve children for part or all of the day, the extent to which decision making should be centralized in state government or devolved to local communities, the degree to which the curriculum should be prescribed by the state, and the issue of teacher qualifications. A number of broader infrastructure issues are then identified and discussed briefly, including teacher preparation, professional development, ongoing technical assistance, site development and expansion, transportation, and program evaluation. The chapter ends with issues that should be of central concern to the pre-K movement over the next decade.

A PROFILE OF UNIVERSAL PRE-K IN NEW YORK

Figure 8.1 shows the scope of New York's UPK program from its first year of classroom operation in 1998 through the 2006–2007 school year, in both state dollars invested and numbers of children served. The data show an increase from $56 million to $255 million over the 9-year period, with a growth in the number of children served from 18,300 to 70,000 during that same period. Note the level of funding between 2002–2006, a period when state administration declined to continue expansion of the program. Governor Spitzer included an additional $146 million in his proposed 2007–2008 budget and pledged a total increase to $645 million by 2011 to serve all of the state's estimated 225,000 4-year-olds (New York Child Care, Inc., 2007).

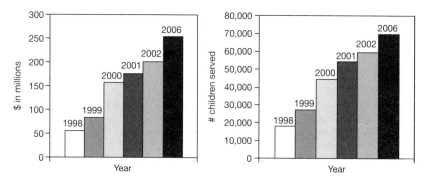

Figure 8.1.   Universal prekindergarten program scope.

When the program was created in 1997, UPK was attached to a larger proposal that included funding for all-day kindergarten, reducing class sizes in K–3, continuing professional development, improving technology, and bonding authority for building improvements throughout public education (Hicks, Lekies, & Cochran, 1999). Authority for the program is vested in the state department of education, which implements the program through hundreds of local school districts. The purpose of UPK is to prepare children for success in kindergarten. But throughout the drafting of the legislation, statewide child care advocacy organizations were actively involved in efforts to ensure that the new program would have the potential to strengthen the existing early care and education system in New York. Table 8.1 shows key provisions included in the legislation (see http://www.emsc.nysed.gov/nyc/upk.html for more information), established in the late 1990s.

In New York, teacher certification can be issued on a temporary basis to individuals with bachelor's degrees, but full certification requires a master's degree. The provision allowing time for teachers who are working toward certification to complete those requirements remains in effect. Data showing compliance with the certification requirements are presented later in the chapter.

Table 8.1.   Key provisions of the universal prekindergarten (UPK) law

Prekindergarten classes for all New York 4-year-olds for a minimum of 2.5 hours per day implemented over a 4-year period, beginning in 1998–1999.

Educational programming that promotes English literacy; meets the social, cognitive, linguistic, emotional, cultural, and physical needs of children; meets the needs of families; integrates preschool children with disabilities; and provides continuity with the early elementary grades.

Attention to support services, parent involvement, assessment, and staff development.

Community collaboration, or contracting out, of at least 10% of UPK funds with organizations outside public school settings, such as providers of child care and early education, early childhood programs, and Head Start.

Required teacher certification by the year 2001–2002 for eligibility to teach in a UPK classroom.

Policy-making power vested in local planning groups and school boards to choose whether to implement a UPK program and, if so, to develop their own separate plans for the delivery of services.

Options of half-, full-, or extended-day services.

Family choice regarding whether to enroll their children in UPK programs.

Until full implementation in 2002, the eligibility of a selected number of districts to participate each year as determined by the state department of education and based primarily on economic need.

State funding for the 1999–2000 school year at a minimum of $2,700 and a maximum of $4,000 per child.

Note: For the 1999–2000 and 2000–2001 years, districts were required to serve a certain percentage of children classified as economically disadvantaged.

It is important to underscore the attention paid to the real needs and circumstances of families and local communities when assessing the legislative provisions. Families are recognized by emphasizing parent involvement, integrating children with special needs, providing access by geographic dispersion of sites beyond the public schools, having extended day programming options, giving families a choice regarding whether to enroll their children, and providing financing that makes the program free or low cost for participants. Recognizing community needs is reflected in policy-making power vested in local planning groups, which are permitted to develop their own separate plans for the delivery of services (within the parameters of the legislation and regulations), the requirement that a portion of funding be contracted out to CBOs, and provision of flexible funding to adjust for the differing economic needs of New York's school districts. From an evaluation standpoint, this systematic attempt to address family and community needs invites an expansion of the standard question: "How is UPK affecting the child's readiness for school?" to encompass a broader inquiry of "How is the UPK program affecting New York's early care and education system as a whole?" This broader question, which has been the focus of the ongoing implementation evaluation conducted by the Cornell Early Childhood Program, guides the organization of this chapter.

ENGAGING COMMUNITY-BASED ORGANIZATIONS

Recognizing that most parents of preschoolers work outside the home and rely on already existing child care settings, the UPK legislation was designed to require local school districts to collaborate with at least some existing service providers by expending 10% or more of their state UPK funds to purchase those community-based services. This decision to include CBOs to deliver pre-K services is not unusual. Nationally, about one third of children in pre-K programs are served in community-based settings. Only two states (Kansas and Louisiana) limit pre-K services to public school settings (Barnett, Hustedt, Hawkinson, & Robin, 2006).

Figure 8.2 shows the distribution of New York's 57,084 UPK children between school-based settings and CBOs during the 2004–2005 school year. Sixty-two percent of UPK children were served in CBOs, far more than the 10% required by the UPK legislation. In New York City, where approximately 60% of eligible children reside, two thirds were in CBOs; upstate, the proportion was just more than half (51%; New York State Department of Education, 2006).

Why did most school districts choose to serve many of their eligible children outside the school when the UPK regulations required a

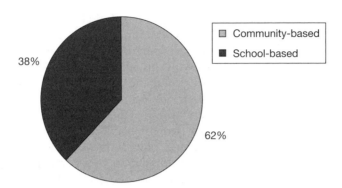

Figure 8.2. Universal prekindergarten site distribution—school and community based.

modest percentage (10%)? One explanation lies in the philosophies of the district leadership regarding where UPK services should be provided. Data on school district philosophies gathered from district UPK program coordinators during the second year of program implementation (1999–2000) are shown in Figure 8.3 (Lekies & Cochran, 2001). The figure indicates that about half of the 54 school districts in upstate New York were philosophically in favor of a balance between school buildings and other CBOs, with the other half leaning a little more toward school buildings than toward CBOs. In New York City, the philosophies were also strongly toward balance, but a quarter of the districts were leaning more strongly toward CBOs. The actual distribution of

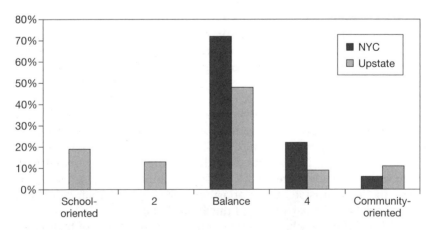

Figure 8.3. School district philosophies regarding location of services.

children upstate and in the city during 2004–2005 mirror these beliefs (gathered 4 years earlier) almost exactly.

Are district philosophies the whole story? No. When asked why they selected the sites chosen, many coordinators indicated that short-age of space in school district buildings was a significant factor (Lekies & Cochran, 2001). The Cornell Early Childhood Program also found anecdotal evidence that some school superintendents were influenced by the fact that they could serve more children with the same revenue by using CBOs because teacher salaries were significantly lower in those settings. Another factor was CBO representatives participating in local planning groups required by the UPK legislation, in which they demonstrated their expertise in early education programming and made the case for CBO involvement (Hicks et al., 1999).

EFFECTS ON COMMUNITY-BASED ORGANIZATIONS

As of 2008, New York was serving approximately 70,000 children in UPK, making it the fourth largest pre-K program in the country, behind Texas, Florida, and Georgia. The program was slated to double in size during 2009–2013. Given the magnitude of UPK in the early care and education arena, it was important to assess its effect on the overall early care and education system in the state, most of which is otherwise financed, located, regulated, and operated outside the public school systems. To do this, the Cornell Early Childhood Program undertook an implementation evaluation strategy that was especially sensitive to the experiences and perspectives of CBOs and contained a number of key elements (see Figure 8.4).

School districts were phased into the UPK program in waves, with Wave 1 consisting of 62 upstate and 32 (all) New York City school districts. The program also expanded gradually within the school dis-tricts (more than 3–5 years) in an effort to accommodate all 4-year-olds whose parents wanted the service. The evaluation began by carefully analyzing the UPK plans submitted by the Wave 1 school districts prior to the first year of implementation and the progress reports they sub-mitted to the state education department during the first 3 years of the program, paying close attention to the roles played by the mandated community advisory committees and the involvement of community agencies. We also conducted in-depth surveys with the UPK coordina-tors in the Wave 1 school districts during the first 2 years of implemen-tation, looking at issues of access, child population diversity, school–community collaboration, classroom practices, teacher preparation and support, and financing. In 2001, a special study was conducted through

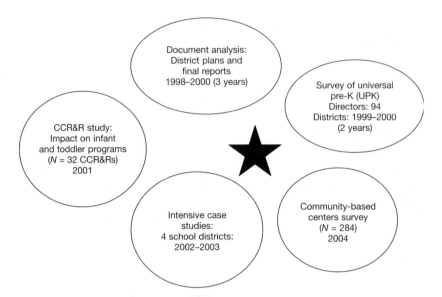

Figure 8.4. Strategies to assess the effects of universal prekindergarten on the early care and education system.

the child care resource and referral network in New York to assess possible effects of UPK on services to infants and toddlers in CBOs. In 2002 and 2003, intensive case studies were conducted in four school districts—one in New York City and three in upstate New York (one urban, one small city, and one rural)—to probe more deeply into issues of universality, collaboration, service quality, and infrastructure supports. The final component of the implementation evaluation—an in-depth survey of the directors of 284 CBOs delivering UPK services—was completed in 2005. Flowing from the emphasis given to understanding how UPK affected the rest of the early care and education system in New York, the findings from this collection of studies provide the basis for the organization of this chapter and the conclusions offered here.

Benefits and Challenges of Involving Community-Based Organizations

A primary reason for surveying the directors of CBOs providing UPK services in New York City and upstate New York was to capture their knowledge and perspectives regarding the ways that participation in

Table 8.2.   Investment indicators for community-based programs

Increased revenues
Reductions in parent fees
Increases in number of children served
Remodeling classrooms
New equipment
New educational materials
Curriculum changes
Hiring more teachers
Hiring assistant teachers/aides
Hiring substitute teachers to facilitate teacher participation in
    professional development
Hiring staff developers or curriculum specialists
Increasing teacher salaries
Increasing salaries of assistant teachers/aides and support staff

the UPK program through local school districts was affecting the early care and education services they provided. We were interested in enhancements and challenges that resulted from participating in UPK. We have created a set of investment indicators based on their responses— aspects of programming that might improve if a new statewide early care and education initiative is undertaken. Changes were selected as indicators only if they were reported by at least one third of the 284 program directors participating in our survey (see Table 8.2).

In New York, more than half of the CBOs included in our survey reported increases in revenue, program changes, curriculum changes, progress with certification, and reductions in parent fees. More than 40% also reported serving more children, hiring more staff, and increasing teacher salaries (Lekies, Morrissey, & Cochran, 2005). A number of other advantages of including CBOs in UPK have emerged from studies summarized previously:

- CBOs provide a better fit with the child care needs of employed parents than part-day, school-based classrooms because they integrate UPK into full-day care. A case study of an urban upstate New York UPK program found that one third of children in UPK were being served in full-day early child care and education settings (Cochran, 2004). This study also documented that a majority of the 4-year-olds not being reached by UPK needed full-day care and were enrolled in family child care settings.

- Using CBOs means that the public schools do not need to find space for UPK in existing buildings or expand buildings in order to accommodate the program. In New York City, this factor was second only to "quality of programming" in explaining why so much emphasis was placed on including community-based UPK sites (Lekies & Cochran, 2001).

- CBOs often provide a better fit with the cultural and ethnic backgrounds of families than public school settings because CBOs are often based in the neighborhood and have been designed explicitly to meet the needs of specific cultural or ethnic groups. Their inclusion as sites expands the early care and education choices available to families and tailors them more specifically to the child-rearing values, norms, and practices of parents (Cochran, 2004).

- The family support and parent involvement alternatives available to families may be expanded. In the previously mentioned urban upstate New York case study, it was possible to compare the parent involvement strategies employed by the public school UPK settings with those used in the CBOs. This comparison revealed that although the different settings share several strategies (e.g., child observation opportunities, activities to do at home, home visits), a number of more intensive strategies were used in CBOs that were not available in the school-based sites (e.g., workshops for parents, parent groups, literacy training, dedicated family worker; Cochran, 2004).

- Staff in CBOs may have a better understanding of developmentally appropriate practices than staff in school settings. Findings from the Cornell case studies suggested that this may be the case, especially at the administrative level. Public school principals are more likely than the directors of CBOs to be grappling with the tension between developmentally oriented and subject-matter-oriented curricular and pedagogical approaches to early education (Cochran, 2004).

Not all early care and education programs in local communities participate in New York's UPK program. We wanted to know how nonparticipants might be affected by the addition of such a substantial new participant in the early care and education system. Telephone interviews were conducted with the directors of 46 non-UPK centers that were located close to school districts with UPK programs. These directors reported perceived reductions in 4-year-olds' total enrollment and greater difficulty with recruiting and competing for teachers since the introduction of UPK into their communities. The changes in teacher recruitment and retention were reported more often by the directors of larger and full-day programs than by those running smaller or part-day programs (Morrissey, Lekies, & Cochran, 2007).

The directors of non-UPK centers were also asked whether their enrollment of infants and toddlers had changed due to the presence of UPK in the school district. The concern was that nonparticipating centers might have had declines in the enrollment of 4-year-olds, leading to a loss of fee income that had partially subsidized infant/toddler care. Eleven percent of directors reported increases in infant/toddler services and none reported decreases. This finding is in accord with a 2001 survey of child care resource and referral agencies in New York (see Figure 8.4) that found the introduction of UPK programming had not affected or increased the overall supply of child care for infants and toddlers in their districts (Lekies, Heitzman, & Cochran, 2001).

When we asked about challenges related to the inclusion of CBOs in the New York UPK program, four ongoing issues were articulated separately or in combination by the various stakeholders surveyed or interviewed through the Cornell UPK implementation studies.

Salary Differential Between Teachers in School- and Community-Based Settings

Surveys in the early 2000s indicated a substantial difference between the salaries of community-based and school-based UPK teachers, both in New York City and in upstate New York. Another study quantified this difference in New York City at more than $10,000 annually (Farrell, cited in Holcomb, 2006). A separate early care and education work force study, with a large sample but limited to New York City, found an even greater teacher salary disparity between the two sectors (community-based median: $36,000; school-based median: $62,000), although some of the community-based teachers in this sample may not have been teaching in UPK-designated classrooms (NYC Early Childhood Professional Development Institute, 2007). Directors surveyed through this study reported significant difficulty retaining certified teachers in the face of competition by public schools.

Monitoring and Ensuring Quality in Community-Based Settings

New York does not require that UPK teachers follow a prescribed curriculum. Curricular decisions are made at the school district level. The state UPK legislation and regulations specify that the curriculum be aligned with state learning standards, ensure continuity with instruction in the early elementary grades, be integrated with the district's instructional program in K–12, and provide an early literacy and emergent reading program based on effective, evidence-based instructional practices. Activities are to be learner centered and designed and provided to promote the child's total growth and development. They are to ensure that

> Children are encouraged to be self-assured and independent through a balanced schedule of teacher-initiated and child-initiated learning activities; instructional materials and equipment are arranged in learning centers that promote a balance of individual and small group activities; and teachers use intentional planning to focus instruction to meet differentiated learning styles of students. (New York State Education Law, 2007)

Regulations also require that school districts establish a process for assessing the developmental baseline and progress of all children participating in the program. This process must provide for ongoing assessment of the development of language, cognitive, and social skills and ensure that the assessment information is used to inform classroom instruction and professional development. Examining annual plans and year-end reports are the primary means used by the state education department to monitor compliance with these requirements. Responsible school district personnel are convened by the state for training and technical assistance at least once a year.

At the school district level, UPK administrators must implement practices to ensure that community-based UPK sites are providing classroom experiences and supplementary services that meet state education requirements. Methods for developing and maintaining a high standard of quality across settings vary from district to district. In general, the primary strategies are joint in-service training for teachers across settings, periodic site visits to community-based classrooms by the district UPK coordinators, and regular technical assistance meetings for UPK center administrators. Most of the directors of CBOs surveyed by the Cornell Early Childhood Program reported that the amount of district monitoring was "just right" and that the school district was highly supportive in general (Lekies et al., 2005). One urban district intensively administers the Early Childhood Environmental Rating Scale–Revised (ECERS-R; Harms, Clifford, & Cryer, 1998) annually in all UPK classrooms to monitor quality (Cochran, 2004).

Infrastructure Needed to Write and Manage Contracts with Community-Based Settings

The process of developing and managing contracts with CBOs is complicated and time consuming. Large urban school districts find that they must dedicate additional staff, which has been a special challenge in New York City where hundreds of community-based UPK service providers are involved.

Need for Policy Innovations to Allow Equitable
Blending of UPK State Funds with Federal and Other State Funds

When state UPK funding comes to a CBO, it is typically combined with funding from other sources to support a full-day early care and education program for the children of working parents. Sometimes this means blending state UPK funds with federal Head Start or state child care financing. In order for this to be accomplished successfully, efforts must be made to align the requirements attached to the various funding sources. When state officials design pre-K regulations, it is essential that they facilitate the blending of these funds with those from other sources and state funds from other agencies. Otherwise, the burden for managing the complex accounting and financial reporting requirements falls on local providers and school district personnel (Holcomb, 2006). An example of collaboration across funding streams is provided by the upstate New York urban school district studied by the Cornell Early Childhood Program. The UPK advisory board negotiated an arrangement with the city's department of social services ensuring that family child care providers would not lose full department of social services subsidies if they released a child to a center-based UPK program for the morning or afternoon (Cochran, 2004).

   The challenges outlined previously are neither insignificant nor insurmountable. Of course, what we cannot know from the New York case is what challenges the pre-K program would have faced had the legislature chosen to restrict program delivery only to school building sites and public school personnel. It would be useful to examine the challenges faced by the two states that limit pre-K services to public school settings and the reasons why several states have decided to expand their service settings to include CBOs.

UNIVERSAL OR CATEGORICAL ACCESS TO PRE-K?

Of the 38 states that funded pre-K programs in 2006, 27 had requirements limiting access to children from low-income families (Barnett et al., 2007). New York took a universal approach when it initiated UPK in 1997, and has maintained that commitment despite political pressure in the governor's office to limit funding to low-income families. State department of education staff advocated strongly for universal provision based on the belief that targeted programs are not successful in the long term and are vulnerable politically (Ochyn & Newland, 2006). Some other advantages to making this policy choice included

- Not having to risk stigmatizing families by forcing them to demonstrate income insufficiency to gain access

- Avoiding the logistical burden imposed by requiring verification of limited income

- Benefiting from the possibility that a preschool program available to all the families of 4-year-olds on a voluntary basis would be more palatable to constituents than one limited only to a segment of those families.

These ideas were discussed by key stakeholders both within and beyond state government during interviews conducted by the author in 1997.

Although universality was an explicit goal of New York's pre-K program, attention was paid to family economic need during roll out, and political circumstances have also constrained the universal implementation of the program. From the beginning, the amount of state funding per child allocated to school districts varied depending on the percentage of children in those districts receiving subsidized school lunches (Lekies & Cochran, 2001; Lekies et al., 2005). Because initial funding was insufficient to serve all school districts, they were invited into the program in waves, starting with the school districts serving the most economically needy families (i.e., all of New York City, the upstate cities, and a number of rural districts). State funds were also increased within school districts over a number of years, and district administrators were required to give first priority to children from low-income families until full funding was available. Flat funding during the period from 2002–2005 prevented expansion of the program into wealthier school districts, creating a categorical program de facto, although more by school district or region than by individual family within the district.

The case of New York illustrates that it is possible to avoid the universal–categorical dichotomy by establishing universal coverage as a policy goal and then implementing that policy with sensitivity to the resource differential that exists among school districts within any state. The pre-K program in New York is perceived as potentially available to all 4-year-olds, but the financing formula recognizes that economic need is greater in some parts of the state than in others.

FULL- OR PART-DAY?

There is some evidence that children who attend an extended-day, extended-year preschool program experience greater improvement in test scores than those who attend half-day programs, although more research is needed to fully understand the relationship between duration of program (length of day, length of year) and readiness for school (Robin, Frede, & Barnett, 2006). The New York program is funded for a portion of the day (minimum 2.5 hours) during the school year. But in

CBOs, UPK funding is often blended with other funds to create full-day programs, and these often run for the full year using teachers that meet UPK qualifications. There are some indications that the UPK resources provided to these programs have an effect that carries over into the non-UPK portion of the day and year.

LOCUS OF CONTROL—CENTRALIZED OR LOCAL?

Local control of public education has a long history in New York. The UPK program reflects this tradition. Local school districts decide who will deliver pre-K services, what curricular approaches will be permitted, how much per-child subsidy will be paid to participating CBOs, and how to organize and carry out the professional development of staff. The general belief among early childhood experts in New York is that this "bottom-up" approach has sparked a considerable amount of innovation at the local level and spawned a strong commitment to UPK among a wide range of local stakeholders (Holcomb, 2006).

It is important to recognize, however, that strong state legislation and regulations set limits on local program design and provided important guidance. All lead teachers were required to be state certified within the first 4 years of program implementation, which, in New York, requires a bachelor's degree at the provisional level and then a master's degree for permanent certification. Districts were required to contract out services for at least 10% of their state funding. District advisory groups that included representatives from specified constituencies had to be involved in program planning. Educational programs had to contain specific elements, and those plans are reviewed annually by the state education department. Districts are required to assess the progress of all children in UPK classrooms, and those findings must be reported to the state education department. The state cannot anticipate or appreciate the full range of program possibilities that exist in local communities. But a firm, ongoing commitment to substantial local autonomy and control can be balanced by a clear set of state requirements and guidelines designed to ensure that UPK complements and enhances existing early care and education services, maintains a satisfactory level of teaching competence at the classroom level, and monitors the progress of all children enrolled in the program.

ONE CURRICULUM OR MANY?

No evidence exists that shows one specific curriculum (e.g., *High/Scope Perry Preschool Curriculum*, *The Creative Curriculum*) is more effective than another at preparing preschool-age children for kindergarten and the early elementary grades (Banks, 2001; Frede & Ackerman, 2007). There is some evidence that certain general pedagogical approaches and emphases may lead to more positive school outcomes over time (child rather than teacher centered, integrated across subject-matter domains, constructivist; Banks, 2001; Frede & Ackerman, 2007).

The school districts in New York are drawing from many sources to develop their curricula. At the same time, state leaders have been clear about their commitments to developmentally appropriate practices and to language and literacy development. At the onset of the UPK program, the state department of education developed, produced, and disseminated a preschool planning guide that stressed a child-centered pedagogical approach grounded in a strong understanding of development (New York State Department of Education, 1998). Surveys and case studies have indicated that these priorities are reflected in the programming carried out by local school districts (Cochran, 2004; Lekies & Cochran, 2001).

Local school districts may specify that all UPK sites use a specific curricular approach. Professional development workshops for UPK teachers and directors that focus on specific learning topics (e.g., literacy, math and science, the arts) are the most common strategies for bringing coherence to the educational program across sites (Cochran, 2004).

TEACHER QUALIFICATIONS

A comparison of the lead teacher qualifications required by the various state pre-K programs shows wide variation, ranging from a master's degree and certification in New York to no requirement in Arizona. The bachelor's degree is the norm, as it is required in 25 states. Fewer than half of the states do not require all pre-K teachers to hold at least a bachelor's degree, and eight states do not require any of their pre-K teachers to hold a bachelor's degree (Barnett et al., 2007).

New York has set a very high bar with its master's degree plus certification requirement. A close look at the situation in New York reveals that a teacher can be employed as a UPK lead teacher with a bachelor's degree and initial certification. These teachers must acquire the master's degree within a specified time period (5 years). In its original regulations, New York UPK provided program sites with a 3-year window (1998–2000) with which to bring existing lead teachers up to the degree and certification requirements. Since then, waivers have been granted to school districts under some circumstances (usually when the district can show that uncertified teachers are engaged in a study plan leading to certification).

Do early child care and education lead teachers need a master's degree in order to do their jobs well? A recent meta-analysis of seven studies examining possible links between teacher higher education background, classroom quality, and young children's academic skills found few and sometimes contradictory relationships (Early et al., 2007). A small secondary analysis of data collected in New York pre-K classrooms had similar findings. The highest scores on the ECERS-R (Harms, Clifford, & Cryer, 1998) classroom rating scale were achieved by teachers with master's degrees and those with only the child development associate (CDA) credential (Cochran, 2004). Those teachers with CDAs were not leading UPK classrooms and, thus, were working with somewhat different role expectations. More research is needed about the aspects of teacher preparation and ongoing professional development that predict higher work performance before definitive statements can be made regarding the optimal ways to prepare early care and education teachers for their work and to support them as they carry it out.

BROADER INFRASTRUCTURE NEEDS

Infrastructure involves much more than simply bricks and mortar when viewed from a systems perspective. The infrastructure issues of teacher preparation, ongoing professional development, state-level technical assistance, site development and expansion, transportation, and large-scale evaluation are discussed next.

Teacher Preparation

Establishing the UPK program in New York prompted the state to re-examine its higher education teacher certification credential that allows teachers to work with children from preschool through the sixth grade (N–6). The N–6 credential was replaced by two alternatives after discussion and statewide debate: early childhood, defined as birth through Grade 2; and childhood, defined as Grades 1–6.

A study of the New York higher education teacher preparation system identified 91 teacher preparation programs in the state that were preparing early care and education teachers and 37 community colleges and 53 programs offering degrees at the bachelor's level and above. In-depth surveys and interviews with the directors of these programs revealed that although a substantial number of colleges have introduced the birth through Grade 2 certificate since the late 1990s, very little attention is being paid to early development and the needs of 0- to 3-year-olds. Emphasis is almost exclusively on 4- to 8-year-olds and on preparing teachers for the relatively well-paid jobs in public education (Lekies & Cochran, 2007). One unanticipated consequence of UPK in New York, then, is a lower profile for early care and education in higher education teacher preparation programs. This same study documented the scarcity of articulation agreements between 2- and 4-year institutions in New York, making it difficult for students (more likely to be from low-income families and from minority communities) to proceed to the bachelor's and master's levels required by UPK. Also evident was the lack of support for the coordinators of these higher education programs and the general shortage of regular faculty positions devoted to them.

Professional Development

As mentioned earlier, professional development is one way to encourage a consistent level of quality across sites within the same school district and across school districts. In New York, the ongoing development of teachers takes place primarily at the school district level. The level of investment in professional development varies considerably from one district to another. Despite the potential for ensuring an acceptable and consistent level of quality across sites, some school districts in New York have not been including community-based UPK teachers in training opportunities provided by the district for school-based teachers (Lekies et al., 2005). Another missed opportunity involves the ongoing development of assistant teachers in UPK classrooms, who usually have little or no formal education beyond a high school degree. When asked what kind of professional development is especially helpful, UPK teachers in New York gave high marks to individual support provided in the classroom by staff development specialists hired by the school district (Cochran, 2004). These specialists may address particular teaching strategies (e.g., literacy-focused) or broader classroom management issues (e.g., children with problem behaviors).

State UPK staff has organized an annual conference designed to provide ongoing professional development for the school district UPK coordinators. No systematic effort is made by the state education department to provide statewide opportunities for the professional development of teachers (e.g., an annual conference), although many school districts do make it possible for their UPK teachers to attend the annual New York Association for the Education of Young Children conference.

Promising Practices Dissemination/Exchange

Giving school districts control over planning was cited earlier as a spark for innovation and creativity. These innovations were evident from the first planning year in the New York UPK program, and the potential for diffusion of these promising practices throughout the state was especially high during the start-up years (Hicks et al., 1999). But the UPK office in the state department of education was seriously understaffed from the beginning and was busy reading and responding to school district plans and reporting progress to the state legislature. An annual statewide opportunity to present and discuss local innovations would provide another means of improving the quality of programming at the local level.

Ongoing Technical Assistance

The small UPK staff in the state education department has managed to provide some ongoing technical assistance to local school districts. When staff members become aware of promising practices being used in a school district, they share the information with other school districts as opportunities arise. The state education department staff has found that regional meetings are effective, especially the face-to-face nature of the sessions. The staff also emphasizes rapid response to districts who call in with questions and has begun putting research articles on a listserv for discussion.

Site Development/Expansion

As the UPK program has begun in local school districts, CBOs have been brought into the program partly because of the services they can offer (e.g., full-day care, culturally appropriate programming) and partly because the public schools simply do not have the space needed to serve all interested families. Typically, school districts have developed criteria to be met by CBOs and then invited CBOs to apply to participate in a UPK program. Often, there were CBOs interested in participating that were unable to meet the criteria set by the school district. In the most forward-thinking New York school districts, the advisory board and UPK coordinator recognized the potential represented by CBOs not yet ready to take on the UPK challenge and spent 1–2 years mentoring those programs until they met the UPK goals and expectations. Sometimes this involved altering the physical design of the classroom and other spaces, and often it meant the provision of new equipment and educational supplies (Cochran, 2004; Holcomb, 2006).

Transportation

School districts in New York are not reimbursed by the state for transporting children who attend pre-K and, therefore, they do not provide transportation to the UPK sites. From the beginning of UPK in New York, district coordinators were aware that the lack of public transportation would be a serious obstacle to making the program accessible to all 4-year-olds (Hicks et al., 1999). Case study analysis of one large up-state urban UPK program revealed that transportation constraints were viewed by the directors of many community-based UPK program sites as the reason why many 4-year-olds, including those enrolled in family child care, were not attending their programs (Cochran, 2004).

Evaluation

Funding for statewide evaluation of UPK was not provided by New York, either at the time the legislation was first passed or later on in the implementation process. One result is that the opportunity to design and complete a statewide impact evaluation that includes a comparison group was lost as comparable children were increasingly attracted into the program as it expanded. Some impact evaluations have been conducted within individual school districts, but there have been no studies across districts and no consistent use of evaluation methods from one district to another.

PRIORITIES FOR THE NEXT DECADE

What will be the priorities in New York UPK during the next decade of the 21st century, and to what extent will these presage developments in the other states? In New York, the first priority for UPK is to become a truly universal program, expanding from the higher need school districts to all of the school districts in the state and from the students who are at risk in middle- and high-resource school districts to all of the 4-year-olds in those districts. Governor Spitzer's promise of an additional $99 million in his proposed 2007–2008 budget and pledge of a total increase to full funding ($645 million) by 2011 was an indication that the political willpower needed to achieve universality was present in New York. Pre-K continues to receive attention and visibility as one of a relatively few public investments that pays for itself in the medium and long term, making it increasingly easy to justify as an expenditure of state revenues.

Universality will become the nationwide norm over the next decade. A number of the largest states (Illinois, Florida, California, Texas) are already moving toward universal coverage, and proposals are pending in others (e.g., a state commission has proposed universal provision in Ohio). Like New York, other states are recognizing that universal coverage can be accomplished without investing the same amount of money per child across the board by using strategies such as a sliding fee schedule based on family income above a specified income floor (e.g., 200% of the poverty level).

I predict that after achieving universality for 4-year-olds, there will be an effort to expand UPK to 3-year-olds. This will not be an easy sell politically, given the $650 million price tag attached to UPK for 4-year-olds, but a strong effort will be made to make the case from a child development and school readiness standpoint. The shortage of space in public school buildings will force continued use of CBOs, and those early care and education stakeholders will lobby hard for expansion in this direction. In New York, there are already indications that some public funding has shifted to 3-year-olds as UPK dollars have become available for 4-year-olds (Cochran, 2004). As in New York, planning bodies in other states continue to talk in terms of 3- and 4-year-olds when articulating pre-K goals, indicating a willingness to think in those broader terms even as they begin with the older part of that cohort. It is quite possible, however, that public funding for 3-year-olds will be limited to lower income families, even in states now committed to universal access for 4-year-olds.

The positive findings throughout the early care and education system in New York, due to the heavy investment in community-based UPK sites, provide a strong argument for designing pre-K as an intentional investment in system-building. Universal prekindergarten can be designed as the addition of a vital component to the overall early care and education system in a way that strengthens the entire system rather than as a separate, self-contained "silo." In New York, this has meant finding ways to collaborate rather than compete with the federal Head Start program, which was originally designed also to serve primarily 4-year-olds. It may be that as true universality for 4-year-olds is achieved in New York, it will become increasingly difficult for Head Start to recruit 4-year-olds, leading to a shift to 3-year-olds. In more general terms, it is likely that concern for the needs of 0- to 3-year-olds will increase as the relative lack of attention to them is made more obvious by the expansion of resources for older preschoolers. The federal Early Head Start program may continue to expand partly in response to this growing discrepancy and in part due to further developments in the understanding of brain development in the very early years (Cochran, 2007).

New York reflects one of the most dramatic demographic shifts underway in American society—the transition to a truly multicultural populace as increasing proportions of infants are born into families whose roots are not in Europe but in Latin countries and in Asia. Already, the majority of infants born in Hawaii and California reflect this pattern, and this will be the case nationwide before the middle of the 21st century (Cochran, 2007). Increasingly, state pre-K programs and the infrastructure supporting them (especially teacher preparation programs) will need to invest attention and resources in ways to accommodate and capitalize on the multiethnic and multicultural nature of the groups of children they serve. This can be done by preparing teachers to work across languages and cultures and by designing educational settings and experiences that emphasize the strengths found in diversity of language and culture.

The final priority deserving attention also flows from a dramatic demographic shift—the movement of the "baby boom" generation into retirement and old age. Between 2005–2025, the number of Americans over the age of 65 will jump from about 35 million to more than 50 million, and the number over the age of 85 will nearly double (Cochran, 2007). This shift will put tremendous financial pressure on the American health care and elder services systems at a time when fewer workers will be paying into the existing Social Security system. If public funds are to continue to flow into early care and education at a level that will provide quality services, then it is imperative that older adults be convinced that this is a wise investment and be educated and organized to exert their political influence to this end. Fortunately, most of these older adults will have grandchildren for whom they will be eager to advocate. Systematic efforts will need to be made to link the early childhood and older adult communities so that the interests of children are not overshadowed by investments at life's end, but instead are understood as contributing to the enhancement of living at every stage of life.

REFERENCES

Banks, R. (2001). *The early childhood education curriculum debate: Direct instruction vs. child-initiated learning.* Retrieved June 5, 2007, from http://ceep.crc.uiuc.edu/poptopics/preschoolcurr.html#ref

Barnett, S., Hustedt, J., Hawkinson, L., & Robin, K. (2006). *The state of preschool: 2006.* New Brunswick, NJ: National Institute for Early Education Research, Rutgers University.

Cochran, M. (2004). *Implementing a State-wide universal Prekindergarten Program: An Urban Case Study.* Ithaca, NY: Cornell Early Childhood Program.

Cochran, M. (2007) *Finding Our Way: The Future of American Early Care and Education.* Washington, D.C.: Zero to Three Press.

Early, D.M., Maxwell, K.L., Burchinal, M., Alva, S., Bender, R.H., Bryant, D., et al. (2007). Teachers' education, classroom quality, and young children's academic skills: Results from seven studies of preschool programs. *Child Development, 78*(2), 558–580.

Frede, E., & Ackerman, D. (2007). *Preschool curriculum decision-making: Dimensions to consider.* Retrieved June 5, 2007, from http://nieer.org/docs/index.php?DocID=142

Harms, T., Clifford, R.M., & Cryer, D. (1998). *Early Childhood Environment Rating Scale, Revised Edition.* New York: Teachers College Press.

Hicks, S., Lekies, K., & Cochran, M. (1999) *Promising practices: New York State universal prekindergarten* (expanded edition). Ithaca, NY: Cornell Early Childhood Program.

Holcomb, B. (2006). *A Diverse System Delivers for Pre-K: Lessons Learned in New York State.* Washington, D.C.: Pre-K Now.

Lekies, K.S., & Cochran, M. (2001). *Collaborating for Kids: New York Universal Prekindergarten 1999–2000.* Ithaca, NY: Cornell University, The Cornell Early Childhood Program, Department of Human Development. Available at http://www.human.cornell.edu/che/HD/CECP/Resources/Reports.cfm

Lekies, K., & Cochran, M. (2007). *Preparing qualified teachers for infants and toddlers: The role and function of higher education teacher preparation programs.* Ithaca, NY: The Cornell Early Childhood Program, Policy Brief.

Lekies, K.S., Heitzman, E., & Cochran, M. (2001). *Early care for infants and toddlers: Examining the broader impact of universal prekindergarten.* Ithaca, NY: Cornell University, Cornell Early Childhood Program.

Lekies, K.S., Morrissey, T.W., & Cochran, M. (2005). *Raising all boats: New York's universal prekindergarten program and community-based programs.* Ithaca, NY: Cornell University, Cornell Early Childhood Program.

Morrissey, T., Lekies, K., & Cochran, M. (2007). Implementing New York's universal prekindergarten program: An exploratory study of impacts. *Early Education and Development.*

New York Child Care, Inc. (2007). *Governor Spitzer proposes pre-k expansion, new investments in children's health, home visits.* Author.

New York State Department of Education. (1998). *Preschool planning guide: Building a foundation for development of language and literacy in the early years.* Albany: The University of the State of New York, Author.

New York State Department of Education. (2006). *Universal prekindergarten annual report to the legislature: 2004–2005.* Albany, NY: Author.

New York State Education Law. (2007). *Amendments to the regulations governing universal prekindergarten.* Albany, New York: Author. Retrieved December 2, 2008, from http://www.emsc.nysed.gov/nyc/upkregulations.eff1.3.08.html

NYC Early Childhood Professional Development Institute. (2007). *Compensation and retention: Challenges for New York City's early childhood workforce.* New York: Author. Available at http://www.earlychildhoodnyc.org/topics/research policyandcommunications.cfm

Ochyn, K., & Newland, L. (2006). *Promoting school readiness through universal prekindergarten.* The Century Foundation.

Robin, K.B., Frede, E.C., & Barnett, W.S. (2006). Is more better? *The effects of full-day vs. half-day preschool on early school achievement.* NIEER Working Paper.

Chapter 9

Emerging Issues in Prekindergarten Programs

Youngok Jung, Carollee Howes, and Robert C. Pianta

In light of the growing awareness of the significance of early childhood development and the substantiality of the achievement gap between subgroups of children, states are moving toward providing high-quality early childhood education to all children, with an emphasis on better serving at-risk children. However, there are multiple challenges to the provision of high-quality early childhood education to all children through statewide universal prekindergarten programs. These challenges include the variation in the definition of high-quality early childhood education and school readiness, the volatility of funding, the difficulty in maintaining program quality, and the intricacies inherent in organizational management systems. Despite these challenges, more than 40 states provide state-funded early education services to eligible children.

The authors of this book offer insights into state and local initiatives that successfully implement large-scale prekindergarten programs and address the concerns related to the implementation of large-scale *universal* prekindergarten programs. In this concluding chapter, we focus on state initiatives to promote program quality and children's learning and on the development and implications for states planning to start or expand prekindergarten programs. We especially emphasize implications that could be generalized to different socioeconomic and geographical contexts of communities and states.

WHAT WE CAN LEARN FROM THREE
CURRENT UNIVERSAL PRE-K INITIATIVES

In describing pre-K initiatives of three states: Georgia, North Carolina, and New York, this book provides valuable and practical advice to states that aspire to provide statewide, voluntary, accessible pre-K programs. The case study of Georgia (see Chapter 6), which is the first state in the United States to provide universal pre-K to all 4-year-old children, illustrates the importance of state-specified program goals and standards: how clearly specified program goals and standards inform and guide local service providers' practices to meet the needs of children, families, and communities. The goal of Georgia's pre-K program is to prepare 4-year-old children for kindergarten by engaging in learning activities that support children's growth in language and literacy, cognition, social-emotional competence, and physical/mental health. To achieve its school readiness goal, Georgia's pre-K program emphasizes the provision of high-quality educational pre-K experiences and provides detailed standards for four key areas of classroom and program function: 1) environment, 2) curriculum, 3) child assessment, and 4) program evaluation. Standards of Georgia's pre-K program are full-day (6.5 hours) instructional services, teachers with at least an associate degree in early childhood education, use of school readiness-focused curricula to guide children's learning, child assessment across an array of school readiness domains, and evaluation of program quality in program administration.

Required by the state standards, the collection of comprehensive data on program quality and children's learning and development has implications for policy-related questions on the impact of state-funded pre-K programs. The evaluation of program quality not only allows the state to monitor program quality and children's experiences in classrooms but also to estimate the extent of which programs make improvements in quality. Georgia's pre-K program adopts a holistic approach to assess children's development, collecting data on children's performance in a wide range of school readiness domains that include language and literacy, cognition, social-emotional competence, approaches to learning, and physical/mental health. Teachers use these results of child assessment to plan instruction and to inform parents about their children's learning and development. Furthermore, the results of program evaluation and child assessment can be used in combination to inform policy makers about the impact of the program on children's school readiness and the associations between the state standards and children's learning and development. In Chapter 2, Schultz reviews other states that require evaluation and child assessment and finds that state initiatives that require both program evaluation and child assessment are more effective in addressing the relations between program quality and child outcomes, monitoring children's progress, developing professional development courses, enhancing teacher education programs, and improving and maintaining program quality.

North Carolina's More at Four Prekindergarten (MAF) Program (see Chapter 7) shows how the state's commitment to pre-K education and its innovative approach to provide funds has had positive effects on the expansion of availability, affordability, and quality of early childhood education. The MAF is a community-based, voluntary, targeted pre-K program for at-risk children designed to improve children's academic readiness for kindergarten, reduce the achievement gap in K–12, and build a high-quality early education program. The state allocated approximately $4,050 per child in 2006–2007 for general operating costs. In addition, the state provides additional funds to build infrastructure to promote program quality, including start-up funds ($500/slot) that may be used to purchase materials to equip high-quality classrooms and professional development funds that pay for scholarship assistance, health insurance for teachers, program evaluation, and professional development. As a result, most of North Carolina's pre-K programs generally meet state-specified standards that reflect many elements of high-quality model programs (e.g., The Abecedarian Project [Campbell, Ramey, Pungello, Sparling, & Miller-Johnson, 2002]), such as small classroom size, full-day instructional schedules, high teacher qualification, use of comprehensive developmental curriculum, and enriching classroom environments.

The case study of North Carolina also brings attention to challenges that states may face in the process of implementing large-scale pre-K programs. In the beginning of the program, MAF encountered many challenges in politics, operation, and finance, such as competition with other early education programs (e.g., Smart Start, Head Start), difficulties in collaboration with other agencies and government divisions, and lack of funding. Despite the challenges, North Carolina quickly established high-quality pre-K programs across the state within its first years of operation (2002–2003) and plans to expand services to more children. The swift establishment of a statewide pre-K program indicates that there is a broad consensus among policy makers and local communities on the importance of children starting kindergarten ready to learn; however, the challenges still abound regarding the expansion and sustainability of the program.

New York State established universal pre-K in 1997 to assist local school districts in providing free prekindergarten to 4-year-olds and to help these children develop pre-academic and social skills needed to succeed in kindergarten through their educational experiences (see Chapter 8). One of the unique features of New York's universal pre-K is that the initiative emphasizes community involvement and requires local school districts to use at least 10% of their grant award to contract for universal pre-K classrooms in community-based programs. Due to public school classroom space constraints, however, school districts are contracting out far more than the mandated 10% of the program to community-based programs: 62% of children served in community-based settings compared with 38% in public schools (2004–2005). Including such a high number of community-based programs brought about remarkable growth in overall pre-K systems, improving infrastructure and increasing family participation. By including community-based programs, New York's pre-K program expands its services to more children; meets child care needs of parents from socioeconomically and culturally diverse populations; relieves public schools' problem of finding space for UPK in existing buildings; improves the quality of educational experiences of children served in community-based programs; and utilizes the expertise of community-based programs in developmentally appropriate practices.

There are also challenges to be found in including community-based programs, including difficulties in recruiting and retaining high-quality teachers for community-based programs, monitoring program quality in community-based settings, developing and managing contracts with community-based settings; and blending UPK state funds with federal and other state funds.

IMPLICATIONS FOR STATES TO START A PRE-K INITIATIVE AND EXPAND THEIR CURRENT INITIATIVES

Although more and more states are joining the universal pre-K movement, debates are still looming on who should be included in state-funded pre-K programs. Advocates for universal pre-K programs argue that all 4-year-old children can benefit from participating in high-quality preschool education and that the lack of school readiness and the achievement gap are observed across all socioeconomic groups (with children from lower income families performing below children from higher income families [Barnett, Brown, & Shore, 2004]). In addition, universal pre-K classrooms are more heterogeneous and diverse, including a wider range of socioeconomic and cultural groups of children than targeted pre-K classrooms.

Advocates of targeted pre-K programs, which limit their provision of early learning experiences to children who are in the most need, emphasize the practicality and cost-effectiveness of such programs. Targeted pre-K programs, which focus on children of low-income and minority families, may meet the specific needs of the disadvantaged children without stretching funding and resources too much. In addition, considering the lack of proper infrastructure that ensures adequate funding and high-quality instructional services, some believe that it is premature to implement universal pre-K.

In Chapter 4, Dotterer and colleagues attempt to address this issue on who should be included in pre-K initiatives. They compare universal pre-K and targeted pre-K programs on classroom characteristics and the pre-academic development of children from low-income families. Their results showed that despite the differences in the socioeconomic and ethnic composition of classrooms (i.e., universal pre-K classrooms had a greater proportion of Caucasian children and a lower proportion of poor children in the class), children in both types of classrooms had similar exposure to socioeconomically and racially diverse groups of children. Review of structural features of classrooms revealed that targeted pre-K programs had shorter classes, teachers with fewer years of education, and smaller teacher–child ratios. In addition, observations of classroom quality revealed that targeted pre-K programs had higher quality than universal programs concerning teaching, provisions of learning experiences, and instruction. Neither program was consistently related to larger child gains during the pre-K experiences, showing no consistent correlations with children's progress in various academic domains. Overall, their findings suggest that variability within the universal and targeted programs is far greater than between the two types of programs. Given that the greater variability was observed within the programs than between the programs and that low-income children in economically integrated preschool classrooms had greater gains in receptive language than low-income children in classrooms with children from mostly low-income families, this chapter suggests that states should focus on increasing diversity within classrooms to promote children's learning and development instead of deliberating on whether to offer universal or targeted pre-K programs.

Currently, state-funded pre-K programs are paid for through an array of state and local school district resources and federal monies (e.g., Title I, Head Start, IDEA). This fragmentation in the funding results in a lack of a common system that informs programs about state standards for program quality and child assessment. State and local practitioners report that this policy fragmentation makes it difficult for them to do the following: respond to multiple funders' different standards, assessments, reporting requirements, and monitoring reviews; manage different forms of data on the performance of children and programs; enhance teachers' effectiveness to identify children's current levels of learning and use researched-based teaching strategies; understand multiple forms of feedback on the performance of children and programs; and enhance continuity between pre-K and elementary education. In addition, the lack of agreement on the state-specified standards for program evaluation and child assessment also creates difficulty in generating ongoing feedback on program participants, the cost of services, and the program's impact on the levels of individual children, programs, local communities, and states.

In order to address the issues related to the funding fragmentation, states are increasingly building state systems to coordinate available services and funds for children, increasing funding for high-quality programs, providing programs with oversight and assistance to improve program quality and child outcomes, and focusing on the development of child-focused standards and assessments. The development of child-focused program standards and child assessments is particularly important because it will provide critical information that will inform key stakeholders regarding the significance and effectiveness of state-funded high-quality pre-K programs and exert influence on policy decisions. In Chapter 2, Schultz recommends that states should be providing more detailed forms of feedback on children's learning and development and on program improvement to address the most critical questions for early childhood programs: 1) How are the children doing? and 2) how are programs contributing to their learning?

Another issue with the funding fragmentation is identifying and blending existing funding sources to generate sufficient dollars to support high-quality, voluntary, universal, state-funded pre-K programs. In general, state pre-K programs are funded with general revenues (e.g., taxes, fees), lotteries, gambling-related funds, and federal funds (e.g., Temporary Assistance to Needy Families [TANF] and Title I). The vast majority of states fund pre-K programs with general revenue, including preschool in the state budget, and distribute funds through a grant/contract method. Lotteries are another popular way to fund preschool programs, and most states have a lottery. However, states' use of other funding sources (e.g., gambling-related funds, federal funds) is limited because of the volatility in funding status. In addition, despite the availability of general revenues and lottery proceeds, there are concerns regarding the uncertainty over the level of funding from these sources for state pre-K because of competition with other worthy educational purposes.

In order to bring together various existing funding sources and secure funding for preschool programs, Mitchell (Chapter 3) suggests that states should establish comprehensive early care and education systems that integrate related policies, services, and support for children birth to age 5. By building comprehensive early childhood systems, states can redirect existing funds as well as identify new sources to raise sufficient funds to support a high-quality, voluntary, universal pre-K program. When determining funding, states must consider whether the funding is secure from fiscal challenges and can be increased as the pre-K program improves in quality and grows to serve all children.

Adding to the complexity of funding pre-K programs is the debate on the intensity, or *dosage*, of pre-K program. Pre-K programs vary in their operating schedules: half day (2–3.25 hours) versus full day (6–6.5 hours) and academic year versus full year. Full-day, year-round programs can better accommodate the needs of working parents who need longer hours of care; however, they are more costly compared with half-day academic-year programs. Findings from the three landmark studies: the Abecedarian Project (Campbell & Ramey, 1994), the Chicago CPC program (Reynolds, 1993), and the High/Scope Perry Preschool Project (Schweinhart, Barnes, & Weikart, 1993) suggest that full-day, intensive, year-round programs are more effective for at-risk children than half-day, less intensive programs. Given the variance in program quality and child characteristics between programs, however, it is difficult to determine the effects of the intensity of the program.

In Chapter 5, Ramey, Ramey, and Stokes provide scientific evidence that full-day programs produce greater benefits for children than half-day programs, improving children's emergent language and literacy skills. They found that children in Louisiana's LA4 who received a full-day program for a full year showed nearly double the academic gains of the children in Maryland's half-day program and Louisiana's half-year LA4 program. In conjunction with other research findings, Ramey, Ramey, and Stokes conclude that full-day programs are more effective, and quality preschool education can definitely improve children's academic performance significantly to levels that place the children at much greater likelihood of succeeding in elementary school than if they had not received such early educational supports.

CONCLUSION

Throughout this book, the authors present scientific evidence on the positive effects of small- and large-scale pre-K programs on children's learning and development that validates the national movement toward providing universal pre-K programs. Regardless of program types, programs that provide high-quality early educational experiences show strong associations with children's growth in language, general cognition, and social competence. Concerns persist, however, regarding the substantial investments of funds and resources that are needed for the provision of high-quality, universal pre-K. This book offers a great deal of valuable advice on how to expand the availability of universal pre-K with given constraints in funding and program characteristics and suggests that states consider taking advantage of existing early childhood education programs and providing services selectively.

REFERENCES

Barnett, S., Brown, K., & Shore, R., (2004). The Universal vs. targeted debate: Should the United States have preschool for all? New Brunswick, NJ: National Institute for Early Education Research.

Campbell, F.A., & Ramey, C.T. (1994). Effects of early intervention on intellectual and academic achievement: A follow-up study of children from low-income families. *Child Development, 65,* 684–698.

Campbell, F.A., Ramey, C.T., Pungello, E.P., Sparling, J., & Miller-Johnson, S. (2002). Early childhood education: Young adult outcomes from the Abecedarian Project. *Applied Developmental Science, 6,* 42–57.

Schweinhart, L.J., Barnes, H.V., & Weikart, D.P. (1993). *Significant benefits: Vol 10. The High/Scope Perry Preschool Study through age 27.* Ypsilanti, MI: The High/Scope Press.

Index

Page numbers followed by *f* indicate figures; page numbers followed by *t* indicate tables.

Abbott Preschool Program, 41
ABC, *see* Arkansas's Better Chance
    for School Success
ABCD model, *see* Applied Biosocial
    Contextual Development
Abecedarian Project, 68, 80–85, 82*t*,
    129, 175
Academic achievement outcomes
    Abecedarian Project, 82–84, 82*t*
    Chicago Child-Parent Centers, 85
    Georgia universal program, 107
    Louisiana LA4 program, 93–98, 94*f*
    Perry Preschool Project, 85–86
    universal versus targeted
        programs, 72–73, 73*t*
Accountability
    education reform initiatives and,
        31
    redefining, 47
    standards-based assessments and,
        34–35, 34*t*
    survey of state-funded programs,
        18–19
Achievement gaps
    as argument for universal
        programs, 66–67
    evidence of, 32
    see also School readiness
Administration and governance
    Head Start, 12
    More at Four program (North
        Carolina), 132–133, 132*f*,
        136–138
    New York universal
        prekindergarten, 148, 148*t*,
        155–156, 159

Smart Start program (North
    Carolina), 59
special education services, 21–22
state-funded programs, 5, 6*t*–8*t*, 12
Age, as eligibility criterion, 13
Alabama
    federal funding, 58
    local funding matches, 60
Alliance of Education Agency Heads
    (Georgia), 120
Applied Biosocial Contextual
    Development (ABCD model),
    91
Appropriations, *see* Funding and
    expenditures
Arizona, tobacco taxes, 56
Arkansas
    child and program assessments,
        45–46
    local funding matches, 60
Arkansas's Better Chance for School
    Success (ABC), 45–46
Assessment
    Bright from the Start program
        (Georgia), 113–116, 117*f*
    challenges and complications,
        36–37
    data management and recording,
        46–47, 115–116, 173–174
    funding for, 40
    future trends, 47
    importance of, 170–171, 174
    readiness assessment of children,
        38–39, 41–43, 44–45, 46
    recommendations, 47
    states' approaches to, 33–36, 34*t*

Assessment—*continued*
 survey of state-funded programs,
  18–19
 universal versus targeted
  programs, 72–73, 73*t*
 see also Program evaluation
Assistant teachers
 professional development, 162
 qualifications, 16, 109, 129

Bachelor's degree requirement for
 teachers, 9*t*–11*t*, 16
Beer taxes, 55
Bilingual programs, 20
BLL, *see Building Language for Literacy*
 curriculum
Bright from the Start program
 (Georgia)
 child assessment, 67–68, 113–116,
  170–171
 comparison with Head Start, 68–69
 curriculum and standards,
  110–113, 112*t*, 170–171
 environmental elements, 108–110
 establishment of, 108
 funding, 14
 program evaluation, 116, 117*f*,
  170–171
 readiness indicators, 117–121
Budgets, state, 52–53, 61, 125, 126*t*,
 127
Build Initiative, 59
Building Language for Literacy (BLL)
 curriculum, 99

California
 eligibility considerations, 13
 income taxes, 57, 61
 lack of program evaluation, 19
 property taxes, San Francisco, 58
 tobacco taxes, 55–56
Carolina Approach to Responsive
 Education, 83
CBOs, *see* Community-based
 organizations
CDA, *see* Child Development
 Associate credential
Chicago Child–Parent Centers, 85,
 129, 175

Child assessment
 Bright from the Start program
  (Georgia), 113–116, 117*f*
 data management and recording,
  46–47, 115–116, 173–174
 importance of, 170–171, 174
 readiness assessment, 38–39,
  41–43, 44–45, 46
 see also Program evaluation
Child Care Developmental Block
 Grant (CCDBG), 141
Child care systems, 145–146
Child Development Associate (CDA)
 credential, 16, 129, 161
Children's Defense Fund, 51
Children's Investment Fund
 (Portland, Oregon), 57–58
Classroom Assessment Scoring
 System (CLASS), 70, 71*t*, 72
Classrooms, spending per, 125, 127,
 141
Colorado
 Denver preschool initiative, 60
 expulsion of students, 14
 lack of program evaluation, 19
 local funding, 25
 sales taxes, 58
Communication ability of students,
 119
Community-based organizations
 (CBOs)
 assessment of program effects,
  151–152, 152*f*
 benefits of using, 153–155
 New York school districts'
  collaboration with, 149–151,
  150*f*, 172
 as prekindergarten sites, 146–147
 site development and expansion,
  163
Concepts of Print, 100
Connecticut
 eligibility considerations, 13
 per-child spending, 24
Cornell Early Childhood Program,
 149, 151
Costs, *see* Funding and expenditures
Criminal incarceration outcomes, 86
Cultural and ethnic diversity
 English language learners, 19–20
 New York universal
  prekindergarten, 154

in targeted programs, 173
see also Economic status
Curricula
Bright from the Start program
(Georgia), 110–113, 112*t*
Infant Health and Development
Program, 83
Montgomery County Public
School System, 99
New York universal
prekindergarten, 155–156,
159–160

Dedicated revenue sources, 60–61
Degree requirements for teachers
Georgia, 109–110
New York, 148, 159, 160–161
North Carolina, 129
survey of state-funded programs,
9*t*–11*t*, 16
see also Professional development
for teachers
Denver, Colorado
preschool initiative, 60
sales taxes, 58
Developing Skills Checklist (DSC),
93, 94*f*
DIBELS, *see* Dynamic Indicators of
Basic Early Literacy Skills
Dosage of programs
Bright from the Start (Georgia), 109
importance of, 175
LA-4 and Montgomery County
programs, 101–102, 102*f*, 175
New York universal
prekindergarten, 153, 158–159
state-funded program survey,
9*t*–11*t*, 14–15
universal versus targeted
programs, 71*t*, 86
DSC, *see* Developing Skills Checklist
Dual self-interest principle, 90–91
Dynamic Indicators of Basic Early
Literacy Skills (DIBELS), 18, 39

Early Childhood Development and
Health Initiative (Arizona), 56
Early Childhood Development
Authority (Kentucky), 56

Early childhood education
child care systems, 145–146
definition (Nebraska), 53
enrollment trends, 3–4
linking to primary school, 33, 37
research evidence, 79–86
standards, 15
state leadership initiatives, 32–33
supports needed, 87*f*
see also Targeted programs;
Universal programs; *specific
programs*
Early Childhood Environmental
Rating System–Revised
(ECERS-R)
Louisiana, 92–93
Montgomery County, Maryland,
92–93
Multi-State and SWEEP studies,
70, 71*t*, 72
New Jersey, 41
New York, 156
North Carolina, 130
Pennsylvania, 40
Early Childhood Mental Health
Consultation Project
(Maryland), 38
Early Childhood Observation System
(ECHOS), 39
Early childhood teachers, 37
Early Language and Literacy
Classroom Observation
(ELLCO), 43, 92–93, 99*f*, 100
Early learning, *see* Early childhood
education
Early Learning Assessment System
(New Jersey), 42
Early Learning Council (Illinois), 59
Early Learning Initiative Program
(Ohio), 43, 59
Early Learning Networks (Seattle), 57
Early Reading First program, 98
ECERS-R, *see* Early Childhood
Environmental Rating
System–Revised
Economic status
diversity, attempts to increase, 74
eligibility and, 6*t*–8*t*, 13, 173
low-income families in targeted
versus universal programs,
70–71, 70*f*, 71*t*, 172–173

Economic status—*continued*
  low-wealth funding formula, 139
  outcomes and, 68
Education aid formulas, 53, 60, 61
Education Management Information
    System (Ohio), 44
Elementary and Secondary
    Education Act of 1965
    (PL 89-10), 52
Eligibility requirements
  English language learners and, 20
  state-funded programs, 6t–8t, 13
Employment outcomes, 82t, 83, 86
English language learners (ELLs),
    19–20
Enrollment
  funding sources, 34t
  in state-funded programs, 6t–8t,
    12–14
  trends in, 3–4, 26–27
Evaluation, *see* Program evaluation
Expulsion from state programs, 14

Families and Education Levy
    (Seattle), 57
Federal funding
  blending of, 141, 157, 174
  for state-funded programs, 25–26
  types of, 52, 58–59, 124
First Things First (Arizona), 56
Florida
  child assessment, 39
  private programs, 26
  state lottery, 54
  universal access, 13–14
Foundation for Child Development,
    142
Frank Porter Graham (FPG) Child
    Development Institute, 125,
    127, 128
Full-day programs, *see* Dosage of
    programs
Funding and expenditures
  blending of funding, 141, 157, 174
  compared to K-12, 24–25
  fragmentation in, 36–37, 173–174
  growth in, 52, 135, 135t, 147, 147f
  half-day versus full-day programs,
    9t–11t

  issues and challenges, 60–61,
    140–143, 173–175
  More at Four program, 55,
    130–135, 132f, 135t, 138–140
  New York universal
    prekindergarten, 147, 147f,
    157, 158, 164
  per-child spending, 9t–11t, 23–25,
    26, 125
  per-classroom spending, 125, 127
  sources of funding, 34t, 52–59,
    60–61, 124, 174
  state initiatives, 33
  state spending trends, 65–66, 125
  survey of state-funded programs,
    9t–11t, 22–26
  for teacher training and
    development, 38–39
  universal versus targeted
    programs, 66
  see also specific states and programs

Gambling-related funds, 55
General revenue of states, 52–53, 61,
    174
Generalizability of funding, 60
Georgetown University, 98
Georgia
  funding for programs, 14, 53, 54
  private programs, 26
  program outcomes, 67–68
  state lottery, 54, 107
  see also Bright from the Start
    program
Georgia Kindergarten Inventory of
    Developing Skills (GKIDS), 121
Get It, Got It, Go!, 44, 100
GKIDS, *see* Georgia Kindergarten
    Inventory of Developing
    Skills
Governance, *see* Administration and
    governance
Grade retention
  Abecedarian Project, 72t
  Louisiana L-4 program, 95–97, 96f
  Perry Preschool Project, 85
Grants
  for distribution of state funds, 53
  as state funding source, 5, 12

Head Start
  compared to Georgia universal
    program, 68–69
  funding, 59, 141
  governance structure, 12
  objection to More at Four program,
    136
  Pennsylvania's incorporation of
    standards, 40
  shift to 3-year-olds, 165
Health considerations, 17, 118
High/Scope Child Observation
    Record, 42
High/Scope Program Quality
    Assessment, 42
High/Scope Study, see Perry
    Preschool Project
Home visits, 17

Idaho, federal funding, 58
IDEA, see Individuals with
    Disabilities Education
    Improvement Act of 2004
IDHP, see Infant Health and
    Development Program
Illinois
  Early Learning Council, 59
  universal access, 13
Inclusion, 21–22
Income taxes, 57
Individuals with Disabilities
    Education Improvement Act
    (IDEA) of 2004 (PL 108-446),
    59
Infant Health and Development
    Program (IHDP), 83–84
Inside the Brain (Kotulak), 81
Institutionalized children, 84
Iowa
  local funding matches, 60
  universal access, 13, 14
It Takes a Village (Clinton), 81

Kansas
  federal funding, 58
  tobacco settlement funds, 56
Kentucky
  special education services, 21
  tobacco settlement funds, 56

Keys to Quality (Pennsylvania), 60
Keystone STARS program, 39–40
Kindergarten Georgia Performance
    Standards (K-GPS), 110, 111,
    112t
Kindergarten Readiness Assessment-
    Literacy (KRA-L), 44

LA4 program (Louisiana)
  comparison with Montgomery
    County program, 101–102,
    102f
  conceptual framework and
    research questions, 91–93
  dosage of programs, 101–102, 102f,
    175
  key findings, 93, 94f, 95–98, 96f,
    97f, 102f
  partnership paradigm, 90–91
  program characteristics, 88–90
Language outcomes
  Louisiana LA4 program, 93, 94f,95
  Montgomery County School
    System, 99–100, 99f
  universal versus targeted
    programs, 73, 73t, 74
LA-UP, see Los Angeles Universal
    Preschool
Learning in Action suggestions
    (Georgia), 110, 111, 112t
Learning standards
  multiple sets of, 36–37, 173–174
  survey of state-funded programs,
    15
Length of day, see Dosage of
    programs
Literacy outcomes
  indicators, 119–120
  Montgomery County School
    System, 99–101, 99f, 100f
  universal versus targeted
    programs, 73, 73t
Local early childhood agencies, 36
Los Angeles Universal Preschool
    (LA-UP), 56
Lotteries, as source of funding,
    53–55, 107, 139–140, 174
Louisiana
  federal funding, 58

Louisiana—*continued*
  tobacco settlement funds, 56
  see also LA4 program
Low birth weight (LBW) infants,
    83–84
Low-income families, *see* Economic
    status
Low-wealth funding formula, 139

MAF, *see* More at Four program
Maine
  education aid formulas, use of, 53
  lack of program evaluation, 19
  per-child spending, 24
Maryland
  child assessment, 38–39
  see also Montgomery County
    Public Schools program
Massachusetts, federal funding, 58
Master's degree requirement for
    teachers, 148, 160–161
Maternal and Child Health Bureau,
    59
Mathematics skills
  Louisiana LA4 program, 94*f*, 95
  universal versus targeted
    programs, 73*t*
Michigan, child and program
    assessments, 42–43
Michigan School Readiness Program
    (MSRP), 42, 46
Minnesota
  lack of program evaluation, 19
  per-child spending, 24
Missouri, funding, 53
Montgomery County Public Schools
    program (Maryland)
  comparison with Louisiana LA4
    program, 101–102, 102*f*
  conceptual framework and
    research questions, 91–93
  dosage of programs, 101–102, 102*f*,
    175
  key findings, 98–101, 99*f*, 100*f*, 102*f*
  partnership paradigm, 90–91
  program characteristics, 88–90
More at Four (MAF) program (North
    Carolina)
  administration, 132–133, 132*f*,
    136–138
  challenges, 135–140, 171

establishment of, 123–124, 127–129
funding, 55, 130–135, 132*f*, 135*t*,
    138–140, 171
program standards and
    characteristics, 129–130
MSRP, *see* Michigan School
    Readiness Program
Multi-State Study of Pre-
    Kindergarten, 69–73, 70*f*, 71*t*,
    73*t*

National Association for the
    Education of Young Children
    (NAEYC), program
    accreditation, 36, 40
National Association of Family Child
    Care, 40
National Association of State Boards
    of Education, 120–121
National Center for Early
    Development and Learning, 69
National Center for Education,
    Development, and Learning,
    125
National Education Goals, 118
National Governors' Association, 59
National Institute for Early
    Education Research (NIEER)
  per-child spending, 60, 125
  as source for state spending data, 51
  survey of state-funded programs,
    4–5, 6*t*–8*t*, 9*t*–11*t*
NCLB, *see* No Child Left Behind Act
    of 2001
NCPC, *see* North Carolina
    Partnership for Children
Nebraska
  constitutional amendment for
    perpetual school funds, 53
  local funding matches, 60
Nevada, English language learners,
    20
New Hampshire, state lottery, 54
New Jersey
  eligibility considerations, 13
  per-child spending, 24
  program quality assessment, 41–42
New Mexico
  child and program assessments,
    44–45
  federal funding, 58

New York
    administration of programs, 148,
        148*t*, 155–156, 159
    assessment of program effects,
        151–152, 152*f*
    benefits of using community-based
        organizations, 153–155
    collaboration with community-
        based organizations, 149–151,
        150*f*, 172
    curriculum, 155–156, 159–160
    dosage of programs, 153, 158–159
    funding, 147, 147*f*, 157, 158, 164
    future priorities, 164–166
    infrastructure needs, 156, 161–164
    investment indicators, 153*t*
    nonparticipant perspective,
        154–155
    program evaluation, 155–156, 164
    site distribution, 149–151, 150*f*
    teacher qualifications and
        preparation, 148, 159, 160–162
    teacher salaries, 155
    universal access, 13, 157–158,
        164–166, 171–172
No Child Left Behind (NCLB) Act of
    2001 (PL 107-110), 31
North Carolina
    appropriations for early care and
        services, 53, 126*t*
    eligibility considerations, 13
    funding, 125, 126*t*, 127
    local level funding, 60, 127, 140
    spending per classroom, 125, 127
    state lottery, 54–55, 139–140
    see also More at Four program
North Carolina Partnership for
    Children (NCPC), 137
North Dakota, federal funding, 58
Nutrition education, 17–18

Office of School Readiness (North
    Carolina), 134–135
Ohio
    child and program assessments,
        43–44
    federal funding, 58, 59
Oklahoma
    education aid formulas, use of, 53
    state lottery, 54
    universal program, 13, 67

Oral & Written Language Scale
    (OWLS), 72
Oregon
    per-child spending, 24
    property taxes, 57–58
OWLS, *see* Oral & Written Language
    Scale

Parents
    Bright from the Start program
        (Georgia), 114
    need for child care systems,
        145–146
    New York universal
        prekindergarten, 154
    participation in program
        governance, 12
    support services for, 17–18
Partners for Learning curriculum, 83
PCMI, *see* Preschool Classroom
    Mathematics Inventory
Peabody Picture Vocabulary Test–
    Third Edition (PPVT-III), 72
Pennsylvania
    federal funding, 58
    funding initiatives, 60
    lack of program evaluation, 19
    program quality assessment, 39–40
Per-child spending
    adequacy of, 60, 141
    compared to per-classroom
        spending, 125, 127, 141
    More at Four program (North
        Carolina), 171
    national average, 26, 125
    survey of state-funded programs,
        9*t*–11*t*, 23–25
Perry Preschool Project, 68, 85–86,
    129, 175
PL 89-10, *see* Elementary and
    Secondary Education Act of
    1965
PL 107-110, *see* No Child Left Behind
    Act of 2001
PL 108-446, *see* Individuals with
    Disabilities Education
    Improvement Act of 2004
Policy initiatives
    assessment approaches, 33–36, 34*t*
    challenges and complications,
        36–37, 140–143

Policy initiatives—*continued*
  New York universal
    prekindergarten, 148, 148*t*
  return on investment concept, 102
  state leadership approaches, 32–33
Policy leaders, 37
Portland, Oregon, property taxes,
    57–58
PPVT-III, *see* Peabody Picture
    Vocabulary Test–Third Edition
Prekindergarten At-Risk program
    (Kansas), 56
Prekindergarten programs, *see* Early
    childhood education; Targeted
    programs; Universal
    programs; *specific programs*
Premature infants, 83–84
Preschool Classroom Mathematics
    Inventory (PCMI), 41
Preschool for All initiative
    (California), 57, 61
Preschool programs, *see* Early
    childhood education; Targeted
    programs; Universal
    programs; *specific programs*
Preschool Yearbooks, 51, 60, 65, 125
Print skills
  indicators, 119–120
  Louisiana LA4 program, 94*f*, 95
Privately administered programs, 12,
    26, 135, 136*f*
  see also Community-based
    organizations
Professional development for teachers
  New York, 160, 162
  North Carolina, 128, 133, 134–135
  survey of state-funded programs,
    16–17
  see also Degree requirements for
    teachers
Program evaluation
  Bright from the Start program
    (Georgia), 116, 117*f*
  importance of, 170–171
  New York universal
    prekindergarten, 155–156, 164
  survey of state-funded programs,
    18–19
  see also Program standards
Program Quality Assessment (PQA)
  Georgia, 116, 117*f*
  Michigan, 43

Program standards
  assessment approaches, 34*t*, 35–36
  Bright from the Start program
    (Georgia), 110–113, 112*t*
  importance of, 170
  lack of agreement, 174
  More at Four program (North
    Carolina), 129–130
  multiple sets of, 36–37, 173–174
  quality, assessment of, 39–46
  survey of state-funded programs,
    15–18
  see also Program evaluation
Project CARE, 83
Property taxes, 57–58
*The Public School Early Childhood
    Study*, 51
Public schools
  linking prekindergarten programs
    to, 33, 37, 112*t*, 120–121,
    142–143
  prekindergarten program
    administration, 6*t*–8*t*, 12
  see also specific programs
Purchases of services contracts, 133

Quality of programs
  assessment of, 34*t*, 35–36, 39–46
  self-assessments, 44
Quality Rating and Improvement
    System (QRIS), 34*t*, 36
Qualls Early Learning Inventory, 46

Readiness, *see* School readiness
Ready for School Goal Team (North
    Carolina), 128
Ready Schools initiative (North
    Carolina), 142–143
Regression discontinuity design, 43,
    67
Return on investment (ROI) concept,
    102
Revenue sources for states, 52–59
Rhode Island
  appropriations for early care and
    services, 53
  Starting RIght program, 53, 59–60
ROI concept, *see* Return on
    investment concept
Romanian children, 84

Sales taxes as funding sources, 55–56, 58
San Francisco, property taxes, 58
SAVS, *see* Self-Assessment Validation System
Schedules, *see* Dosage of programs
School readiness
assessment of children, 38–39, 41–43, 44–45, 46–47
essential components, 110
Georgia definition of, 117–118
indicators of, 117–121
North Carolina definition of, 128–129
support sources needed, 87f
School Readiness Rating Scale (Michigan), 42
Schools, *see* Public schools
Seattle, local property taxes, 57
SELA, *see* Support for Early Literacy Assessment
Self-Assessment Validation System (SAVS), 41
"Sin" taxes as funding sources, 55–56, 61
Site visits, 18
Smart Start program (North Carolina)
administration and governance, 59
funding for, 53, 126t, 136–137, 142
National Technical Assistance Center, 59
overview, 128
Social and interpersonal skills, 119
South Carolina, per-child spending, 24
Special education services
Louisiana LA4 program, 97–98, 97f
Perry Preschool Project, 85–86
in state-funded programs, 20–22
Spending, *see* Funding and expenditures
Staff, *see* Teachers
Staff–child ratios, 9t–11t, 17, 71t
Starting RIght program (Rhode Island), 53, 59–60
State agencies, 36
State Early Childhood Comprehensive Systems, 59
State-funded programs, survey results
data collection, 4–5
definition, 5

early learning standards, 15
eligibility requirements, 6t–8t, 13
English language learners, services for, 19–20
enrollment, 6t–8t, 12–14
funding and expenditures, 9t–11t, 22–26
governance and administration, 5, 6t–8t, 12
length of day, 9t–11t, 14–15
monitoring and accountability, 18–19
program structure and standards, 9t–11t, 15–18
special education services, 20–22
transportation services, 19
State-Wide Early Education Programs Study (SWEEP), 69–73, 70f, 71t, 73t
Support for Early Literacy Assessment (SELA), 41
Support services, provision of, 17–18
SWEEP, *see* State-Wide Early Education Programs Study

Targeted programs
arguments for, 68–69, 172–173
compared to universal programs, 68–69, 69–74, 70f, 71t, 73t, 173
funding, 66
see also More at Four program (North Carolina)
Taxes as funding sources, 55–56, 57–58
Teacher Education and Compensation Helps (T.E.A.C.H.), 126t, 128, 133
Teachers
assistant teachers, 16, 109, 129, 162
elementary school, 37
parent–teacher conferences, 18
professional development, 16–17, 128, 133, 134–135, 160, 162
qualifications and training, 9t–11t, 16–17, 109–110, 129, 148, 159, 160–162
salaries, 130, 155
staff–child ratios, 9t–11t, 17, 71t
training scholarships, 126t, 128, 133
universal versus targeted programs, 71t

Technical assistance, New York
    universal prekindergarten, 163
Temporary Assistance for Needy
    Families (TANF), 58–59
Tennessee
  local funding matches, 60
  state lottery, 54
Test of Early Reading Abilities
    (TERA), 100–101, 100f
Texas
  education aid formulas, use of, 53
  English language learners, 20
  lack of program evaluation, 19
Title I funds, 52, 59, 137
Tobacco settlement funds, 56
Tobacco taxes, 55–56, 61
Training, teacher, see Degree
    requirements for teachers
Transportation services, 19, 163–164

Universal programs
  arguments for, 66–68, 157–158, 172
  compared with targeted programs,
    69–74, 70f, 71t, 73t, 173

expansion to 3-year-olds, 165
funding, 66, 158
states providing, 13–14
see also Bright from the Start; New
    York

Vermont, education aid formulas,
    use of, 53
Voluntary Prekindergarten (VPK;
    Florida), 54

West Virginia
  education aid formulas, use of,
    53
  universal access, 13, 14
Wisconsin, education aid formulas,
    use of, 53
Woodcock-Johnson III Tests of
    Achievement, 72, 73t
Work Sampling System (WSS), 38, 46,
    114–115
Wyoming, special education services,
    21